THE GOSPEL

A Redemption and Restoration **Story**

MIKE O'DOWD

The Gospel: A Redemption and Restoration Story
Copyright © 2021 by Mike O'Dowd

Published by Deep River Books
Sisters, Oregon
www.deepriverbooks.com

Cover design by Jason Enterline
ISBN—13: 9781632695512
Library of Congress Control Number: 2020924987

Printed in the USA
2021—First Edition
29 28 27 26 25 24 23 22 21 10 9 8 7 6 5 4 3 2 1

To my son Ben and my daughter Jessica. May your mom and I be blessed to rejoice over you in glory, amidst many sons and daughters the Father will draw to himself through you according to the gospel of Jesus Christ . . . according to his story.

Table of Contents

Introduction

What is the gospel? The apostle Paul teaches in Romans 1:16 that "it is the power of God for salvation to everyone who believes." In the preceding verse, Paul indicated to the church in Rome, "I am eager to preach the gospel to you." The gospel, therefore, can be expressed in a message—and in that message resides the very power of God to bring salvation to those who believe it. But what is the content of this message, and what does it mean to believe this message that brings salvation to the hearer? If a person's salvation hinges on belief in this message, then the answer to these two questions are vital. One of the implications of Romans 1:16 is that belief in an *errant* message will not bring the power of God into a person's life to save them. So then, what is the gospel?

I came to Christ as an adult, and most of my Christian life was spent worshipping and serving God in a Southern Baptist tradition. Within that tradition, I have seen "the gospel" presented in a variety of ways. It was not unusual over the course of years to hear a sermon on a biblical text unrelated to the gospel that would, without fail, take a turn to an invitation that sounded something like: "If you've never invited Jesus into your heart, won't you do so today and be saved?" Is that the gospel? Is that the content of the message that Paul teaches "is the power of God for salvation"?

I've been in other settings as well, where the gospel is preached as caring for the poor or intervening within our culture to bring justice to those who are powerless to do so. In other words, in these settings

7

the gospel isn't a message but rather the act of liberating the poor and oppressed from their circumstances. Is *that* the gospel? Before you dismiss the notion of the gospel as action rather than message, consider Peter's admonition to the church in 1 Peter 4:17: "For it is time for judgment to begin at the household of God; and if it begins with us, what will be the outcome for those who do not obey the gospel of God?" Still, I would contend that Peter's train of thought leads to the conclusion that someone who genuinely embraces the gospel message by faith should see their life progressively transformed to reflect the character of the gospel message's central person: Jesus Christ.

It may seem that I'm belaboring a point most Christians would be in agreement over, but if this is what you're thinking, try polling the folks at your church with the question, "What is the gospel?"—and enjoy the variety of answers you get!

Fortunately Paul, at least in a sense, gives us the answer to the question "What is the gospel?" in 1 Corinthians 15. In verse 1 of that chapter, he writes to the Corinthians, "Now I would remind you, brothers, of the gospel I preached to you, which you received, in which you stand. . . ." Once again the Scriptures present the gospel as a message that can be preached and received by those who hear it. Paul perhaps indicates here an answer to one of the two vital questions asked above—What does it mean to believe this message that brings salvation to the hearer?—when he says "which you received, in which you stand," or as the New Living Translation reads, "You welcomed it then, *and you still stand firm in it.*" The nature of belief that brings salvation to the hearer is a belief in the gospel which perseveres—a point Paul adds some muscle to in what he says next.

In verse 2, still speaking of the gospel, Paul goes on to say, "and by which *you are being saved, if you hold fast* to the word I preached to you—unless you believed in vain." Again, the implication in Paul's caution to the Corinthians here is that a failure to "hold fast" to the gospel is an indication of vain belief, whereas genuine belief results in ongoing change in the life of the hearer ("you are *being* saved"). The gospel is a message "by which you are being saved." In other words, the gospel "is the power of God for salvation," and that salvation is an ongoing experience of being saved in the life of the believer, just as Peter indicates in his phrase "obey the gospel of God." It would seem then that the nature of belief that brings salvation to the hearer is a belief in the gospel that perseveres and brings the life change over time, marking the believer as one who is "being saved."

And from that affirmation of the gospel as a message which brings ongoing and enduring salvation, Paul then reminds the Corinthians of the message. In verses 3–5 he writes, "For I delivered to you as of first importance what I also received: that Christ died for our sins in accordance with the Scriptures, that he was buried, that he was raised on the third day in accordance with the Scriptures, and that he appeared to Cephas, then to the twelve." So then, here is the gospel in its simplest yet still complete form. We are sinners, and in accordance with the Scriptures Christ died for our sins, was buried, and was resurrected on the third day. Paul then goes on to state that these details of what Christ accomplished according to the gospel, most notably his resurrection, was thoroughly attested to by eyewitnesses, most of whom were still alive at the time of Paul's writing to the Corinthians.

It's a very simple message but it comes loaded with implicit detail. The gospel doesn't say that just anyone died for our sins, was buried, and rose again. *Christ* did these things, and he did so "in accordance with the Scriptures." *It is the marvelous wonder of the person and work of Jesus Christ, and the marvelous wonder of the biblical account that both prophesies and depicts Christ's person and work, that is the focus of this book.* The gospel truly is a redemption and restoration *story*. In fact, it is the greatest story ever told, and unlike many great stories it isn't fictional; it's true!

The gospel message that "is the power of God for salvation" is simple in terms of the content we embrace through faith, and so are saved. In the chapters ahead, I'm not making the case that perfect knowledge of the biblical account from Genesis to Revelation and how it interrelates to reveal Christ and his work is necessary for someone to come to saving faith in Jesus Christ. Again, I'm not trying to make the case that the gospel is a complex message. But the Scriptures teach repeatedly that the gospel is the power of God to both save us and to keep saving us through the course of his work of bringing us to salvation, for "he who *began* a good work in you will *bring it to completion* at the day of Jesus Christ," as Paul teaches in Philippians 1:6. And that "day of Jesus Christ" is the day our Lord Jesus returns to resurrect his church, bringing God's work of salvation in us to its Christlike completion. As John says in 1 John 3:2, "Beloved, we are God's children now, and what we will be has not yet appeared; but we know that when he appears we shall be like him." Paul gave us his concise statement of the gospel in 1 Corinthians 15:3–4, but he also explained the gospel from Romans 1:16 to the end of chapter 11—more than ten chapters! And as he did, he relied upon the Scriptures' account of this redemption and restoration story from the beginning of creation to the end of history, and into eternity.

My heart and purpose in writing this book is not to engage academic arguments over the content of the gospel message and the nature of saving faith. My heart and purpose is a pastor's heart and purpose: to share the amazing gospel story in its dizzying breadth and depth, "in accordance with the Scriptures," to the people I dearly love. These are my sisters and brothers in Christ who have been my eternal joy and family at every stop along the way where the Lord has assigned me and my family. And at every stop along the way, a constant has been a lack of understanding about this amazing gospel story.

Some years back, I was teaching a young married class of believers at our church in south Georgia. We had just begun studying 1 Peter and we were in chapter 1, verses 3–5, where Peter writes "Blessed be the God and Father of our Lord Jesus Christ! According to his great mercy, he has caused us to be born again to a living hope through the resurrection of Jesus Christ from the dead, to an inheritance that is imperishable, undefiled, and unfading, kept in heaven for you, who by God's power are being guarded through faith for a salvation ready to be revealed in the last time." When we got to the part where Peter teaches about our inheritance as an unshakeable salvation that God is preserving for us by his power, "ready to be revealed in the last time," the discussion took an interesting turn. Peter is referring to our future resurrection here—the culmination of our salvation; the second exodus of God's people of all time, through their resurrection from the dead, into the eternity he has promised and prepared for us "in accordance with the Scriptures." To a person, this class of twenty-five people or so had no idea what I was talking about. How could this happen? How could followers of Jesus Christ be so deficient in their understanding of their own salvation? I'm not sure, but it's happened before.

In 1 Corinthians 15, Paul was reemphasizing the gospel to the Corinthians because of his concern over their belief in the resurrection—not Christ's resurrection, but *their* resurrection. Paul makes the case to the Corinthians that if there is no hope in a future resurrection to eternal life for them, their faith is futile. And it's futile because it fails to understand the fullness of the gospel as it unfolds for us in the Bible "in accordance with the Scriptures."

As the author of Hebrews describes it, our salvation is "such a great salvation" (Hebrews 2:3)—one in which we receive an everlasting "kingdom that cannot be shaken" (Hebrews 12:28). The gospel is an amazing story which is both rooted in and forms the very heart of the biblical story. It is a story of the work of our great God and Savior Jesus Christ, which has the power to bring the very life of Jesus Christ to the life of a believer, and to grip us with his infinite vigor for the hope of his coming kingdom. The story ends with his work of redemption and restoration complete. It ends with "such a great salvation" fully and eternally realized in the eternal lives of believers, with a new heaven and a new earth. As the Father declares in Revelation 21:7 (NASB), "He who overcomes will inherit these things." It's a glorious ending and a marvelous journey through the Scriptures in getting there.

Turn the page, enjoy the journey, and rejoice along the way that this inheritance is "an inheritance that is imperishable, undefiled, and unfading, kept in heaven for you, who by God's power are being guarded through faith for a salvation ready to be revealed in the last time."

Chapter 1

In the Beginning
(Genesis 1:1–2:3)

The journey begins with this amazing gospel story unfolding where every good story begins: in the beginning! The Bible is often referred to as the greatest story ever told, and not coincidentally it follows the classic plot line of great stories. Genesis 1 and 2 begin with the introduction of the hero and main characters in the ideal setting that reflects the hero's purpose and will. In fact, in the very first line of the Bible, the hero—God himself—is introduced as the very creator of the setting, along with the main characters: the men and women he created in his image after his likeness. And so, as you would do with any great story, it's time for introductions. It's time to get to know God, man, and woman.

They say first impressions matter. A husband likely remembers when he first met his wife, and vice versa. Yet, because marriage proposals are typically more intentional than first encounters, a woman likely very clearly remembers how her husband proposed. I suspect she was paying attention when he popped the question. People pay attention when introductions and proposals are significant. In light of that, if God has intentionally chosen to reveal himself to us, and the very first line of his message begins an introduction of himself in a very particular way, shouldn't we pay attention to it and attach a particular significance to it? The emcee approaches the microphone and announces, "Ladies and gentlemen, introducing someone truly significant!"

God: The Sovereign Creator of His Very Good Creation

In twenty-first-century American Christian circles, any mention of a focus on Genesis 1 and 2 often leads to the presumption that a lengthy discussion on modern science and the Scriptures is about to ensue. For the record, I take Genesis 1 and 2 literally—that God created the heavens and the earth in six days and rested from that creative work on the seventh day. For whatever it's worth, I have a Bachelor of Science degree and four master's degrees and I can make an intellectually satisfying argument for this position, which I'd be happy to share with you over coffee some time.

But my convictions over Genesis 1 and 2 are not grounded in intellectually satisfying arguments from science in light of the Scriptures; they're grounded in the fact that the God who introduces himself in Genesis 1 and 2 knows me by name and has proven himself to be faithful and true to his word at every turn, even when I have been faithless. As the psalmist says, "Oh, taste and see that the LORD is good" (Psalm 34:8)! And because he makes himself known to us as the God who is good all the time we can, by faith, hold to what the author of Hebrews affirms: "By faith we understand that the universe was created by the word of God, so that what is seen was not made out of things that are visible" (Hebrews 11:3). Therefore, in order to get to know God in this time of introduction, focus on what Genesis 1 focuses on: what God teaches about himself through his work of creation, beginning with the fact that he created everything.

This is emphasized in Genesis 1:1 to 2:1 like bookends to God's introduction of himself. In 1:1 he "created the heavens and the earth" and in 2:1, "Thus the heavens and the earth were finished." As if to emphasize that this work of creation included everything, Genesis 2:1

concludes "and all the host of them." And because God created every-thing, an inference to be made from this text is that God transcends his creation.

But what does it mean to say, "God transcends his creation"? The word "transcend" means "to rise above or go beyond the limits of" something.[1] God exists and has eternally existed apart from his creation. He is not a created being and is therefore not subject to or bound by the limits of his creation—the limits of time and space and the laws he designed into his creation. Therefore, as he chooses to, he can act within his creation supernaturally. In other words, he can act within creation in ways which are impossible for any other being, most notably in the very act of creation itself.

The Hebrew word translated "create" in Genesis 1:1 is only used of God in the Scriptures,[2] and coming back to a verse quoted earlier—Hebrews 11:3—God did the impossible in creation. He brought the entire universe into being from nothing for "By faith we understand that the universe was created by the word of God, so that *what is seen was not made out of things that are visible.*" This connects back to Genesis 1 and 2 to affirm another dimension of God's nature: God's word alone has the power to bring his perfect will to pass. In Genesis 1:3, the scripture reads "*And God said,* 'Let there be light,' and there was light."

Read through your copy of the Scripture and notice how this refrain "And God said," followed by the result, is repeated throughout Genesis 1. In verse 6, God speaks and an entire atmosphere is created. In verse 9, God speaks and the entire surface of the earth takes form. In verse 11, God speaks and all the earth's dry land blossoms with vegetation. In verse 14, God speaks and the void of the entire cosmos is filled with celestial bodies which serve the purpose of ordering life on the earth. In verse 20, God speaks and the sea and sky are filled with life. In verse 24, God speaks and all the living creatures which inhabit the land come forth from the earth. Finally, in verse 26, God speaks to himself and creates humanity. Just his word alone has the power to speak the entire universe into existence; therefore, everything must be under his control. And if that is so, then God is sovereign over all the universe.

Think of the significance of this to the original audience for the book of Genesis. Moses is the inspired human author of Genesis writing to God's people Israel. These people lived for four hundred years as slaves in Egypt, a nation which took everything in God's creation and did what the apostle Paul warned in Romans 1:25 that the faithless of every generation do: "they exchanged the truth about God for a lie and worshiped and served the creature rather than the Creator." The Egyptians made gods out of the beasts of the field, the creatures of the sea and sky, and the celestial bodies in the heavens—and as the Scriptures teach, the people of Israel learned from their idolatrous oppressors well and were prone to follow their example. One of God's messages to his people Israel in Genesis 1 wasn't how light from stars a billion light years away could be seen at the time of creation (and remember, he transcends his creation). It is that those very stars are created entities that function according to his good will and purpose, and as such, they possess none of the power the Egyptians attributed to them as they made them into gods. In essence, one of the messages the Lord gives to his people Israel in Genesis 1 is, "Don't fear their gods and don't worship them! Rather, set yourself apart from them and worship Me alone." Even in the principle of setting ourselves apart as his people, God teaches us about himself through his work of creation—that our sovereign God makes true distinctions.

Separating one thing from another occurs throughout Genesis 1. The waters are separated from dry land and also separated from each other within the atmosphere. But most notably, in 1:4, the text says "And God saw that the light was *good*. And God separated the light from the darkness." The first time God characterizes his work as "good" is with the creation of light, and he immediately separates it from the darkness. Throughout the Scriptures, light and darkness represent the distinction between good and evil; therefore, it is not coincidence that it is also the first distinction God makes in all the Scriptures.

Our sovereign God alone is the One who can make the true distinction between good and evil, and his people of all ages are called to faithfully follow him by embracing his distinctions as our most deeply held convictions.

But there's one more very significant point about our sovereign God which Genesis 1 introduces: God's creative work brings about *redemption*. Once more, Genesis 1:2 reads *"The earth was without form and void."* This phrase, *"without form and void,"* is fascinating. In the Hebrew, it reads וָבֹהוּ תֹהוּ (remember to read it from right to left!) which essentially means that it was good for nothing. It was a wasteland. In its beginning form, God begins with an earth that is useless in its form and devoid of any worthy content. You might say that he starts with an earth that, left to itself, is a thoroughly lost cause. But if you read Genesis 1 and the first few verses of Genesis 2 very carefully, you'll notice that God, in a very orderly fashion by the way, transforms the formless wasteland of earth in Genesis 1:3–13 into a useful and fruitful form he calls good. And in giving it this form, he prepares the earth to receive the fruitful and multiplying life he subsequently creates to fill the empty void.

God begins with an empty wasteland in Genesis 1:2, and by his creative handiwork, redeems it entirely as Genesis 2:2–3 indicates: "And on the seventh day God finished his work that he had done, and he rested on the seventh day from all his work that he had done. So God blessed the seventh day and made it holy, because on it God rested from all his work that he had done in creation." Summing up Genesis 1:1–2:3 in light of God's redemptive work, theologian Allen Ross writes, "God's creative work brings about redemption. It begins by taking a formless and void waste place and ends with a marvelous creation at rest, blessed and sanctified by God. *The pattern of God's redemptive work first begins to unfold at creation*" (emphasis mine).[3]

There is much more to learn about God from Genesis 1 and 2, but in the interest of time, let's shift the introduction to the other main characters of the greatest story ever told: the men and women created in his image, after his likeness.

Humanity: The Representatives of the Sovereign God

Genesis 1:26–28 states:

> Then God said, "Let us make man in our image, after our likeness. And let them have dominion over the fish of the sea and over the birds of the heavens and over the livestock and over all the earth and over every creeping thing that creeps on the earth."
>
> So God created man in his own image,
>
> in the image of God he created him;
>
> male and female he created them.
>
> And God blessed them. And God said to them, "Be fruitful and multiply and fill the earth and subdue it, and have dominion over the fish of the sea and over the birds of the heavens and over every living thing that moves on the earth."

Mindful of the role humanity plays in God's story, there are two things that merit our particular focus. First, humanity is the pinnacle of God's creative work. Notice the distinction in how man is created. Up to this point in the text, God speaks and brings things into being. But in creating humanity, God speaks to himself: "Let *us* make." This may be the first allusion to God as Trinity in the Scriptures, but even if the "us" has another reference, God stops to keep an audience with himself before creating humanity, and this argument for humanity's exalted place in God's created order grows stronger when we see that humanity is unique in all creation as God's chosen representatives in it.

The Scripture says we are made in his image, after his likeness. It is profoundly difficult to nail down exactly what this says about our nature. Some scholars take this to mean that since God is Spirit, being made in his image and likeness must entail the fact that we possess a spirit. But this is difficult to hold to in light of Genesis 9:6, where God commands Noah and his sons after the flood, "Whoever sheds *the blood* of man, by man shall *his blood* be shed, *for God made man in his own image.*" God makes the fact that humans are his image-bearers the basis for capital punishment here, because of violence inflicted upon a person's *body.* This very strongly points to the conviction that God created us as whole persons and that it is as whole persons that we are made in his image and likeness. Given the context of Genesis 1:26–28, this means we have been given the capacity to visibly represent the invisible God in his creation as beings with a *physical, moral,* and *ethical* capacity to do so. Let's consider a physical capacity first.

After declaring to himself in Genesis 1:26, "Let us make man in our image, after our likeness," God then gives humanity the responsibility to exercise dominion over the world. This is clearly a responsibility that practically demands our physical presence, as the command to "Be fruitful and multiply and fill the earth" in verse 28 further suggests.

But with this physical presence, we are also charged to exercise authority in a way *morally* and *ethically* pleasing to God. In verses 26 and 28, God granted us dominion—authority to rule—over the earth and all that is in it. The sovereign God would not have granted us dominion without the expectation that it would be exercised according to his will and purpose. Remember that it is a very good creation (at this point) and that in verse 28, God commanded humanity to *"subdue"* it. In other words, God is commanding humanity to subject the earth to the actions of their will, but if God's creation is very good and humanity was commanded to subdue it, then *the actions of humanity's will to subdue the earth must entail the kind of stewardship which maintains a very good creation.*

To sum up, then, I take our role as image-bearers to mean that we were created as whole persons with the capacity and expectation that we represent God's will and purpose, faithfully exercising his ruling authority he has delegated to us to tend to his creation—a role which is unique to humanity as the pinnacle of his creation.

So then, having given some consideration to the opening scene in God's story, how does this apply to us today? *What is the significance for us today in light of the Genesis 1 and 2 account in God's story?*

To begin with, remember that this is the *ideal*. The biblical story, like every great story patterned after it, will soon run into the villain and the conflict which attacks and distorts the hero's ideal setting. But from that point on, the biblical story and the narrative of this book will roll steadily toward God's work of redemption and restoration. *The gospel is ultimately the account about God's work of restoring the ideal we see in Genesis 1 and 2 to an even greater height, and what God has done on our behalf to save us for that restored ideal in eternity.* The final chapters in this book will show that God has saved us to rule and reign with him forever as his representatives—as completed new creations in Christ—in the meaningful existence of tending to his creation once again made very good in a whole new way.

A second point of significance for us *now* is to embrace the Sovereign God of creation. God's introduction of himself as creator to his people Israel in Genesis 1 and 2 is just as relevant to his people the church today. In Genesis 1 and 2 we learn that God created everything. As Hebrews 11:3 teaches, take this by faith and don't fall—pun intended—for worldly alternative explanations. He is sovereign and transcends his creation. He is not limited in his good intentions toward us by a world that often limits us in troubling and despairing ways. His word has unlimited power; it can be trusted, and he can be trusted to act according to his word. In Matthew 5:5 Jesus says, "Blessed are the meek, for they shall inherit the earth." The meek are those who rest in God's power rather than trust in their own, and Jesus' promise is that the meek will ultimately inherit this earth. God's word is powerful and perfect in its timing, and can be trusted all the time. The meek know this and live it.

We also learn from Genesis 1 and 2 that our God makes true distinctions, most notably between light and darkness/good and evil. Hold fast to the distinctions God makes, lest we find ourselves under the stern warning of Isaiah 5:20: "Woe to those who call evil good and good evil, *who put darkness for light and light for darkness.*"

Lastly, and maybe most wonderfully, these first two chapters of the Scriptures teach us that God is a God of redemption. He is about the business of taking what is lost and broken and making it very good, blessing it, and making it holy. Or, as Paul says in Philippians 1:6, "he who began a good work in you will bring it to completion at the day of Jesus Christ." With respect to ourselves, a final point of significance for us today is to represent the Sovereign God of creation.

We know the whole story, so we also know that we are fallen and marred image-bearers. Nonetheless, we are new creations in Christ and God is about the work of transforming us into the character of the perfect image bearer: our Lord Jesus Christ. And as such, our role in this story is as the "advance party." We go into a world made hostile toward God—as we'll see in the next chapter—bearing the gospel message that can save men and women *from* the consequences of their role in the rebellion against God and *for* the role he longs for each of us to have with him in eternity. As Paul says in 2 Corinthians 5:20, "we are ambassadors for Christ, God making his appeal through us. We implore you on behalf of Christ, be reconciled to God." As ambassadors for the King of kings, we represent him physically, morally, and ethically wherever we go upon this earth, bearing his gospel message. We must bear it as his messengers in a way that faithfully represents the One who sends us.

Chapter 2

The Calamity of the Fall
(Genesis 3:1–19)

In his book *Finishing Strong*, Steve Farrar writes, "Sin will take you farther than you want to go, keep you longer than you want to stay, and cost you more than you're willing to pay."[4] This quote clearly points to one aspect of sin: it has an appeal at first glance which tends to blind us to its long-term consequences—which greatly outweigh its initial appeal. But one interesting thing about this quote is subtle: the notion that *sin itself is personified as something that has power and a wicked motive*. This is actually consistent with what the Bible teaches about sin, and this aspect of sin will be fleshed out more in the next chapter with the story of Cain and Abel in Genesis 4.

But in Genesis 3, sin enters into God's very good creation through Adam and Eve as an invitation—an invitation for them to declare independence from their Creator and submit to an alternative authority which sin, crafty in its ways, disguises as an invitation to be their own boss. This is the heart of temptation: an invitation to rebel against God. On the front end, sin is an easy master because "it's all about me." In the end, though, as Paul teaches so thoroughly in Romans 5–7, sin binds us to its power as its slaves, and having so bound us, leads us to death.

Sin has a motive. Sin has an agenda. And as we follow the action driven by this motive and agenda in Genesis 3, we'll begin with God's plan for man that Satan, sin personified, seeks to destroy, and then move to the response of man to that plan with this response's lasting and disastrous consequences to humanity. But even in the midst of this great calamity—of the pinnacle of his creation rebelling against him—Scripture reveals the gracious response of God, in a promise that brings hope despite our rebellion. But there is no rebellion—no declaration of independence—without a prerequisite submission to, and dependence upon, an authority. The great lie in every rebellion is that, once it begins, either no authority or a better authority will rise to take its place. Adam and Eve embraced this great lie, as an act of rebellion against God and his plan for humanity.

God's Plan for Man (Genesis 2)

God's introduction of himself, his creation, and man as the pinnacle of his creation established the ideal setting of his very good creation. In Genesis 2, God's plan for man in this very good creation unfolds in greater detail. God has fashioned his creation so that humanity would have every good thing for his own provision and in 2:15, God charges man *"to work it and keep it."* God also charges man with the privilege of naming every living creature God has made. This is significant, as the act of naming something in the Scriptures indicates the authority of the one who names over the things named.

God also blesses man with the gift of woman and blesses them both with the divine institution of marriage in 2:23–25. In these verses, we see a portrait of an intimate relationship of husband and wife that is unique in all creation. The very names given to them indicate this relationship was designed for the two to complete one another. Genesis 2 then gives us a picture of man and woman in intimate relationship with one another and with God, unashamed and serving him in meaningful work in his creation while exercising dominion over it—and in so doing, enjoying the blissful dependence upon their Creator who has lavished the fullness of his blessing upon them. And all this is given with one condition, as Genesis 2:16–17 indicates: **"And the LORD God commanded the man,** *saying, 'You may surely eat of every tree of the garden, but of the tree of the knowledge of good and evil you shall not eat, for in the day that you eat of it you shall surely die.'"* The tension rises: How will humanity respond to a life of meaningful service, blissful dependence, and simple obedience?

The Response of Humanity (Genesis 3:1–7)

The account in Genesis 3:1–7 states:

> Now the serpent was more crafty than any other beast of the field that the LORD God had made.
>
> He said to the woman, "Did God actually say, 'You shall not eat of any tree in the garden'?" And the woman said to the serpent, "We may eat of the fruit of the trees in the garden, but God said, 'You shall not eat of the fruit of the tree that is in the midst of the garden, neither shall you touch it, lest you die.'" But the serpent said to the woman, "You will not surely die. For God knows that when you eat of it your eyes will be opened, and *you will be like God,* knowing good and evil." So when the woman saw that the tree was good for food, and that it was a delight to the eyes, and that the tree was to be desired to make one wise, she took of its fruit and ate, and she also gave some to her husband who was with her, and he ate. Then the eyes of both were opened, and they knew that they were naked. And they sewed fig leaves together and made themselves loincloths.

The prime ingredients for any good rebellion is the temptation of an alternative. In this passage, temptation comes through the serpent's proposition of independence in verses 1–5. In verse 1 we're introduced to the serpent, a beast of the field. The creature here is clearly a serpent, but just the simple fact that the creature speaks with humans indicates that the serpent is something more. In Revelation 12:9 and 20:2, he's plainly identified as Satan, and although Genesis 3 offers no explanation, Scripture teaches that Satan is a fallen angel with powers commensurate with the ability to either appear as a serpent or to possess an actual serpent and present himself through it. Either way, the creature speaking in verse 1 is to be taken by the reader as Satan, who is introduced through a conversation he strikes up by questioning God's command.

In appearing in the form of a serpent, Satan comes as a creature under Adam and Eve's dominion, as Genesis 1 teaches. The implication of this is that, by deceiving them into submitting to his will, Satan will usurp man's dominion. In the fall, then, Satan gains the dominion given to man. This is why we often see the Scriptures refer to Satan as the ruler of this world and why Satan, in his temptation of Jesus in the wilderness in Matthew 4:8, offers Jesus "all the kingdoms of the world and their glory" and Jesus doesn't dispute his authority to do so.

One of the terrible consequences of the fall is that humanity, apart from being delivered from the power of sin through saving faith in God, now exercises his dominion under the authority of Satan. Satan is, after all, in the rebellion business, and the rebellion begins in verse 1 as he says "Did God actually say . . . ?" Satan begins by suggesting the possibility that God's command is open to question, and he begins by distorting the facts of what God prohibited as he inaccurately recalls God's command as "You shall not eat of *any* tree in the garden" when God had actually said in Genesis 2:16–17, "You may surely eat of *every* tree of the garden" except "the tree of the knowledge of good and evil." *Satan distorts God's command by eliminating the freedom he gave in it and, in its place, universally applies the prohibition*. Almost as if he already knows the inclination of Eve's heart, he reveals how Eve has distorted God's command.

Verses 2–3 read "And the woman said to the serpent, '*We may eat* of the fruit of the trees in the garden, but God said, "You shall not eat of the fruit of the tree that is in the midst of the garden, *neither shall you touch it, lest you die*."'" Notice what Eve does here. She engages in a threefold distortion of God's command. She says "We may eat" whereas God said "You may surely eat." Like Satan, Eve diminishes the sense of freedom in what they were permitted to do, whereas God was emphatic in assuring them of that freedom. Like Satan, she expands the prohibitions in God's command when she says "neither shall you touch it" with respect to the tree; God spoke nothing of such a prohibition. Finally, she weakens the penalty for disobedience in saying "lest you die" (suggesting probability) whereas God expressed certainty with "you shall surely die."

And so, just as Satan tapped into Eve's apparent issues with God's prohibitions, he then shifts in verse 4 to the matter of consequences—an opening Eve gave him in sharing her own perspective. Satan denies the consequences of disobeying God's command: "You will not surely die." Take note of what Satan has to work with heading into verse 5. In twisting God's word—and particularly, the prohibition in his command—Satan reveals in Eve that *she perceives God has restricted her freedom in ways he has not, and has prohibited her in ways beyond what he truly has.* Furthermore, she reveals to Satan that *she has diminished the consequences of disobedience to the Lord God in her own mind.* God's command is the focus of this temptation, and Satan has drawn out Eve's doubt over every dimension of his command. Satan is now ready to attack God directly, as he attributes false motives to God in giving his command.

In verse 5 Satan says, "God knows that when you eat of it your eyes will be opened, and you will be like God, knowing good and evil." Satan's explanation of God's motive in giving the command in Genesis 2 was that God was jealous and was holding them back from their *true* destiny, which verse 5 indicates was to be like him—one they could arrive at if they cut the cord and took matters into their own hands. Independence Day! Come join the rebellion! And bring a friend!

As we know, Eve succumbed to the temptation and enlisted her husband in the act. In verse 6 Eve now saw the prohibited tree through her own eyes as good, delightful, and desirous. She saw and she took, and as the end of verse 6 indicates, "she also gave some to her husband who was with her, and he ate." Adam was there the entire time, quiet and willing. You get the sense he didn't even need the temptation, as if he'd already convinced himself this was the right thing to do. And now, remember what Steve Farrar said: "Sin will take you farther than you want to go, keep you longer than you want to stay, and cost you more than you're willing to pay."

Despite what the serpent promises, the man and woman suffer the consequences of their desire for independence. Satan's promise of sin was that they would be like God, but in verse 7 their knowledge of good and evil leaves them naked and ashamed, and in their independence, left to provide for themselves out of their own resources: pathetic, fig-leaf loincloths. And as the remainder of Genesis 3 reveals, the cost of their sin was more than any of us could pay.

The Five Calamities of the Fall (Genesis 3:8–13, 16–19)

The sin introduced into God's very good creation through Adam and Eve affects everything, as Genesis 3:8–13 and 16–19 shows:

> And they heard the sound of the LORD God walking in the garden in the cool of the day, and the man and his wife hid themselves from the presence of the LORD God among the trees of the garden. But the LORD God called to the man and said to him, "Where are you?" And he said, "I heard the sound of you in the garden, and I was afraid, because I was naked, and I hid myself." He said, "Who told you that you were naked? Have you eaten of the tree of which I commanded you not to eat?" The man said, "The woman whom you gave to be with me, she gave me fruit of the tree, and I ate." Then the LORD God said to the woman, "What is this that you have done?" The woman said, "The serpent deceived me, and I ate." . . .

> To the woman he said, "I will surely multiply your pain in childbearing; in pain you shall bring forth children. Your desire shall be contrary to your husband, but he shall rule over you."

> And to Adam he said, "Because you have listened to the voice of your wife and have eaten of the tree of which I commanded

you, 'You shall not eat of it,' cursed is the ground because of you; in pain you shall eat of it all the days of your life; thorns and thistles it shall bring forth for you; and you shall eat the plants of the field. By the sweat of your face you shall eat bread, till you return to the ground, for out of it you were taken; for you are dust, and to dust you shall return."

These calamities stand out in the text, beginning with the fact that *creation was subjected to a curse of futility*. In verses 17–18, the ground that was intended to be a superabundant source of blessing to humanity has become cursed because of sin, bringing forth thorns and thistles. In Romans 8:20–21, Paul teaches us that this curse encompassed all of creation: "For the creation was subjected to futility, not willingly, but because of him who subjected it, in hope that the creation itself will be set free from its bondage to corruption." And humanity doesn't escape the effects of this bondage to corruption.

Humanity's relationship with creation became dominated by pain and toil. In verses 17–19, Adam's reality is that whatever comes forth from the earth will come only through pain and the sweat of his brow, as a cost of rebellion and independence. But it's not simply humanity's relationship with creation that has been distorted.

Humanity's relationship, one to another, became dominated by adversity. Notice in verses 12–13 that Adam and Eve's relationship digresses into the blame game. They both confess to their sin but only after seeking to shift blame: Adam upon his wife and Eve upon Satan. But the price of sin paid in broken human relationships is not temporary but enduring, as verse 16 shows: "To the woman he said, 'I will surely multiply your pain in childbearing; in pain you shall bring forth children. Your desire shall be contrary to your husband, but he shall rule over you.'" Sin brings institutional adversity into the most intimate of human relationships. Notice in verse 17 that as God describes the cursed nature of Adam's relationship to creation, he explains the root cause for this as, "Because you have listened to the voice of your wife." The one created as his helper—the one created to complete him—is now the cause for his grief. Not that he needed a cause, for he is cause enough unto himself.

A person's relationship with one's self was broken. In verse 10, Adam is introduced to fear in its unhealthy sense. Fear is an emotion which devours the living soul we were created to be. By implication, all of the unhealthy devouring emotions entered into humanity at the fall. And in verse 16, we see that woman, who was promised the blessing in Genesis 1 of multiplying God's image-bearers to fill the earth and rule it, now sees that promise of life within herself become a promise of multiplying pain through childbirth. But there is one final, and most significant, calamity of the fall.

Humanity's relationship with God was broken and, therefore, life was lost. In verses 8–11, Adam and Eve hide from God's presence in fear over the sin of their rebellion—their disobedience to his *one command*. The relationship now broken, the consequence God assured Adam and Eve of should they disobey—"you shall *surely* die"—is also assured in verse 19 as Adam is told his new destiny: "By the sweat of your face you shall eat bread, till you return to the ground, for out of it you were taken; for you are dust, and to dust you shall return."

As you move through chapter 3 toward the end, verses 22–24 teach one essential fact: eternal life was part of the blessing of creation, but in Adam and Eve's fallen state, eternal life in intimate relationship with God was no longer possible, and so, God would no longer permit it . . . *on Satan's rebellious and sinful terms*, terms the Scriptures teach and we have all embraced.

In sum, Genesis 3 is a profoundly tragic story, and as I preached through this chapter on one occasion, I was moved to try and capture the nature of the tragedy through the following poem.

No measures can we take
When the earth shudders and shakes
When the levee breaks
And the floods rage
There is no escape

No fruit is born
From seed in famine's dust
Hands set to a rusted till
Still plough if you will
Still plough if you must

A guilty tormented heart
Did I blame you?
Did you blame the devil?
I confess in part yet
Sometimes I can't tell between the two

So you and I joined together
A one-flesh duel
At your worst a thorn, at my worst a tyrant
The wedding song goes silent
As the band plays the fool

My God, my God, why have you forsaken me?
It must have been you, to be sure
For now your image I can plainly see
Looks like me no more
So from your bonds, I am set free

Free to notice everything's broken
Free to reject you even exist
Free to cherish a thought I've spoken
That you could ever even be missed

Free to live with any conviction

Free to suffer and dare to proclaim

"I'm free to live without contradiction

That the One I reject is the One who I blame."

Free to go my own way and stumble

Free to ignore the still small call

"I oppose the proud but give grace to the humble

And pride comes before the fall"

So then, as Genesis 3 comes to a close, we see that God bars the way to eternal life for fallen man—with the implication that God, and God alone, must make the way back to eternal life with him possible. But take hope, for in the midst of the despair, hopelessness, and calamity of Genesis 3, God is neither silent nor indifferent.

The Response of God (Genesis 3:14–15)

The Lord God said to the serpent, "Because you have done this, cursed are you above all livestock and above all beasts of the field; on your belly you shall go, and dust you shall eat all the days of your life. I will put enmity between you and the woman, and between your offspring and her offspring; he shall bruise your head, and you shall bruise his heel."

Verses 14–15 present a dual curse: in verse 14 a curse upon the serpent as a beast, and in verse 15 a curse upon Satan. We are at the point in the biblical story where the villain has attacked the hero's plans, introducing conflict into the story. The conflict is hard to fully discern until you get to God's elaboration of the conflict between two individuals in verse 15: "he shall bruise your head, and you shall bruise his heel." From the earliest days of the church this verse has been taken to describe Christ's

ultimate victory over Satan on our behalf, to win for us the redemption that can bring us back into an eternal life relationship with God.
Satan will bruise the heel of the offspring of a woman—the miraculously virgin-born son of Mary—in that Christ will suffer death but not
the finality of it, as his resurrection proved. But Christ will bruise Satan's
head: an image meant to convey a final victory.

Here, in the midst of our rebellion against God—our rejection of
him—God shows us that there is hope in his provision for us still. God
would make a way for us to be restored to an eternal life that we all
choose to abandon because, like Adam and Eve, we are all willful participants in the rebellion. In Romans 3:23 the scripture teaches *"all have
sinned and fall short* of the glory of God," and in Ephesians 2:3 that we
are all *"by nature* children of wrath." These points are impressed upon us
well by the following story.

A prominent twentieth-century author on the topic of preaching,
Haddon Robinson, writes in his book *Biblical Preaching*:

> The law can prompt us to sin. I am told that several years ago
> a high-rise hotel was built in Galveston, Texas, overlooking the
> Gulf of Mexico. In fact, they sank pilings into the gulf and built
> the structure out over the water. When the hotel was about to
> have its grand opening, someone thought, *What if people decide to
> fish out the hotel windows?* So they placed signs in the hotel rooms,
> "No fishing out the hotel windows." Many people ignored the
> signs, however, and it created a difficult problem. Lines got
> snarled. People in the dining room saw fish flapping against the
> picture windows. The manager of the hotel solved it all by tak-
> ing down those little signs. No one checks into a hotel room
> thinking about fishing out of the windows. The law, although
> well-intentioned, created the problem.[5]

In a similar vein, Paul writes in Romans 7:7, "What then shall we
say? That the law is sin? By no means! Yet if it had not been for the law,

I would not have known sin. For I would not have known what it is to covet if the law had not said, 'You shall not covet.'" But Satan seized what was already in a proud and rebellious heart by tapping into that heart's proud rejection of God's command, as Paul continues in verse 8: "But sin, seizing an opportunity through the commandment, produced in me all kinds of covetousness." This is our nature and we know it. And the point for all of us in this part of the story is to not shift blame or deny the consequences of death and eternal separation from God. The point is for us to embrace the truth that we all share in Adam's sin and guilt, and to embrace what God has done to restore us to himself on the only terms possible: his terms.

The Hero and the rest of the main characters have now been introduced. We started with the Hero's perfect initial conditions, and we've seen how the villain has seemingly succeeded in foiling the Hero's purposes and plan. Now this redemption and restoration story shifts gears, as the rising conflict between the hero and the villain play out.

Chapter 3

Grace Abounds in the Great Divide (Genesis 4:1–16)

In Genesis 4:7 God warned Cain, "sin is crouching at the door. Its desire is contrary to you, but you must rule over it." Sounds predatory!

I once read a story a Christian songwriter shared that illustrates this insidious nature of sin. She had shared with a close colleague about a great deal she found on a brand-new laptop on an internet auction site. Her friend responded with the caution about things that are too good to be true. When she assured him she was confident in the offer, he repeated his caution to her—an insistence which annoyed her, as she assured him she wasn't born yesterday.

She made the transaction, only to quickly discover she had been scammed out of $1,300. She felt foolish, and in her foolish pride she avoided her friend in every way so as to avoid the "I told you so" moment. Over time, she grew to resent this friend who simply sought to guard her from harm. In her own mind, he became "that jerk." Eventually though, a mutual obligation brought them together on an airline flight, during which her friend inquired about how the great deal on the new laptop turned out. Cornered, she was faced with the choice to save face and lie or make the confession her pride led her to dread. She chose to confess and quickly rediscovered that "the jerk" was once again her teasing but deeply empathetic buddy. "Sin is crouching at the door." It was clearly crouching in this woman's life, but she ultimately chose not to give it the deadly foothold it desired.

In the previous chapter we saw how sin brought great divides into the reality of human existence, but we also saw that God's grace abounds in the great divide as he immediately foreshadowed his plan to rescue us. The terrible consequences for Adam, Eve, and all humanity remain as a result of sin, but clues in Genesis 3 such as Adam and Eve's imperfect confessions and their acceptance of God's sacrifice on their behalf to replace their fig-leaf loincloths point to the way of the faithful that we'll see develop in Genesis 4: a way that restores relationship with God, preserving the faithful for an eternity God will ultimately bring to pass at the end of human history, reversing the devastation we brought upon creation and ourselves because of our sin. We've already seen how the villain—Satan—attacked the hero's plan, introducing conflict into God's ideal setting, and this conflict moves us into the rising action of the biblical story. This conflict happens immediately in the biblical narrative, between Cain and Abel in Genesis 4. Cain represents the way of the faithless—a man who chose to follow Satan's way by choosing to remain in rebellion against God, and so came into a direct clash with God and his people.

This chapter approaches Genesis 4 topically, considering these two ways—the ways of the faithful and the faithless—in light of the marks of character which distinguish and divide them, and in light of the distinguishing marks of God's character that bridge this great divide. Satan has launched his first attack, and it was highly destructive as it corrupted all of creation with sin now "crouching at the door" in the life of every man and woman, waiting to seize the opportunity to do further damage. But in Genesis 4, God's image-bearers still have a choice, and in turning to him by faith God's grace abounds toward them in this battle. The effects of his grace can be seen in the way of the faithful.

The Way of the Faithful

The first indication of this way found in Genesis 4 is in the hope and trust of Eve. In verse 1 the scripture reads, "Now Adam knew Eve his wife, and she conceived and bore Cain, saying, 'I have gotten a man with the help of the LORD.'" Recalling the last chapter, God's gracious promise of hope in Genesis 3:15 was that a conflict would play out in human history between the offspring of a woman and the offspring of Satan, and this conflict ultimately plays out at two levels in the Scriptures' account of history. One level is between the division in humanity of the followers of God and the followers of Satan, the ruler of this world. At the individual level, God's representative in the conflict, who will ultimately bring victory over Satan, is the offspring of a woman, Jesus Christ.

At this point, Eve does not have this specific understanding of God's redemptive plan, but she does have his promise, and she trusts in it . . . and hopes in it. In Genesis 4:1, it may be that her joy is grounded in the hope that God's promised redeemer and champion who will deliver humanity from the curse of our sin would come through her. This possible interpretation becomes stronger in verse 25 of chapter 4 as Eve, following the birth of her third son Seth, says, "God has appointed for me another offspring instead of Abel, for Cain killed him." Eve still holds to this hope of a redeemer and recognizes the faith distinction between Cain and Abel, as she now attaches that hope to the birth of Seth rather than Cain as a replacement for her faithful son Abel: a son who reveals to us further the way of the faithful through his actions and attitude.

Abel is the first hero of faith mentioned in Hebrews 11: "By faith Abel offered to God a more acceptable sacrifice than Cain, through which he was commended as righteous, God commending him by accepting his gifts. And through his faith, though he died, he still speaks" (Hebrews 11:4). It was faith in God that drove Abel's actions and attitude in his offering, but what made them more acceptable? In Genesis 4:3–5, the scripture states, "In the course of time Cain brought to the LORD an offering of the fruit of the ground, and Abel also brought of the firstborn of his flock and of their fat portions. And the LORD had regard for Abel and his offering, but for Cain and his offering he had no regard." There's clearly a contrast between the two offerings, and the contrast gives us the insight we need. Both Cain and Abel's offerings and attitudes seem to conform to their perspectives toward God. Abel took great care to ensure he was offering his best. Cain appears somewhat indifferent, as if he was simply discharging a duty.

As Hebrews 11:4 indicates, Abel's faith example still teaches us. It teaches us that, even from the very beginning of human history, genuine faith is demonstrated by giving God our best with an attitude that longs to do so. But it is this very faith-driven action and attitude that provokes the conflict between the faithful and the faithless. The power of sin wielded by the ruler of this world leaves its marks on all of creation, but particularly in the way of the faithless.

The Way of the Faithless

We see these marks of the power of sin in Cain. Cain, the first human born to a woman, becomes human history's first murderer, showing us the speed and intensity in which sin's effects escalated in our history— an escalation we see in Genesis 4 and which continues exponentially to the time of the flood, as we'll see in the next chapter. In Cain, sin moves through Satan's willing rebel; and sin's target in this battle is the well-being of the faithful, an assault fueled by the fact that the faithless become angry at God's approval of the faithful.

In Genesis 4:1–5, God regarded Abel's offering and rejected Cain's. It was not a result that should have surprised Cain, as his indifference revealed his lack of regard for the Lord, but nonetheless, as verse 5 concludes, "So Cain was very angry, and his face fell." Cain felt he was worthy of God's commendation without having to meet God's expectations, and in the "me, myself and I" world that sin promotes, Cain is angry over being unfavorably evaluated and disinterested in being corrected. A timeless mark of the character of the way of the faithless is in how they disregard warnings against sin.

In verses 6–8 of Genesis 4, God challenges Cain over his reaction, and in verse 7 God essentially tells Cain that he wasn't commended or accepted because he didn't do what was right. The implication is that

Cain has chosen his sinful course but could choose otherwise; the danger in his present choice is that "sin is crouching at the door. Its desire is contrary to you, but you must rule over it." *In other words, by choosing sin—by choosing to rebel against God's will and his ways—Cain is inviting a powerful force into his life which desires to do him harm and subject him to its authority.* The wording of the Hebrew text in verse 7—and in particular, potential meanings for the word "crouching"—may indicate that sin, as personified here, is being referred to as if it is "some sort of demonic entity."[6] God is warning Cain of the dangerous forces his choices are inviting into his life and urging him to turn from them. But instead of engaging with God on the matter, in verse 8 Cain flatly disregards God's warning and instead directs his attention toward his murderous intentions. In a clear work of premeditation, he speaks to his brother for the purpose of luring him to an isolated setting, then rises up against him and kills him. So, having acted upon his sinful choices, Cain then demonstrates that the faithless deny responsibility for the consequences of their sin.

Verse 9 of Genesis 4 reads "Then the LORD said to Cain, 'Where is Abel your brother?' He said, 'I do not know; am I my brother's keeper?'" Just as God questioned Adam and Eve in Genesis 3 to elicit a confession, he does so here with Cain. But unlike Adam and Eve, Cain not only denies his crime but does so with an attitude. It's almost as if Cain is saying to God, "If you think he needs a keeper, why don't you do it?" But as verses 10–14 show, denying responsibility does not keep us from accountability. Even then, Cain's reaction to God's judgment against him reveals that the faithless reject accountability for their sinful deeds.

In Genesis 3, five calamities from the fall come as a result of sin entering into creation through Adam and Eve's sin, and in verses 10–16 of Genesis 4, at least four of these calamities come into play in Cain's life in a way that represents a stunning escalation over Genesis 3. For example, in verse 10 God's reacts to *the sin-driven break in human relationships,* saying to Cain "What have you done?" But unlike in Genesis 3, this reaction is not just against broken thoughts and emotions but a reaction to broken thoughts and emotions moving to the finality of murder. And in verses 11–12, *the break between man and creation* intensifies, as that which was rendered difficult in Genesis 3—obtaining fruit from the ground—is now made even harder for Cain.

Finally, in verses 13–14, *the internal breakdown of humanity* intensifies as Cain, in contrast to Adam and Eve, demonstrates no repentance nor any desire (or need) for forgiveness. Instead, he complains about his punishment—which graciously does not include his own death—and part of his complaint at the end of verse 14 reveals a striking, self-centered hypocrisy as Cain tells the Lord, "I shall be a fugitive and a wanderer on the earth, and whoever finds me will kill me." The man who has just killed his own brother in cold blood and copped an attitude with God for being questioned about it is now complaining that he might meet the same fate at the hands of another. There is not a hint of a sense of accountability in Cain's response, and as verse 16 indicates, Cain thus experiences a fourth calamity of the fall: *separation from the presence of the Lord,* as "Cain went away from the presence of the LORD and settled in the land of Nod, east of Eden."

If you put the whole text together in terms of the character sketch of a faithless man named Cain, here's the picture it paints: he worships halfheartedly; angrily sulks when called to account; engages in cantankerous outbursts against God; commits the most heinous of crimes out of pride, anger, and resentment without showing any remorse, repentance, or need for forgiveness; and he shows no gratitude for God's grace. He is a man of all-consuming self-interest and self-pity. He is the consummate portrait of someone who has opened the door to the crouching power of sin, invited it in, and barred the door to God's gracious intervention in his life. But in the great divide sin makes exponentially greater in Genesis 4, grace abounds all the more.

God's Grace Abounds in the Great Divide

One of the great fallacies in the understanding of many Christians is that the Old Testament is all about law and judgment while the New Testament is all about grace and forgiveness. The fact of the matter is that each—law, judgment, grace, and forgiveness—abound in both testaments. Furthermore, you cannot begin to fully understand God's grace until you see it in the Old Testament, because it appears there in such abounding ways in the face of the Scriptures' most vivid portrayals of the deepest of human depravity.

Cain was profoundly depraved and rejected God with the highest of hands, yet God shows us from the very beginning of human history that his grace always abounds. Notice in Genesis 4 that, despite Cain's indifference towards God, the Lord clearly invited Cain into opportunities to seek him through worship. Despite Cain's murderous intention so deeply seated that even a warning from God was thoroughly ineffective, God still intervenes in Cain's life to warn him anyway. And despite having murdered anyway, even under these circumstances, and having demonstrated a complete lack of repentance, God still spares his life. And in verse 15, God demonstrably intervenes on Cain's behalf to protect him from the very consequences he so coldheartedly brought upon his brother Abel.

As we move through these Old Testament passages we'll be considering, if we pick up nothing else from them, I pray we pick up a deep and unshakeable realization that God's grace is an overflowing and abundant grace, even to the point of making you shake your head in joyful wonder over how gracious he is! And so, with grace coming to the fore here, a few points of application for us in light of that grace are in order.

Walk in Light of God's Grace

In Titus 2:11–12, Paul writes "the *grace* of God has appeared, bringing salvation for all people, *training us* to renounce ungodliness and worldly passions, and to live self-controlled, upright, and godly lives *in the present age*." Again, contrary to what is often believed about God's grace, grace doesn't ignore our sin. Rather, God's grace responds to sin with a redemptive purpose, seeking to turn us from sin's deadly course. And it *is* a deadly course. In Romans 1, Paul reveals how it works in the life of a person who, like Cain, persists in rejecting God's gracious overtures to them. Three times in five verses, Paul shows a progression with the phrase "God gave them up." He "gave them up" to "the lusts of their hearts," then "to dishonorable passions," and finally to "a debased mind." There comes a time when God ceases to reach out to those who oppose him, giving them over to their own way: the way of the faithless. But that action of God is not our determination to make. We are called to be avenues of his grace to the Cains in our lives. And so, in following God's example with Cain, consider these three ways in which God's grace was extended to Cain, beginning with this exhortation: never cease to extend grace's invitation.

God knew Cain's heart better than Cain knew Cain's heart, yet God extended an invitation to Cain to worship him. We may grow weary of the constant rejection or indifference our friends, neighbors, loved ones, family members, or other companions show toward the things of God. You invite them to church, with no response. Likewise, to a Bible study. You share the gospel and they could care less. You intervene in their lives to meet their needs as God calls his people to do, yet having tasted and seen the goodness of God, they still chase after the ways of the world. Regardless, we need to take heart that in the marvelous mystery of how grace turns people to God, he is the one who produces the results; we are simply called to be faithful in these things. But discouragement understandably comes, and in those moments, take heart: God knows our discouragement.

If you have someone in your life who breaks your heart because your outreach to them is not only rejected but angrily opposed, don't forget Genesis 4. Even God's immediate presence and directly spoken word was ineffective in turning Cain away from his dreadful and sinful course. Even when God gave Cain an opportunity to come clean, Cain responded to God with disdain. I suspect many of you have gone through this same routine with people you dearly love. God knows your pain and heartache, and his all-sufficient grace extends to us as well in these trials with our lost and wandering loved ones. And when they wander beyond your reach, know that sometimes grace casts us out as a last recourse.

This may have been what Paul was telling the Corinthian church in 1 Corinthians 5:5 when he commanded them, regarding an unrepentant, sexually immoral man, "to deliver this man to Satan for the destruction of the flesh, so that his spirit may be saved in the day of the Lord." Cain was cast from God's presence, but God cast a form of protection over him to preserve his life; perhaps to buy him time under the dominion of Satan as Paul taught—to suffer consequences that might break sin's hold upon him and cause him, like the prodigal son, to turn back to God.

Grace doesn't ignore sin, and sometimes even brings its consequences heavy to bear as a last recourse. When this happens with someone you know and love, recognize that it may be God's grace in action and pray for them. Pray for their preservation and pray that, in the midst of their preservation, they might come to understand as the prodigal son did when he said "Father, I have sinned against heaven and before you. I am no longer worthy to be called your son" (Luke 15:18–19). We know from the Scriptures that when a heart becomes so humbled, broken, and contrite, and calls out to God, grace comes running. And as we continue this redemption and restoration story, grace remains front and center.

Chapter 4

Grace Rescues the Righteous from Wrath (Genesis 6:1–22)

Wickedness is the prevailing feature in human nature. In all of us. As products of an American culture which embraces, as an article of faith, that we're all inherently good, this assertion of wickedness rubs us the wrong way. We're likely to say "That's not me!"

A World War II vet who became a pastor after the war once reflected on his experience in liberating Jewish prisoners from the Dachau concentration camp. The horrors he witnessed brought him to a sustained sense of rage. He was consumed by the absolute evil of it all until he witnessed a fellow soldier named Chuck escort twelve Nazi prison guards to a boxcar for an interrogation but then immediately executed them instead. When Chuck emerged from the boxcar he smiled maliciously and said, "They all tried to run away." No disciplinary action was taken and the pastor recalled he had a nauseating fear that the captain might call on him to escort the next group of guards—and an even more dread fear that if he did, he might do the same as Chuck. He said, "The beast that was within those guards was also within me."[7]

Kay Warren had a similar insight when she visited Rwanda after the 1994 genocide there: "The first time I visited Rwanda, I went looking for monsters. . . . I had heard about the 1994 genocide that had left one million people dead—tortured, raped, viciously murdered—and somehow

I thought it would be easy to spot the perpetrators. I naïvely assumed I would be able to look men and women in the eyes and tell if they had been involved. I was full of self-righteous judgment. What I found left me puzzled, confused, and ultimately frightened. Instead of finding leering, menacing creatures, I met men and women who looked and behaved a lot like me."[8]

Wickedness is an innate feature of our fallen humanity. In this chapter, we'll focus primarily on Genesis 6. In so doing, we're going to see that our wickedness invites God's judgment and wrath, and drives us to our greatest need: God's grace—a grace that rescues us from our nature, and so rescues us from the wrath our nature is deserving of.

Humanity's Wickedness Invites God's Judgment and Wrath

And it's an open invitation because, once again, wickedness is the prevailing feature in human nature. It is the feature of our nature that is present in every person in every age. It's an assertion we love to question, but as the above stories show there is ample evidence to support this assertion in our human experience. So then, we shouldn't be surprised that there is ample evidence in the Scriptures' account of the human experience as well, beginning with the truth that this assertion is evident in its near-universal outcome.

Verses 1–2 of Genesis 6 read "When man began to multiply on the face of the land and daughters were born to them, the sons of God saw that the daughters of man were attractive. And they took as their wives any they chose." Two key groups—the sons of God and the daughters of man—need to be identified here. You may be familiar with the range of interpretations on verse 2. One which is popular is that the sons of God are angelic beings who interbred with women to produce a pre-flood super humanity described in Genesis 6:4. But the problem with this interpretation is that no explicit mention of angels has been made in Genesis up to this point and Genesis 6 is focused exclusively on judgment against humanity, not angels. Another problem with this interpretation is that there is a flow in the message of Genesis 4–5 that gives a very simple, different, and compelling explanation—one that doesn't involve speculation about angels.

Remember from Genesis 4 how Abel and Cain represented the two categories of humanity: the way of the faithful and the way of the faithless. In the second half of Genesis 4, Cain's lineage reproduces his character of worldly people, culminating in his sixth-generation descendant Lamech who tells his two wives in 4:23–24: "Adah and Zillah, hear my voice; you wives of Lamech, listen to what I say: I have killed a man for wounding me, a young man for striking me. If Cain's revenge is sevenfold, then Lamech's is seventy-sevenfold." Cain's legacy in a fallen world is that he reproduced a character in the culture who was even more wicked and violent than himself. Cain and his lineage represented the ways of humanity and humanity's fallen nature.

In contrast, if you follow along beginning in verse 25 of chapter 4, there Eve acknowledges the ways of God reflected in Abel rather than Cain, and sees Seth as Abel's replacement. From that point on, Seth's lineage represents the ways of God reflected in the lives of the faithful. In 4:26, Seth's son Enosh is born and "At that time people began to call upon the name of the LORD." As you continue to read Seth's lineage in chapter 5, there is no description of the worldly ways that proliferate in Cain's line, and in 5:22, Seth's descendant Enoch walked with God and never experienced death because God took him.

Continuing to 5:28–32, Seth's descendant Lamech (not the Lamech of Genesis 4) fathers Noah, a man described in Genesis 6 as a righteous man who walked with God. But also notice Lamech's faith in Genesis 5:28, as he says of Noah "Out of the ground that the LORD has cursed, this one shall bring us relief from our work and from the painful toil of our hands." Just as Eve demonstrated faith in God in her hope that Seth might be the Lord's promised man to deliver humanity from the curse of the fall, so Lamech had the same faithful hope that Noah might be the one the Lord promised. The narrative in Genesis 4–5 presents the two branches of humanity: those who faithfully follow the ways of God, and those who follow the worldly ways of man.

I believe the sons of God and the daughters of man represent those two branches of humanity, and like Eve in the garden, the sons of God liked what they saw and took it, with the result that we see in Genesis 6:4: "the sons of God came in to the daughters of man and they bore children to them." God's people joined themselves to the ways of the world, producing a worldwide culture of worldly, mighty men of renown, just as we see in Cain's lineage. Cain's wicked lineage overwhelmingly prevailed as the representatives of humanity's true nature. This assertion is evident in God's striving against it.

In the NIV, verse 3 reads "Then the LORD said, 'My Spirit will not contend with humans forever, for they are mortal; their days will be a hundred and twenty years.'" Note here that God is not reducing human lifespan to 120 years; he is setting a time limit on his Spirit's work of contending with human wickedness. But the very fact that the Spirit of God must contend against us is evidence of the force with which human nature's wickedness prevails. But there is also evidence of its force in the very heart of God; this assertion is also evident in God's grieving over it.

In verse 5, the text describes the breadth and depth of humanity's wickedness, so much so that verse 6 states "And the LORD regretted that he had made man on the earth, and it grieved him to his heart." The prevailing wickedness in human nature is so great that it brings God to withdraw his Spirit from contending with it and moves his heart to grief and regret. In a very real way then, God's response to our wickedness is primarily grounded in who he is. Wickedness invites God's judgment and wrath, and we discover the justifiable merits of his judgment and wrath in Genesis 6 in at least two ways.

To begin with, God's judgment and wrath against us is *merited on the basis of his assessment*. Verses 5 and 12 begin with "The Lord saw" and "God saw." In verse 5, he specifically saw what God alone can see and assess: "that the wickedness of man was great in the earth, and that every intention of the thoughts of his heart was only evil continually." In verses 11–13, God's assessment continues along similar lines. He saw that the earth was totally corrupt and filled with violence—not unlike, by the way, the description in Genesis 4 of Cain's sixth-generation descendant Lamech, a man of unparalleled violence. God is a God of love, mercy, compassion, and kindness, but he would not be faithful to any of those aspects of his nature if he failed to act against world-wide wickedness. We do violence to the nature of God when we fail, as Paul teaches in Romans 12:19, to "leave room for the wrath of God, for it is written, 'Vengeance is Mine, I will repay,' says the Lord." Judgment and wrath are necessary aspects of God's nature, and so God's judgment and wrath is also affirmed as *merited on the basis of his actions*. As 2 Peter 3:7–9 (NASB) teaches:

> But by his word the present heavens and earth are being reserved for fire, kept for the day of judgment and destruction of ungodly men.

> But do not let this one fact escape your notice, beloved, that with the Lord one day is like a thousand years, and a thousand years like one day. The Lord is not slow about his promise, as some count slowness, but is patient toward you, not wishing for any to perish but for all to come to repentance.

God is slow to act in judgment, and Peter is addressing the human tendency to conclude that God therefore never acts in judgment. In Matthew 24:38–39, Jesus taught that this was the mindset of those in Noah's world as he says "For as in those days before the flood they were eating and drinking, marrying and giving in marriage, until the day when Noah entered the ark, and they were unaware until the flood came and swept them all away." The flood was a complete, worldwide judgment, as Genesis 6:17 states: "For behold, I will bring a flood of waters upon the earth to destroy all flesh in which is the breath of life under heaven. Everything that is on the earth shall die." In other words, everyone on the earth merited judgment. Our prevailing wickedness makes this a prevailing truth today, pointing us to our greatest hope and our greatest need.

God's Grace Alone Rescues Humanity

You might stop and say "What about Noah? Isn't he the exception?" Start in Genesis 6:8 in search of the answer to that question. After God declares his intention to blot out every living thing from the face of the land in verse 7, the text states in 6:8, "But Noah found *favor* in the eyes of the LORD." This word "favor" is the translation of the Hebrew word for "grace." Before the descriptions of Noah's righteous character in the text, the Scriptures teach that Noah first experienced God's grace. In the marvelous mystery of God's grace, even righteous Noah would be the victim of this flood apart from God's grace, because God's grace is unmerited and effective in transforming human nature.

By its very definition, God's grace is unmerited—even for Noah. In the sequence we see throughout the Scriptures, God's grace precedes everything. And for those who respond to it by faith and faith alone, God's Spirit effectively works to redeem our wicked nature, as we see in Noah in verse 9: "Noah was a *righteous* man, blameless in his generation. Noah walked with God." The word "righteous" here is always used in Genesis to describe persons who stand in contrast with the wicked because they abide by God's standards. In other words, this is not addressing a righteousness imputed or credited to Noah, but indicating a true assessment of Noah's character. And so, in the redemption sequence that we see throughout the Scriptures, God's grace precedes everything, and by faith transforms us, and the evidence of that transforming grace is obedience to God's will: the fruit of his effective grace.

Let's put ourselves in Noah's shoes. Surrounded by a world that is totally corrupt and filled with violence and indifference toward God, Noah alone—with the possible exception of his family—is walking with God. God tells Noah, "A worldwide flood is coming as a judgment; you've got about a hundred years. Build this ark I'm describing to you that will hold a representative pair of every living thing, an ark that's about half the size of a modern aircraft carrier." And in 6:22 we see, "Noah did this; he did all that God commanded him." God's grace bore the fruit of real righteousness in Noah's life, a life of radical obedience. This is the pattern of real redemption the Scriptures affirm from beginning to end—a testimony of his effective work in our lives that serves to give us the assurance he longs for us to have.

God's Grace Rescues the Righteous from Wrath

Noah was delivered from the worldwide destruction of the flood. Lot was delivered from the destruction of Sodom. Rahab was delivered from the destruction of Jericho. Daniel was delivered from the destruction of Judah. In 2 Peter 2, Peter describes God's deliverance of Noah and Lot from wrath and concludes that if God rescued these men, even as he acted in judgment, "then the Lord knows how to rescue the godly from trials, and to keep the unrighteous under punishment until the day of judgment" (2 Peter 2:9). The Scriptures teach that a final day of judgment is yet to come, and that God's grace rescues the righteous from wrath. For believers, there are two applications of this point that are particularly relevant.

The first is to *live mindful of his coming wrath*. In Genesis 6, the great decline in the moral character of the world came because the sons of God saw that the daughters of man were attractive, and so they took any wives they chose. The world degraded into moral chaos, leading to a time of great judgment, because the way of the faithful was diluted into nothing through their embrace of the ways of the world. In a very ominous statement alluding to his future coming in judgment, Jesus says in Luke 18:8, "Nevertheless, when the Son of Man comes, will he find faith on earth?" Likewise, speaking of the time preceding his return, Jesus says in Matthew 24:12, "And because lawlessness will be increased, the love of many will grow cold." God's acts of judgment throughout the Scriptures teach us patterns of how he will act at the time of final judgment. The flood, Sodom and Gomorrah, Jericho, the destruction of Judah, and the like teach us that God, when he chooses to act in judgment, acts swiftly and terribly, and that he does so at points in time when his ways are thoroughly abandoned over a prolonged period of time. Like Noah, should we find ourselves in the time leading up to the final judgment, living as God's truly faithful people will demand that we persevere in obedience in a time when we will be a very distinct minority in a godless world, where lawlessness will increase and the love of many will grow cold. The time to start living and keep living such a life of radical obedience is today; and so, *live confident that God will rescue his people from his coming wrath.*

Noah was delivered through wrath. Lot was delivered from wrath. In both cases, God protected the righteous from the consequences of his wrath. In 1 Thessalonians 5, Paul challenges the Thessalonian church to the deepest level of commitment to their Christian walk in light of the coming final judgment and then encourages them: "For God has not destined us for wrath, but to obtain salvation through our Lord Jesus Christ" (1 Thessalonians 5:9). Can God be trusted to deliver us?

At this point in our journey through this story of redemption and restoration, the attack on God's plan for creation has risen to a climax. Evil has seemingly won, reducing the odds in the battle down to Noah versus the world. But despite the circumstances, Noah lives a life of radical obedience that reflects a deep trust in God and a confident conviction that the battle is truly no contest. God's grace, moving effectively through Noah, delivered him through the flood. And from Noah, through his son Shem, a line of descendants came which included Abraham, Isaac, Jacob, Judah, David . . . and the Son of David, Jesus Christ. Lamech's hope that his son Noah might be God's promised deliverer was true, in a sense. It just took a while!

Despite the endless opposition of the world and unseen powers and principalities, God's path to our final redemption and restoration has not missed a beat, even through a worldwide flood. Unlike your stock market investments, his past history is indicative of his future performance. Trust him.

Chapter 5

A Race Divided Is Grace Provided
(Genesis 10–12)

There was once a CEO of a Fortune 500 company who pulled into a service station to get gas. He went inside to pay, and when he came out he noticed his wife engaged in a deep discussion with the station attendant. It turned out she knew him. In fact, back in high school before she met her eventual husband, she used to date this man. The CEO got in the car and the two drove in silence. Feeling pretty good about himself, the CEO broke the silence saying, "I bet I know what you were thinking. I bet you were thinking you're glad you married a Fortune 500 CEO, and not some service station attendant."

His wife quickly replied "No, I was thinking that if I'd married him, he'd be a Fortune 500 CEO and you'd be a service station attendant!"[9]

Pride has a way of distorting our perspective, and it's accompanied by some particular attitudes and emotions. It tends to go hand-in-hand with the attitude, "I am both successful and the source of my success." But in a way that was illustrated wonderfully by this CEO's wife, pride also tends to go hand-in-hand with an underlying fear: "I'm just a fraud, and what awaits me is not inevitable successes, but rather that humbling moment which reveals me to be the fraud I truly am."

We tend to think of our needs from the perspective of the good things God can bring us by his goodness and grace. But as an old friend and Christian brother of mine once shared with me after a very difficult period in his life, he was thankful for how God, by his grace, kept him from the worst of himself. If you're a follower of Jesus Christ and pride is a sin problem in your life, expect that grace will meet your need through that humbling moment when grace separates you from your proud attitude and any basis for pride in the first place. This is a principle of grace working on an individual level, but what's interesting about the biblical text from parts of Genesis 10–12 is that this principle of God's grace works corporately on a grand scale as well.

God's work of redemption and restoration takes an interesting twist in these three chapters from Genesis, as he reveals a new entity in his plan for redemption: the nations. In God's plan, the nations serve to purposefully divide humanity, to keep us from the worst of ourselves while at the same time creating the civilizational framework of nations through which God will bring eternal blessing. In his hymn "We've a Story to Tell to the Nations," H. Ernest Nichol writes "We've a song to be sung to the nations that shall lift their hearts to the Lord. A song that shall conquer evil, and shatter the spear and the sword." In God's plan of redemption, the nations' hearts will be lifted and man's evil will be overcome. This dichotomy of purpose toward the nations is evident in how God brings the nations into being.

The Nations: Part of God's Plan for Our Redemption

Genesis 10 explains how the nations originated from the three sons of Noah, culminating in verse 32: "These are the clans of the sons of Noah, according to their genealogies, in their nations, and from these *the nations spread abroad on the earth* after the flood." Chapter 10 teaches us how the nations came to be spread across the earth, but in verses 1–9 of chapter 11, we learn more details as to how. More importantly, we also learn why: the nations are a redemptive measure to restrain the sinfulness of humanity.

We typically think of unity as a good thing, and rightly so, but when unity serves the purpose of rebelling against God's will in order to exalt the will of man—i.e., corporate pride—there are few things more destructive. And in verses 1–4 of chapter 11, we discover that left unrestrained, humanity embraces the destructiveness of pride.

In Genesis 9:1, after the flood, God renews his creation mandate from Genesis 1 as he commands Noah, "Be fruitful and multiply and fill the earth." But by the time humanity gets to verses 1–4 of chapter 11, the entire human race is unified in rebellion against this command. With a common language, they gather in one place—with every intention of staying in one place. The key question is "Why?" Two points from verse 4 give us a pretty clear picture of why—pride and fear: "Then they said, 'Come, let us build ourselves a city and a tower *with its top in the heavens*, and let us *make a name for ourselves*, *lest we be dispersed* over the face of the whole earth.'"

We see humanity's pride, not unlike what we still see today, in its building projects. To build a tower that reaches the heavens, and the desire to make a name for themselves, reveals not only humanity's desire to put themselves in God's place, but also humanity's hubris in thinking it's possible.

But this picture of unity in God-supplanting pride is driven just as much by a sense of fear: "Lest we be dispersed over the face of the whole earth." Ironically, unified humanity sees itself as a God-substitute, yet fears the loss of control, security, and blessing they perceive would come by heeding God's command. *Loss of control, security, and blessing are timeless motivations for rejecting God's will and way, and rejecting God's will and way are timeless explanations for human tragedy and sorrow.* When these motivations are embraced by people on a grand scale, tragedy and sorrow are embraced on a grand scale. Therefore, in Genesis 11:5–9 God divided humanity into nations, to restrain us from the sin of pride.

Humanity sought to undertake its greatest work of reaching the heavens, yet in a bit of divine sarcasm, verse 5 reduces our best down to the insignificance our best truly represents, as "the LORD came down to see the city and the tower." At the end of Genesis 3, after Adam and Eve had acquired the knowledge of good and evil on their own terms, God, by his grace, barred humanity from access to the eternal life he created us to have—because such a life lived out of our sinful nature, apart from relationship with him, would become an eternal horror. In a very similar way, in Genesis 11:6, God saw humanity, unified in their proud pursuit of control, security, and blessing, as an act of rebellion against his will, as only the beginning of their misfortunes—misfortunes he clearly indicates will escalate. As he says at the end of verse 6, "nothing that they propose to do will now be impossible for them." And so in verses 7–9, God divides them by denying their ability to communicate with one another, and then brings about what he commanded them to do in Genesis 9:1 as he disperses them "over the face of all the earth." And so, coming back to verse 32 of chapter 10, this is how and why the nations came to be "spread abroad on the earth." The creation of the nations was an act of God's common grace, to keep us from the worst of what our corporate pride could bring.

But there's one more dimension of common grace the nations bring that I think is important for us to know: the nations restrain humanity from the proliferation of wickedness. Remember that the creation of nations follows relatively quickly after the pre-flood history of humanity living without this civilizational structure: no nations and no government. And as we saw in the previous chapter, this resulted in such widespread evil that God acted in worldwide judgment through the flood. In Romans 13:1–4, Paul writes:

> Let every person be subject to the governing authorities. For there is no authority except from God, and *those that exist have been instituted by God.* Therefore, whoever resists the authorities resists what God has appointed, and those who resist will incur judgment. For r*ulers are not a terror to good conduct, but to bad.* Would you have no fear of the one who is in authority? Then do what is good, and you will receive his approval, for *he is God's servant for your good.* But if you do wrong, be afraid, for he does not bear the sword in vain. For *he is the servant of God, an avenger who carries out God's wrath on the wrongdoer.*

With the nations came the ruling authorities, which Paul teaches have been instituted by God as an agent of his wrath against wickedness. I don't think it's an unreasonable inference to make that God, longing to bring salvation to fallen humanity by coming into the world at the right time through Jesus Christ, established the nations and their ruling authorities as an act of common grace to temper the wickedness of humanity, so that his final act of worldwide judgment could be deferred long enough for his plan of redemption to fully unfold. In other words, the nations emerge in God's redemptive plan as a central feature of that plan. But the nations represent more than just God's common grace as a restraining force. The Scriptures also teach that the nations are an object of God's work of eternal redemption, perhaps most notably in the relationship between the nations and the church.

If the church is Christ's chosen vehicle to spread the gospel, the nations are the roads the church travels. This is evident in the very clear connection Christ makes between the church and the nations in his Great Commission to the church in Matthew 28:19: "Go therefore and make disciples of all nations." The nations not only restrain the sinful impulses of fallen humanity, but also serve as the impetus for the church to go and do the work of being fruitful and multiplying, filling the earth with redeemed humanity. And not just for the present time: redeemed nations will endure as a feature of eternal civilization!

This is a fascinating, mysterious, and wonderful point: it seems we will still live as a civilization of nations in eternity. In Revelation 21:24–26, John describes the New Jerusalem on the new earth and says of the city, "By its light will *the nations* walk, and *the kings of the earth* will bring their glory into it, and its gates will never be shut by day—and there will be no night there. They will bring into it the glory and the honor of *the nations.*" But God's story of how he uses the nations to bring about redemption doesn't stop here—there is one nation which stands out in his plan.

A Great Nation to Bring Eternal Blessing to All the Nations

Genesis 12:1–3 reads, "Now the LORD said to Abram, 'Go from your country and your kindred and your father's house to the land that I will show you. And *I will make of you a great nation*, and I will bless you and make your name great, so that you will be a blessing. I will bless those who bless you, and him who dishonors you I will curse, and in you *all the families of the earth shall be blessed*.'" Up to chapter 10 of Genesis, God's plan of redemption primarily focused on his promise from Genesis 3 to bring humanity's deliverer—the one who would save us from the consequences of our sin—as a male offspring of a woman. After this, through Genesis 9, the message focused on the two branches of humanity as demonstrated by representative individuals: the way of the faithful who embraced both God's promised deliverer and the need for him, and the way of the faithless who embraced worldly ways. So then, the redemption story focused on individuals and remained somewhat vague about the true and full nature of the promised deliverer. But in Genesis 10–12 we see two notable turns in God's redemption story, beginning with the fact that God's plan of redemption to the nations broadens in scope.

We've already looked at this from the perspective of the nations' restraining role, and we've glimpsed as well at how the nations themselves are also objects of redemption. But in Genesis 12:3, God tells Abram "in you all the families of the earth shall be blessed." The word "families" here is the Hebrew word for "clan"; in Genesis 10 we saw that all the nations of the earth originated as clans descended from the sons of Noah. In essence, the great turn in God's plan of redemption that we encounter in Genesis 10–12 is the true scope of God's plan. His eyes are on individuals, yes, but individuals seen through the lens of the full diversity of humanity— every tribe, tongue, and nation. And it is from a great nation which arises from Abraham's descendants that the blessing to the nations comes, as seen in 12:2 where God promises Abram "And I will make of you a great nation." The role of nations virtually explodes onto the scene of God's story of redemption and restoration in Genesis 10–12.

And yet, just as we see his word broaden our salvation perspective, at the same time God's work of redemption narrows in scope to one man. In Galatians 3, Paul teaches that God's promise to Abram that the nations would be blessed through him was God preaching "the gospel beforehand to Abraham" (v. 8), and that this blessing would come through Abraham's seed—i.e., the offspring of Abraham's descendant: the promised Savior Jesus Christ. The lens in the biblical story is sharpening the focus on God's promised deliver. Our rescuer. Our Savior.

The biblical story this book seeks to trace continues to follow the rising action, and as it does we'll notice that this connection between the larger community of the great nation God will make of Abraham and the narrow focus on the Savior who will come from this nation will go hand in hand. But how does a message predominantly about the nations and a great nation possibly apply to us?

Learn the Lessons of a Race Divided and Grace Provided!

We actually started a first point of application at the beginning of the chapter: humanity was divided into nations as God's gracious response to the dangers brought on by corporate pride and fear. Through the nations, God precluded humanity from arriving at the worst potential that pride and fear could bring. As a first point of application, I want to encourage you to yield to the obstacles God casts before our pride. Allow me to illustrate this with a personal story.

Back in 2001, while on staff as an instructor at the Air Force's Air University, I served as director for the flagship course in the Air Force's master's program, for officers moving into command and staff positions. When I was given the position, I immediately selected a team of officers and led them through a complete redesign of the course. As the time approached to teach the course, I was literally brimming with pride of authorship when it came time to prepare the entire faculty to teach it.

During one of those faculty prep sessions, an instructor sitting in the back of the room asked a loaded question of the member of my team who was instructing—a question that called into question the value of the particular part of the course being presented. In retrospect, it was a great and helpful question; but as this future pastor who was, at the time, a very regenerate fighter pilot with a vibrant workplace ministry to many people who were present at this session, I immediately verbally cut down the guy in the back row right at the knees. I used choice words skillfully that thoroughly and publicly humiliated a fellow officer. It was a great testimony.

If you've never had the Holy Spirit set his hand on you so heavily that you felt your soul would be crushed while he's causing the words "You're wrong!" to ring in your mind, good! (That's an experience that is good to avoid.) I immediately stood up and pleaded for that guy's forgiveness—not because I wanted to but because I didn't think I'd survive if I didn't!

I could have precluded it all by not doing some things, but most notably by not placing my confidence solely in my abilities, and by not putting my trust in the fact that my future well-being depended on being a "somebody" who did the kinds of things the right people would notice. This guy made a great point with his question, and in my pride I attacked him out of the fear that he had made a great point with his question. Please feel free to hold this story against me as the Lord leads you.

But first, let me close with one other point of application: yield to God's call to redeem the nations.

I don't want to belabor this point; I simply want to make an important conceptual connection between the text we've looked at in this chapter (selections from Genesis 10–12) and the church's mission. In Acts 1:8, Jesus tells his disciples, "you will be my witnesses in Jerusalem and in all Judea and Samaria, and to the end of the earth." He's telling them that the commission to take the gospel to the nations will follow a progression—a progression that will happen by heeding his command to "go!" Most church folks love the idyllic picture of the church in the early chapters of Acts but miss the fact that the church, by lingering in Jerusalem, was being disobedient to this command to go.

In this chapter's text, God scattered humanity when they failed to heed his command to fill the earth; to go. In Acts, he does the exact same thing. Stephen's calling and ministry in Acts 6–7 provokes a violent response against him and then, as Acts 8:1 records, "there arose on that day a great persecution against the church in Jerusalem, and they were all scattered throughout the regions of Judea and Samaria." God's work of redemption and restoration in this world involves his command to his people to go. A church that resists its responsibility to its Jerusalem, its Judea and Samaria, and the ends of the earth is a church that may find itself brought to obedience the hard way. God has promised an amazing eternity to us as his people, the church, and we ought to live in light of that—as we'll see in the next chapter.

Chapter 6

Live in Light of God's Future Promises
(Exodus 19:1–6)

On the third new moon after the people of Israel had gone out of the land of Egypt, on that day they came into the wilderness of Sinai. They set out from Rephidim and came into the wilderness of Sinai, and they encamped in the wilderness. There Israel encamped before the mountain, while Moses went up to God. The LORD called to him out of the mountain, saying, "Thus you shall say to the house of Jacob, and tell the people of Israel: 'You yourselves have seen what I did to the Egyptians, and how I bore you on eagles' wings and brought you to myself. Now therefore, if you will indeed obey my voice and keep my covenant, you shall be my treasured possession among all peoples, for all the earth is mine; and you shall be to me a kingdom of priests and a holy nation.' These are the words that you shall speak to the people of Israel." (Exodus 19:1–6)

In Genesis 10–12, the nations simply burst onto the scene in God's story of redemption and restoration, and God promises to bring blessing to the nations through the great nation God would bring through Abraham's descendants: the nation of Israel. This shift to the nations represents a significant turning point in God's restoration and redemption story. There-fore, over the next several chapters we're going to see the significance of this turning point play out, as the focus of God's work of redemption narrows to the nation of Israel and then expands once again to Israel's role in blessing the nations. All the while, we'll see the work of God's promised redeemer begin to emerge as the source of blessing to both.

In Exodus 19:5, God promises the people of Israel, "you shall be my *treasured possession* among all peoples." That phrase "treasured pos-session" speaks of a prized piece of property, a sense the New Living Translation brings out in its translation: "you will be my own *special trea-sure.*" Who among us wouldn't long to hear God utter those words to us!

As a father of an adopted daughter, it reminds me of the great lengths adoptive parents typically go to bring the treasured possession of a new son or daughter into their home. In Exodus 19, we're going to see the great lengths God goes to bring his people Israel to himself. In this great prelude to God giving his people Israel the terms of his covenant relationship with them, we see that God promises they will be his treasured possession on the basis of what he has done, what he is doing, and what he will do. This is the wonderful assurance of our covenant-keeping God. We know he is faithful in his promises because we know he has proven to be faithful—a point God himself makes to his people Israel in Exodus 19.

God Confirms His Present Work through the Fulfillment of His Promises

God's confirming work in the lives of his people confirms that his promises have no expiration date. Some six hundred years or so before the events of Exodus 19, God made this promise to Abraham in Gen-esis 17:7–8: "And I will establish my covenant between me and you and your offspring after you throughout their generations for an everlasting covenant, to be God to you and to your offspring after you. And I will give to you and to your offspring after you the land of your sojournings, all the land of Canaan, for *an everlasting possession, and I will be their God.*" Notice that what God is promising both Abraham and his descendants is the promise of an everlasting relationship with God, in the land that he will give them as an everlasting possession. But back in Genesis 15:13, God also told Abraham his descendants would live for a period of four hundred years in a foreign land, become oppressed there, and ultimately be delivered by God from that oppression and back into the Promised Land. The story of the book of Exodus begins toward the end of that four-hundred-year oppression. As Exodus 2:23–25 states:

> During those many days the king of Egypt died, and the people of Israel groaned because of their slavery and cried out for help. Their cry for rescue from slavery came up to God. And God heard their groaning, and God remembered his covenant with Abraham, with Isaac, and with Jacob. God saw the people of Israel—and God knew.

Remember, God's promise to Abraham, Isaac, and Jacob was a promise of an everlasting relationship with God in the land he would give them as an everlasting possession. Exodus 3–19 gives us the account of God raising up Moses to deliver Israel out from their bondage in Egypt and into the wilderness of Sinai—a journey that would ultimately end with his people Israel brought into this Promised Land. And it is the sum of his work of delivering his people through Moses that God reminds the people of Israel of in Exodus 19:4: "You yourselves have seen what I did to the Egyptians, and how I bore you *on eagles' wings* and brought you to myself." This work of bringing his people to himself is done with the utmost tenderness of care.

The metaphor of the eagles' wings is a picture of the loving compassion, protection, strength, and watchfulness of God. Just as young eagles are carried on adult wings and brought out of their nests and taught to fly, so the Lord lovingly carried and safely delivered Israel. It's a picture beautifully described in Deuteronomy 32:9–11:

> But the LORD's portion is his people, Jacob his allotted heritage. He found him in a desert land, and in the howling waste of the wilderness; *he encircled him, he cared for him, he kept him as the apple*

of his eye. Like an eagle that stirs up its nest, that flutters over its young, spreading out its wings, catching them, bearing them on its pinions.

God's work of delivering his people through Moses was part of his work in keeping an age-old covenant promise to Abraham, Isaac, and Jacob, but in his present work of bringing his people into his presence in the wilderness of Sinai, God's confirming work confirms that his promises know no delays.

Back in Exodus 3:11, before he had embraced his God appointed role as Israel's deliverer, Moses asked God "Who am I that I should go to Pharaoh and bring the children of Israel out of Egypt?" From Moses' perspective, this task was an insurmountable challenge. Pharaoh was the ruler of a superpower which was presently enslaving the people of Israel. How could Moses possibly bring about their deliverance—and even if he could, what next? Israel had grown to a nation of more than a million people in Egypt; if bringing them out of Egypt seemed impossible, bringing such a number of people into the wilderness beyond Egypt was maybe even more impossible. How could the lives of more than a million people be sustained in a barren desert wilderness?

But even in light of these harsh realities, in Exodus 3:12 God gives a promise in response to Moses' question: "But I will be with you, and this shall be the sign for you, that I have sent you: when you have brought the people out of Egypt, you shall serve God on this mountain." The mountain God is referring to here is the mountain in the wilderness of Sinai, where Moses and the people of Israel are led in Exodus 19:1–2: "On the third new moon after the people of Israel had gone out of the land of Egypt, on that day they came into the wilderness of Sinai. They set out from Rephidim and came into the wilderness of Sinai, and they encamped in the wilderness. There Israel encamped before the mountain."

It's interesting, to say the least, that God had promised Moses to bring them to this mountain after the people had come out of Egypt.

It's a task with a whole bunch of impossible steps. Deliver a slave nation from a superpower. Part the Red Sea so they can cross on dry land and then destroy the superpower's pursuing army through the closing of the sea—all along the way to a wilderness that cannot possibly sustain them. Yet it is to this place that God promised to bring them, so he could meet them there. Notice the emphasis on the wilderness in verses 1–2. The phrase "they came into the wilderness of Sinai" is stated twice, followed by "they encamped in the wilderness. There Israel encamped before the mountain." God brought the people of Israel to himself through the impossible and into the impossible, and he did so right on time.

I love the NIV's rendering of verse 1: "On the first day of the third month after the Israelites left Egypt—on that very day—they came to the Desert of Sinai." Not only is the impossible not a hindrance to God keeping his promises, but one might suspect he chooses to make and keep his promises in the midst of the impossible so that we might not err by attributing his work to some other source. God's work confirms that his promises know no delays. We should live in light of this truth.

God's Present Work Should Move the Faithful to Live in Light of His Future Promises

Exodus 19:5 begins, "Now therefore," capturing the sense in the Hebrew text that, given the fact that God has made great promises to his people Israel and has kept them fully right up to the present time, the faithful can be assured that his promises will result in a future under his great care and blessing. Verses 5–6 read: "'Now therefore, if you will indeed obey my voice and keep my covenant, you shall be my treasured possession among all peoples, for all the earth is mine; and you shall be to me a kingdom of priests and a holy nation.' These are the words that you shall speak to the people of Israel."

The first part of God's promise to Israel is conditional: "If you will indeed obey my voice and keep my covenant, you shall be my treasured possession among all peoples." We've already talked about Israel's place as God's treasured possession, but this status is contingent upon obedience to him. We know that, as a nation, Israel failed to keep covenant with God and was exiled from the land he had promised Abraham, Isaac, Jacob, and their descendants as an everlasting possession. This might lead us to conclude as Paul did (for the sake of argument) in Romans 11:1: "I ask, then, has God rejected his people?" In other words, has God turned from his own promises? Paul answers his own question, "By no means!" which essentially means "that's impossible!" This word "treasured possession" is only used a few times in the Old Testament, and the Lord's use of it in Malachi 3:16–18 helps us understand that God hasn't rejected and won't reject his people because of their national failure:

> Then those who feared the LORD spoke with one another. The LORD paid attention and heard them, and a book of remembrance was written before him of *those who feared the LORD and esteemed his name. They shall be mine*, says the LORD of hosts, in the day when I make up my *treasured possession*, and I will spare them as a man spares his son who serves him. Then once more *you shall see the distinction between the righteous and the wicked, between one who serves God and one who does not serve him.*

Just as we have seen throughout our tracing of God's story of redemption and restoration, humanity walks along two paths before the Lord. In our Malachi text, this distinction is noted as between the righteous and the wicked, where the righteous are those who fear the Lord, esteem his name, and serve him. The people of Israel always reflected this twofold way, and as the Lord says here in Malachi, the righteous shall be his in the future day when he makes up his treasured possession. The covenant God mentions in Exodus 19:5, which he is about to enter into with his people Israel, is—as he promised to Abraham, Isaac, Jacob, and their descendants—an everlasting covenant lived out in relationship with him in the land he promised as an everlasting possession. A future day yet remains for *believing* national Israel where, "You shall be to me a kingdom of priests and a holy nation."

Notice this is future tense. God *will* bring this to pass. God's promises have no expiration, and they don't delay. They happen and they happen on time: his time. I know I have spent a lot of time in this chapter looking at texts outside Exodus 19, but given the nature of the text and how it fits into God's story of redemption and restoration, consideration of these texts is necessary. As the action rises in the biblical story, the foreshadowing to the future redemption and restoration intensifies.

Two more texts outside Exodus 19 help us better understand the timing and truth of God's promise to Israel here to make them "a kingdom of priests and a holy nation." In Romans 9:6–8, after making the argument that the fullness of God's promises to his people Israel remain in effect despite appearances to the contrary, Paul teaches:

> But it is not as though the word of God has failed. For not all who are descended from Israel belong to Israel, and not all are children of Abraham because they are his offspring, but "Through Isaac shall your offspring be named." This means that it is not the children of the flesh who are the children of God, but the children of the promise are counted as offspring.

And as we know, despite the seeming impossibility of the promise that a son named Isaac would be born to an elderly Abram and Sarai, Abram "believed the LORD, and [the Lord] counted it to him as righteousness" (Genesis 15:6). God's eternal promises to Israel will come to pass to those who are true children of Abraham, who reflect Abraham's faith in the Lord. This promise will be realized by a faithful remnant.

Later on, in Romans 9:27, Paul quotes from Isaiah as part of his argument that God's promises remain in effect: he will keep his promises to *faithful* Israel. The entire Isaiah passage that Paul quotes in part reads:

> In that day the remnant of Israel and the survivors of the house of Jacob will no more lean on him who struck them, but will lean on the LORD, the Holy One of Israel, in truth. *A remnant will return*, the remnant of Jacob, to the mighty God. For though

your people Israel be as the sand of the sea, *only a remnant of them will return.* Destruction is decreed, overflowing with righteousness. For the Lord GOD of hosts will make a full end, as decreed, in the midst of all the earth. (Isaiah 10:20–23)

Eternity will have a kingdom of priests; a holy nation; a uniquely treasured possession among all the nations of the earth. The remnant of Jacob *will* return—God has decreed it. He will make a full end of it, in the midst of all the earth. This is his timeless and on-time promise to the faithful remnant of his people Israel.

But for we who have been grafted into these promises, how should this teaching on Israel's great and unique place in God's plan of redemption and restoration shape our Christian walk? I come back to the main point of this chapter.

Live in Light of God's Future Promises

And in light of humanity's dark history toward God's people Israel, we who have been grafted in ought to honor God's chosen people. Sadly, the church has been part of this dark history. Perhaps foreseeing the potential for this, Paul warns the church in Romans 11:17–18: "But if some of the branches were broken off, and you, although a wild olive shoot, were grafted in among the others and now share in the nourishing root of the olive tree, *do not be arrogant toward the branches.* If you are, remember *it is not you who support the root, but the root that supports you.*"

I'm not suggesting that a certain people group be given *carte blanche* to do wrong, but I am suggesting that the attitude of the church toward the Jewish people ought to align with the attitude God already has toward his people as his "treasured possession among all peoples." That wonderful result will be to God's glory; therefore, it ought to be our great desire to be a faithful partner in his work of redeeming a faithful remnant for that day when he brings his promises to Israel to full fruition.

Secondly, we must serve the Lord as a royal priesthood and a holy nation. Similar to Exodus 19:5, Peter applies this status to the church in

1 Peter 2:9. The role of a priest is to stand between God and people to help bring the people closer to God and to help make God's truth, justice, favor, discipline, and holiness known to them. Taking God's expectations of Israel in this role as a model, Christians are called to: 1) live as examples of God's character, so that people might observe it and be drawn to him; 2) proclaim the truth of God and invite people to embrace him by faith, entering into an everlasting covenant relationship with him; 3) intercede in prayer on behalf of others, for the sake of bringing them into this covenant relationship; and finally, 4) preserve, honor, and exalt his word for the divine revelation it truly is before all the world. These are intentions we must act upon through a life of obedience. As we'll see in the next chapter, they are good intentions because they are rooted in the intentions of the only One who is truly good.

Chapter 7

Our Best Intentions Are the Lord's Intentions (2 Samuel 7:1–17)

In Isaiah 55:8–9, the Lord gives us great insight into the nature of perspective: "For my thoughts are not your thoughts, neither are your ways my ways, declares the LORD. For as the heavens are higher than the earth, so are my ways higher than your ways and my thoughts than your thoughts." As his people, a fundamental fact we have to embrace is that our perspective is vastly different than his—a point Peter makes with respect to time when he says, "But do not overlook this one fact, beloved, that with the Lord one day is as a thousand years, and a thousand years as one day" (2 Peter 3:8).

An economist who read this verse was amazed and talked to the Lord about it. "Lord, is it true that a thousand years for us is like one minute to you?" The Lord said "yes," so the economist replied, "Then a million dollars to us must be like one penny to you." The Lord said, "Well, yes." Feeling like he had gained some perspective, the economist then asked, "Will you give me one of those pennies?" and the Lord said, "All right, I will. Wait here a minute!"[10]

Now this economist may not have had the best of intentions, but even with our best intentions we can often wander outside his will. Zeal for the Lord is a wonderful thing, but when our zeal is misguided we need his correction. We need his perspective. As finite beings seeking to serve him, our perspective is often bound by our present circumstances. But as his redeemed people whom he leads as he wills to serve his eternal purposes, our present circumstances and the sense of the future those circumstances can lead to is woefully inadequate as the basis for our best intentions toward our Lord. As theologian J. I. Packer puts it, "We are to order our lives by the light of his law, not our guesses about his Plan."[11] In other words, we need to walk by faith, ordering our intentions around the principles of his Word, which serve not as a spotlight on the end of the road but as a lamp to our feet and a light to our path.

The focus for this chapter is 2 Samuel 7 and what it teaches us about intentions. The central human figure in this passage is King David, and in it David's intentions receive God's loving correction that informs David's understanding in a way that places all of David's life in its divine perspective: as a life which God blesses according to his will—not only to bless David, but to bless Israel for all eternity. As we dive into the text, we'll discover that David's circumstances moved him to presume upon God's plans, albeit with good intentions.

David's Intention: To Sincerely Serve the Lord through His Own Understanding

> Now when the king lived in his house and the LORD had given him rest from all his surrounding enemies, the king said to Nathan the prophet, "See now, I dwell in a house of cedar, but the ark of God dwells in a tent." And Nathan said to the king, "Go, do all that is in your heart, for the LORD is with you." (2 Samuel 7:1–3)

God's blessing of David with a royal palace and rest from the constant press of battle was clearly a time where David experienced a great turn of fortune, but it also discontented David. As he tells the prophet Nathan in verse 2, "See now, I dwell in a house of cedar, but the ark of God dwells in a tent." David doesn't clearly come out and say it, but what follows makes it plain that it seemed inappropriate to David—the Lord's servant—to be living in greater luxury than his Lord and master, and that David felt compelled to act to move the Lord out of his tent and into some better digs! And in verse 3, Nathan—a prophet of the Lord—seems to share David's perspective and affirms it without seeking the Lord's direction.

It's hard to argue the intentions of these men. David clearly seeks to honor the Lord, and the goodness of David's intention seems so self-evident to Nathan that he affirms it without question. But both men had sufficient direction from the Lord in his word to convince them otherwise. In fact, the entire twelfth chapter of the book of Deuteronomy is dedicated to this message God has for his people: all decisions on the manner and place that his people are to worship him are his and his alone. David's sincere intentions were encroaching upon the will and plan of God—and, as one might imagine, God opted to intervene on his own behalf.

The Lord's Objections Correct David's Understanding

> But that same night the word of the LORD came to Nathan, "Go and tell my servant David, 'Thus says the LORD: Would you build me a house to dwell in? I have not lived in a house since the day I brought up the people of Israel from Egypt to this day, but I have been moving about in a tent for my dwelling. In all places where I have moved with all the people of Israel, did I speak a word with any of the judges of Israel, whom I commanded to shepherd my people Israel, saying, "Why have you not built me a house of cedar?"'" (2 Samuel 7:4–7)

The Lord corrected David's understanding swiftly. In verse 4 the Lord brought his correcting message to his prophet Nathan "that same night," and in verse 5 he commands Nathan "Go and tell my servant David." Up to this point, David is only referred to as "the king," and the text does so three times. But in verse 5, David is "my servant"—a reference the Lord only uses in the Scriptures for his faithful servants. It gently and lovingly reminds the king that he is, above all, the Lord's servant, and that both the initiative to build a temple and the choice of the person for the task must come from God and not from an individual king. God makes this point in the form of a question to David in verse 5: "Would you build me a house to dwell in?" He then demonstrates the folly of David's intentions with a history lesson, reminding David in verses 6–7 that he has never dwelt among his people in anything other than the tent he commanded them to build and that he has never commanded any of Israel's leaders to change those dwelling accommodations.

In fact, God may also be impressing upon David an important dimension of his character that David's good intentions reveal he might have failed to grasp. God's emphasis on the great duration of time—some four hundred years by the time of David's reign—in which he has chosen to humbly dwell amongst his people, indicates that David's discontent for the Lord's humble accommodations is not a perspective the Lord shares. In John 1:14, John teaches that the eternal Son of God "became flesh and dwelt among us." Not unlike the Lord contentedly dwelling in a tent for the sake of his people Israel, Jesus took on the humble dwelling of human form for our sakes.

In 2 Samuel 7:8–17, the Lord shifts the conversation away from David's misguided intentions to serve him and toward the Lord's intentions, both for David's sake and for the sake of all Israel.

The Lord's Intention: To Bless David's House according to His Will (2 Samuel 7:8–17)

As finite beings seeking to serve God, our perspective is often bound by our present circumstances. In the remainder of 2 Samuel 7, the Lord gives David divine perspective by setting his entire life in the context of God's eternal purposes. He begins by showing David that his blessing of David's house encompasses all of David's life and responsibilities, past, present, and future. This progression through time follows the text, beginning in verse 8 where we see that the Lord had blessed David in the past.

In verse 8 the Lord commands Nathan to tell his servant David "Thus says the LORD of hosts, I took you from the pasture, from following the sheep, that you should be prince over my people Israel." In other words, "David, this is your life. From pasture to prince; from following sheep to leading a nation. I didn't work through you because you came from greatness; I worked through you because you were humble and faithful." There were many trials in David's life from pasture to prince, but the Lord's purpose for David put those trials in context, and the Lord was blessing David in the present.

In the first part of verse 9, God reminds David that his present peaceful circumstances in verse 1 which led David to act in the first place served the purpose of confirming to David, "I have been with you wherever you went." For the Lord, it was far more important that David have the perspective that his circumstances were confirmation of the Lord's blessed presence rather than as a catalyst for David to build him "a house of cedar." The Lord's presence in David's present was an exhortation to faith. David's future held a great promise for himself and his people, whom he served as king. The Lord would bless David, and through him bless Israel in the future.

In the second half of verse 9 the Lord tells David "I will make for you a great name, like the name of the great ones of the earth." Very much like the Lord promised Abram, David would become great. In fact, as you read through the Old Testament, the Lord himself used David as the standard by which every king who followed him upon his throne in Jerusalem would be measured. But it was not greatness for greatness' sake. In verse 10 and the first half of verse 11, the Lord revealed to David that his rule would bless Israel. For the first time since the time of the judges—some four hundred years—Israel would know peace, stability, and freedom from the affliction of enemies, and in a way they had yet to experience. Most of us would likely be very content to limit our perspective of our purpose and significance in this life *to this life*—to the kind of impact God had made and promised to continue to make through David. But from God's perspective, when he moves in the life of his people, the effects outlive us.

The Lord's blessing of David's house extended beyond David's life. In the second half of verse 11, the Lord comes back to the topic of a house—but not for himself, as he tells David: "Moreover, the LORD declares to you that the LORD *will make you a house.*" In verses 12–15, the Lord foretells of the reign of David's son Solomon. In verse 12, the Lord promises David that he will establish the kingdom of a son from his own body; and in verse 13, the Lord tells David that his son is the Lord's choice to build a house for his name. Solomon, as we know from the Scriptures, built the temple in Jerusalem, and I think it's interesting that the building project David elevated to the greatest importance is something the Lord mentions only after he describes the great nature of the blessing he will bring to David and his people Israel. More importantly, the Lord directs the work of the temple for the sake of his people.

Having been brought into the land and finally delivered from the threat of foreign affliction, his people Israel are no longer wanderers in tents. Circumstances have changed. They have settled, and so the Lord has determined to move from a tent to a more permanent dwelling in line with his promises to his people to settle them in the land. And David's house—i.e., the reign of David's descendants—would be established forever (as we'll see in a moment when we look at verse 16); this is an unconditional promise.

The Lord's promise to David in verse 13 that Solomon's throne would be established forever confirms to David that this promise will not be undone by succession. The Lord's promise to David in verse 14 that he will discipline Solomon for his iniquity confirms to David that this promise will not be undone by the moral failure of his successors; and the Lord's promise to David in verse 15, "my steadfast love will not depart from him, as I took it from Saul, whom I put away from before you," reaffirms this point and assures David that no other house will ever supplant his in the Lord's plan for Israel. And it is an eternal plan.

The Lord's blessing of David's house continues unto eternity. In verse 16 the Lord tells David, "And your house and your kingdom shall be made sure forever before me. Your throne shall be established forever." The Lord's promise of an enduring house for David became Israel's assurance that God would once again lift the nation up and cause it to flourish anew. Despite the circumstances of trial and tribulation and judgment the nation would experience because of their covenant disobedience, the faithful among the Lord's people Israel—even through the centuries—could hold to the hopeful perspective the Lord had given them in this promise to David. And this long-awaited hope came to pass as the angel Gabriel proclaimed to Mary in Luke 1:31–33: "And behold, you will conceive in your womb and bear a son, and you shall call his name Jesus. He will be great and will be called the Son of the Most High. And the Lord God will give to him *the throne of his father David, and he will reign over the house of Jacob forever,* and of his kingdom there will be no end." Amen.

The Lord created the nations, and through the nation Israel, he promised to bless all the nations of the earth. From Abraham's descendants would rise a redeemer to bring this blessing to pass. So now, in our story of redemption and restoration, we see that the Lord narrows the focus further as Abraham's descendant David becomes the one through whom the Lord will raise up this redeemer.

Applying the Circumstances of This Promise

There is much here to apply for God's people who are zealous for him. But as his zealous people, we must be zealous in truth. Zeal for God lived out through a passionate personal identification with the interests of Christ's kingdom, as Christ has made those interests known through his word, is honoring to him and a great blessing to the church. But as we saw with David and Nathan, zeal has a quality that captures our fancy in a way that can cause us to miss how it may be misguided. We always need to filter zeal through the sobering quality of the truth before we hand zeal the reins. And should we need to correct a zealous endeavor, we should do so in the gracious way the Lord did with David: by correcting misguided intentions *without destroying the zealous heart.* After all, great change for good often comes through God's inspiration of his zealous servants, and as a second application of this chapter's text, we need to embrace the necessity for change in the life of Christ's church.

The message in 2 Samuel 7 addressed the need for change in Israel's corporate worship, through the temple the Lord directed Solomon to build. The culture had made the transition from sojourners to permanent residents. Commenting on this, the *Pulpit Commentary* makes the point that a change in worship was a necessary adaptation so that the truth of God's word would be "more effective in its influence on a different state of society"[12]—not as change for change's sake but as a recognition that the nature of human culture changes.

As the dynamics of a culture change, the setting changes in a way that requires modifications in form and methods, which hold fast to the truth while adapting to the changing developments of human society. Few of us will walk to church this coming Sunday, which means the community we live in is much broader than the community of a local church two hundred years ago. Few of us are still sitting in high-backed and sided pews which block our view from one another. If you sing hymns on Sunday morning, it's most likely with musical accompaniment, and with lyrics other than the text of the Psalms. There was a time when this would have been revolutionary rather than old-fashioned. And by the way, it's likely you're also reading those lyrics off a projected screen, not out of a hymnal. Some of us now read the biblical text from a cell phone or tablet. For a church to remain both faithful to the truth and relevant and effective in its ministry, it must adapt to the changing ways in which people live in society. This doesn't happen naturally or effortlessly, as we have a remarkable propensity to cling to traditions long after we've lost track of why the underlying practices were established in the first place.

The US standard railroad gauge is 4 feet, 8½ inches, a standard brought to America by England. The English used this gauge because the tools used to build their first railways were the tools used to build wagons, which just so happened to have 4 foot, 8½-inch wheel spacing. This spacing was a concession to the reality that the roads in Britain still retained the deep ruts left by Roman chariots during the time when Britain was under Roman rule—chariots which also had 4 foot, 8½-inch wheel spacing. The Roman standard was derived after trial-and-error efforts of early chariot builders. They determined the best width that would accommodate two horses' behinds was 4 feet, 8½ inches.

When the company Thiokol built the booster rockets for the space shuttle, the engineers who designed the rockets had to ship them by rail. If you're following along, you'll realize that the design for an essential part of the space shuttle program was limited by the width of the back-sides of two Roman horses!

Always remember that the life of your church—which is in fact Christ's church—like the life of David and his people in 2 Samuel 7, is a life lived in the progress of an eternal redemption context. Like David, we must not get ahead of the light God gives to our path, *but neither must we seek to focus the light of his direction backward in order to keep our wheels in the ruts left in the path.*

Chapter 8

Fresh Hope for Dry Bones
(Ezekiel 37)

Imagine a nation no longer in existence, apart from the remains of their long dead dry bones. Then these long dead dry bones come together, take on human form, and become reanimated by the breath of life God pours into them like a blowing wind. A wind that blows where it wishes, and you hear its sound, but you do not know where it comes from or where it goes, and seemingly, in an instant, they become a nation . . . born again! Can you imagine such a scene? Hopeless one moment, and in awestruck wonder at the Lord the next. We're hard-pressed to find an experience which helps us relate to such an occasion.

But maybe an amazing orchestra created out of recycled trash from an impoverished city's landfill can at least get our hearts moving in the right direction.

When you think of an orchestra, you probably picture a refined group of musicians with their carefully selected and maintained quality instruments. But try instead to picture in your mind an orchestra made up mostly of kids who play instruments made out of trash from the dump. This is the Recycled Orchestra from Cateura, Paraguay. Cateura is more like a slum alongside a landfill than a town. Every day, about three million pounds of solid waste gets dumped in the landfill, and many families of Cateura scratch out a living scavenging trash from it in order to resell what they can. But the real treasure in this landfill can be found in ordinary trash resurrected to new life as musical instruments. A violin made out of cans, wooden spoons, and bent forks. A cello which uses an oil drum for its body. Drum heads made from old X-ray film. A saxophone made out of a drainpipe, melted copper, coins, spoon handles, cans, and bottle caps.

The Recycled Orchestra was founded by Favio Chavez, who worked in Cateura as an environmental engineer and was inspired to teach music to the many children of Cateura in his spare time. Ultimately, word of the orchestra made its way to Paraguayan filmmakers and then beyond Paraguay. They went from being a community-based group to being the toast of international development ventures and media around the world![13]

Now it is one thing to throw away trash carelessly and restore it to something beautiful and wonderful. It's altogether another thing to throw away people carelessly. Who cares about the contents of a landfill? Evidently some people do to the point of restoring trash into works of beauty. Psalm 116:15 reads, "Precious in the sight of the LORD is the death of his saints." Who cares about the bones of dead people? Evidently the Lord our God, who has not forgotten his precious saints and the wondrous work of restoration he will make of them.

Do you feel dried up today? Is your hope on the wane? Do you feel disconnected from fellowship? Are you in need of revival? If so, then I hope that in the text from Ezekiel 37 you'll take heart in a message that even old, long-dead dry bones are not beyond the power of God to experience true and everlasting revival. There is fresh hope for dry bones, and the Lord teaches us this in a stunning, dramatic fashion through his vivid depiction of Israel's resurrection.

As we'll see, a time yet remains in redemption history when the Lord will resurrect his people Israel and restore them as a nation. Though any hope for this may presently seem no more hopeful than the prospects a pile of rubbish has in a poor city's dump, what man can make beautiful from lost things pales in comparison to the handiwork of the God who makes all things new. And he will do a new work in Israel.

The Lord God Will Resurrect His People Israel

Abraham and his descendants—God's people Israel—have a very prominent place in God's plan of redemption and restoration. The nation of Israel was created to be a blessing to the nations, but it was also created, as the Lord promised them, to be his treasured possession. Israel would be a nation which would enjoy an everlasting covenant relationship with the Lord, uniquely lived out forever in a specific place—the land he promised them—and under a specific authority: the house, throne, and kingdom of David. In other words, this was a promise of everlasting life as a nation of real people, to be experienced in a real place as a real kingdom.

But the logical problem in all of this is that every one of these real people—even today—fit at least one of the following conditions which seem to contradict the Lord's promise: they're not in the land, they're not under the rule of a descendant of David in the land . . . and they're dead! It's hard to argue this is a promise being kept, or even a promise which can *be* kept.

A resident of Greenville, South Carolina once received a letter from Health and Human Services, telling her "Your food stamps will be stopped, effective March 1992, because we received notice that you passed away. May God bless you. You may reapply if your circumstances change." How can a dead person collect public assistance? How can a dead nation receive such promises? Circumstances have to miraculously change, and the Lord has a plan to do just that.

In Ezekiel 37:2, after the Lord had placed Ezekiel in a valley full of bones, Ezekiel writes "And he led me around among them, and behold, there were very many on the surface of the valley, and behold, they were *very dry*." I absolutely love the movie *The Princess Bride*. One of my favorite lines from the movie is when Miracle Max describes Wesley, the movie's hero, as "only mostly dead." Well, when Ezekiel says these bones were "very dry," he's making the point that these are the bones of people who are *very* dead—a point reinforced by the Lord's question and Ezekiel's answer in verse 3: "And he said to me, 'Son of man, can these bones live?' And I answered, 'O Lord GOD, you know.'" Ezekiel's answer reflected the careful balance between his awareness that this was humanly impossible and the fact that he was standing in the presence of an almighty God for whom all things are possible. Ezekiel knew that if the bones could live, it was a matter only God knew and that only God could bring to pass.

As if on cue, in verses 4–6 the Lord tells Ezekiel to speak his word to these bones, and declares that by his word that they will live. He then explains to Ezekiel the manner in which he will make this happen—a two-stage process, the first stage being that the Lord will resurrect his people in human form.

Imagine the suspense for Ezekiel. What happens next? Consider reading verses 7 and 8 out loud to try to get the sense of how startling this was to Ezekiel: "So I prophesied as I was commanded. And as I prophesied, there was a sound, and behold, a rattling, and the bones came together, bone to its bone. And I looked, and behold, there were sinews on them, and flesh had come upon them, and skin had covered them. But there was no breath in them."

This event wasn't a metaphor to be spiritualized. What Ezekiel saw was full of sound and sight as bones rattled and these remains of long-dead people meticulously took on human form from the inside out. And take note that, just as Paul teaches in 1 Corinthians 6 and 15, this is a resurrection to life—not out of thin air or even dust, *but of a particular dust*: the real remains of real people. But as Ezekiel observes at the end of verse 8, "there was no breath in them." A body alone does not a living person make. The Lord will resurrect his people as living souls.

In verses 9–10 the forms of these people don't come to life until they receive the breath of life. Once again it is the Lord's word which brings these people to life. There's an interesting play on words in these verses as the Hebrew word for "breath," "wind," and "spirit" are the same word (רוּחַ, pronounced *roo-ach*); the context determines the interpretation. "Breath" and "wind" are the meanings in verses 9–10, but in verse 14, where the Lord is explaining to Ezekiel what he just saw, he says "I will put my *Spirit* within you, and you shall live." The two-stage pattern—form and breath—that the Lord follows for raising his people back to life here is also the pattern we see in Genesis 2:7 when God creates Adam, and when he was done creating Adam, as the King James Version so beautifully puts it, "man became a living soul."

The miracle God shows Ezekiel here is a miracle brought to pass by the power of God's word and the working of his Spirit to raise dead people back to life as whole persons; as living souls. But because we have the benefit of reading ahead, I have made assumptions about who these resurrected people are and why God raised them. But if you're Ezekiel living this in real time, these events beg an explanation, and so the Lord explains this vision of resurrection to Ezekiel in verses 11–14, first by telling Ezekiel the answer to the "who" question.

It is Israel who will be resurrected. In verse 11, these bones are the whole house of Israel; and in verses 12-13 this resurrection will be experienced by the people from their own graves wherever they may be buried. We know this because the Lord tells Ezekiel in verse 12 that after he has resurrected the people, "I will bring you *into* the land of Israel."

This leads us to the answer of the "why" question. Israel will be resurrected in order to bring the Lord's covenant promises to them to pass. Ezekiel is writing to the people of Israel after the last of the nation had been exiled from the land by the Lord as a result of their centuries-long covenant disobedience. As verse 11 describes, as a nation they are dead; they have lost all hope of becoming a nation again or of seeing God's covenant promises fulfilled. They are scattered among the nations and separated from one another. And it is in light of this hopeless spiritual condition of a nation that the Lord explains to Ezekiel in verse 14 that he will resurrect his people, give them his Spirit so that they can truly live, bring them into the land he promised, and they will know him. And as the rest of chapter 37 teaches, this resurrection is the redemption of a nation.

The Lord God Will Restore the Nation of Israel

In verses 15–20, the Lord has Ezekiel take two sticks, representing his divided people Israel, and has him join them together as one in his hand. Then, in the sight of these people in exile, the Lord commands Ezekiel to explain the meaning of this object lesson, beginning with the fact that the Lord will restore Israel to national unity.

In verse 21 the Lord tells his people that he will gather them back into the land of promise from wherever they have been scattered to. Having gathered them, he says in verse 22, "I will make them *one nation in the land*, on the mountains of Israel. And *one king* shall be king over them all, and they shall be no longer two nations, and no longer divided into two kingdoms." If you remember from your study of the Old Testament, the kingdom of Israel was first divided under the reign of Solomon's son Rehoboam, very soon after Solomon died. It was a division driven by pride, greed, foolishness, and rebellion; and in its wake, this division of Israel led to rampant idolatry, particularly in the northern kingdom of Israel. For Israel to experience a sustained restoration to national unity, a spiritual restoration had to accompany it. The Lord has a plan to bring this to pass; he will restore Israel to national purity.

In verse 23 the Lord declares that he will act to save his people. He will cleanse them from all idolatry and transgressions; and in verse 24, with a resurrected David as king to shepherd them once again, they will walk before the Lord in obedience. As we saw God promise his people Israel in Exodus 19:6, they will be "a kingdom of priests and a holy nation." And unlike with Israel's past attempts to reflect this high standard in their own strength, the Lord's final work of restoration in unity and purity for Israel will be a lasting work. The Lord's restoration of Israel will be everlasting.

The Hebrew word for "forever" or "eternity" is עוֹלָם (pronounced *oh-lahm*) and it is used five times in verses 25–28. In verse 25, it is used to convey that generations of the faithful will dwell in the land forever with David as their prince forever; and in verses 26 and 28, it is used to convey that they will live in an everlasting covenant relationship with God, with his sanctuary in their midst forevermore. Forever in the land. Forever with David as their prince. Forever in covenant relationship with the Lord. Forever with his sanctuary in their midst. This last point is so significant that Ezekiel dedicates the last nine chapters of his book to the Lord's vision of this sanctuary and its construction—complete with how David, the prince, and his people will dwell forever in relation to it, and how they will come into it to worship the Lord in his very presence.

I don't deny the prophetic significance of the relatively recent restoration of Israel as a nation and the great return of Jews into the land, but please don't mistake what we presently see for the restoration God promises. When Christ returns to establish his worldwide kingdom, he will, as he teaches in Matthew 24:31, "send out his angels with a loud trumpet call, and they will gather his elect from the four winds, from one end of heaven to the other." When we see the *elect remnant* of Israel, including those resurrected, gathered into the Promised Land by the Lord's very evident doing—with the resurrected David as prince among them, and Jesus Christ, the Son of God and the Son of David, seated upon David's everlasting throne within the Lord's sanctuary restored in their midst—then, as the Lord says in Ezekiel 37:28, "the nations will know that I am the LORD who sanctifies Israel." Until then, Israel remains, in a very real sense, in a state of exile.

Ezekiel 37 was originally given by the Lord, through Ezekiel, to hopeless exiles—exiles who had become driven to say, as the New Living Translation puts it in verse 11, "We have become old, dry bones—all hope is gone. Our nation is finished." So, for us, I'll ask again the questions I asked at the start of the chapter: Do you feel dried up today? Is your hope on the wane? Do you feel disconnected from fellowship? Are you in need of revival?

Embrace the Hope God Has Given You!

Ezekiel 37 gives a vivid picture of God's power to transform his people, but it's a work so stunning that it seemingly leaves us with a lack of life experiences to help us grasp it. Even a trash heap turned orchestra seems to fall well short as a parallel. But in Romans 8:11 Paul teaches, "If the Spirit of him who raised Jesus from the dead dwells in you, he who raised Christ Jesus from the dead will also give life to your mortal bodies through his Spirit who dwells in you." In other words, life-giving resurrection power dwells in each follower of Jesus Christ!

A minister visiting Italy saw the grave of a man dead for centuries. He died rejecting Christ yet was fearful of the resurrection he knew Christ promised to bring, so he placed a huge stone slab put over his grave to preclude any possible resurrection. But evidently, when he was buried, an acorn must have fallen into the grave, which eventually grew up through the grave, split the slab, and is now a towering oak tree. Observing this ironic scene the minister asked, "If an acorn, which has power of biological life in it, can split a slab of that magnitude, what can the acorn of God's resurrection power do in a person's life?"[14]

In my time as a pastor I've seen God's resurrection power convict people young and old to faithfully obey Christ's command to be baptized. I've seen a man on his deathbed embrace the opportunity to finish his race of faith by sharing the gospel to all who came to visit him. I've seen a young man and his grandparents rejoice at how God had transformed their lives at the same time; young and old both finding the fresh hope of new life through faith in Christ. I'm certain you have the same kind of stories you can tell—people among us who have known God's resurrection power to "give life to their mortal bodies through his Spirit."

In Romans 5:3–5, Paul teaches that this work of the Holy Spirit's resurrection power to transform our character proves itself in our lives, especially in the midst of tribulation and struggle, giving the believer a hope which does not disappoint. Therefore, as his people the church, we know there's fresh hope for dry bones because we see it in ourselves and one another.

Conversely, we need to refrain from false hope. Ezekiel was a prophet to a people in exile, yet some who heard Ezekiel also saw the partial return from exile God brought to pass under the rule of the Persians. It was a return which seemed like the restoration of the kingdom God had promised through the prophets. But in truth, reality paled in comparison to the promises. In Ezra 3:12, some of those returnees who were old enough to remember the former temple wept when they saw the foundation of the temple the people laid after their return from exile. The Lord had promised through Ezekiel a glorious temple in the restored kingdom, yet the one they were building fell miserably short even of the standard of the previous temple.

The Lord begins the work of transforming us in this life, sometimes even in great leaps. But every Christian will struggle with sin and its pitfalls until Christ resurrects us. The transformation we see in ourselves and one another are signposts of coming glory, but we will always retain the capacity in this life to disappoint one another. This is true for your pastor, your spouse, your parents, your mentor, etc. God alone, who is transforming us by the power of his Holy Spirit into the likeness of his Son Jesus, is the basis for our hope which won't disappoint. We need to give one another the grace of not placing one another in that place of fresh and living hope which God alone must hold in our lives.

Chapter 9

Walk Like We're Walking in His Kingdom Come (Isaiah 2:1–5)

The word that Isaiah the son of Amoz saw concerning Judah and Jerusalem.

It shall come to pass in the latter days that the mountain of the house of the LORD shall be established as the highest of the mountains, and shall be lifted up above the hills; and all the nations shall flow to it, and many peoples shall come, and say: "Come, let us go up to the mountain of the LORD, to the house of the God of Jacob, that he may teach us his ways and that we may walk in his paths." For out of Zion shall go forth the law, and the word of the LORD from Jerusalem. He shall judge between the nations, and shall decide disputes for many peoples; and they shall beat their swords into plowshares, and their spears into pruning hooks; nation shall not lift up sword against nation, neither shall they learn war anymore.

O house of Jacob, come, let us walk in the light of the LORD. (Isaiah 2:1–5)

Cell phones are a prominent way in which we connect with our world today, and they're also a prominent distraction. In one sense, we've become more distracted by these additions to our lives because of our unhealthy propensity to multitask with our phones, especially while driving. But in a more substantive sense, cell phones are equally distracting in a very different way. Because of the way they connect us to other peoples' lives (or at least a perception of their lives), emotional and spiritual distractions often arise in the form of jealousy over what other people have or are doing—jealousy over what we're missing.

We live in a culture of endless distractions and access to endless distractions. One result of this is a kind of social anxiety that greatly amplifies a fear of missing out. This is particularly prominent in today's culture, because of the widespread use of social media and the distorted perceptions social media creates. For many of us today, our contentment is under assault by our perceptions of how poorly we're doing. Everybody else's lives seem to be moving along so wonderfully—a scourge in our day-to-day existence that seems to feed itself through the pathologies in our spirit. You could call this the social scourge of living in the land of endless distraction and opportunity, and it's the condition God's people Israel were experiencing that drove the occasion for this chapter's text from Isaiah 2.

Our story has focused intensely over the last three chapters on God's plan of redemption and restoration for his people Israel, but now we're going to shift gears toward God's plan for the nations. But even as we do, we'll see that God still has Israel in mind. The nations will serve as a foil to challenge his people to a faithful walk—a foil which can either spur repentance or jealousy.

"Walk like we're walking in his kingdom come" is a challenge to the church today, but one that mirrors an identical challenge to Israel in Isaiah 2, as God gives his people Israel a vision of the faithfulness of the Gentile nations in the last days—for the purpose of provoking them to faithfulness as well. Isaiah's vision transports the people of the southern kingdom of Judah to the end of the age, featuring a kingdom a jealous God longs to lure his *treasured possession* into through some tough love: namely, an unflattering comparison with the faithful Gentile nations. By way of a vision, Isaiah makes what must have been a startling declaration to Judah.

The Lord Will Redeem the Nations in the Last Days

Verse 1 and the first part of verse 2 in Isaiah 2 read, "The word that Isaiah the son of Amoz *saw concerning Judah and Jerusalem*. It shall come to pass in the latter days." The events that follow will come to pass at the end of the present age and the beginning of the age to come. Note that Isaiah "saw" this word, which means he's likely writing as a result of a divine vision. Also note that his concern is for Judah and Jerusalem, a point we'll return to later in the chapter. But suffice to say for now, Isaiah reveals the wonderful truth that God will not only redeem his people Israel but will also redeem the nations as well, and that it will be a thorough and lasting redemption. Just as we are transformed from the inside out, beginning with a change in our inward convictions, the Lord will transform the nations' convictions and will begin this work by transforming their perspective of him.

The Lord will prove himself to be victorious and exalted in the eyes of the nations. Verse 2 describes what must have been a vivid vision of a transformation within the land of Israel: "It shall come to pass in the latter days that the mountain of the house of the Lord shall be established as the highest of the mountains, and shall be lifted up above the hills; and all the nations shall flow to it." The temple mount in the city of Jerusalem today is surrounded by terrain which rises above it. In the ancient Near Eastern world, pagan temples were usually built on the highest place available so they would be closer to heaven—a fascination of the nations we know the people of Israel shared because of the Scriptures' frequent accounts of their worship on high places. But the depiction of the supreme exaltation of the Lord's dwelling place will symbolically demonstrate to the nations the superior glory and greatness of the Lord and his ultimate triumph as the one true object of worship, so much so that "the nations shall flow to it." That word "flow" literally means "to flow like a stream"—in this case, a stream flowing uphill! The Lord will exalt himself as the irresistible object of worship in the eyes of the nations, and as a result the nations will long for his presence, his word, and his ways.

Verse 3 reads, "and many peoples shall come, and say: 'Come, let us go up to the mountain of the Lord, to the house of the God of Jacob, that he may teach us his ways and that we may walk in his paths.' For out of Zion shall go forth the law, and the word of the LORD from Jerusalem." The verse begins by reiterating the point that the nations will flow up to the Lord's sanctuary; they will have an irresistible longing to be in his presence . . . as a community. Why? Because in his presence, they will, as a community, learn his ways and how to walk according to those ways. And how can they do that? Isaiah closes verse 3 with the explanation: they will receive his word and his law in his presence. As it always does by God's grace, God's living and active word will pierce to the very core of the peoples' being, transforming the nations. The Lord will transform the nations' character, and just as the peoples of the nations sought him as a community, so too will they be transformed as a community. As people who have recognized the Lord as supremely exalted in all of the universe, the nations will submit to the Lord.

The first half of verse 4 reads, "He shall judge between the nations, and shall decide disputes for many peoples." Notice what this statement implies: the issues that set nations in conflict with one another don't disappear automatically, but rather are resolved as a result of people who have sought the Lord, received his teaching from his word, and now possess the heart, mind, and will to embrace his judgments. In other words, they will embrace, as a community, the will of God because they respond to his mediation with renewed minds. And having been renewed, the nations will abandon conflict and embrace peace, but unlike history's human efforts to produce peace, this won't be an uneasy peace with deeply suspicious former enemies casting jaded eyes upon one another. This will be an enduring peace embraced by the transformed community of nations, and they will prove their intentions as true.

They will offer this proof first by abandoning the instruments of war. "They shall beat their swords into plowshares, and their spears into pruning hooks." And having traded their weapons for the tools of a gentle economy, they will abandon the most devastating instrument: war. They will abandon the ways of war in a lasting sense, as verse 4 concludes: "neither shall they *learn* war anymore." How remarkable is this transformation?

In a 2003 *New York Times* article entitled "What Every Person Should Know about War," it is cited that "Of the past 3,400 years, humans have been entirely at peace for 268 of them, or just eight percent of recorded history." Isaiah 2, therefore, may be describing the most stunning transformation of corporate character human history will ever experience. But in a text which Isaiah tells us is a message "concerning Judah and Jerusalem," the people of Israel are remarkably absent from this future account of God's majestic and exalted presence and work in the land he has promised his people. I believe Isaiah 2:5 teaches us why.

Israel, the Blessing to the Nations, is Provoked to Faithfulness by the Nations

In our story, we've seen how God scattered the nations from the tower of Babel for the sake of their future redemption and then promised Abraham that the great nation which would arise from his descendants would be the source of blessing to the nations. Now this blessing is being foretold, through this breathtaking vision to Isaiah. But where is the Lord's people Israel? Why is their role in God's plan ignored?

In Romans 11:11–12 Paul, explaining Israel's national failure to embrace the Messiah and the role that failure plays in God's plan of redemption and restoration, says this: "So I ask, did they stumble in order that they might fall? By no means! Rather, through their trespass salvation has come to the Gentiles, so as to make Israel jealous. Now if their trespass means riches for the world, and if their failure means riches for the Gentiles, how much more will their full inclusion mean!"

Despite all the mystery this verse entails, it's safe to say that it shows us that God's plan does pit, in a sense, his people Israel against the Gentile nations for their mutual benefit; and in the mystery of his grace, this also entails a provocation to jealousy. Coming back to Isaiah 2, the house of Jacob finally comes into the picture in verse 5 where, after showing his people the stunning salvation of Gentile nations which will be seen in their land, the Lord commands his people to "come, let us walk in the light of the LORD." In other words, "come and obey my word and its commands," and this can't help but stir up some jealousy because, as

Isaiah 2 indicates, the Lord has shown his people that the nations will walk *as Israel was commanded to walk.*

Through Isaiah, the Lord has given his people a vivid picture of the future obedience of the nations as a challenge to the house of Jacob to walk in his ways. The nations are not yet coming to Jerusalem to be taught by the Lord, but Israel already has his word. How unthinkable then that Israel should continue to walk in darkness.

Many scholars, in light of the flow of the message in this part of Isaiah, believe that this text was given to Israel during the reign of Uzziah—a time when the people of the southern kingdom of Judah experienced great military power, peace, and prosperity not seen since the reigns of David and Solomon. Perhaps not unlike our culture today, this future vision of the kingdom of heaven had little appeal to a people who had their own glorious kingdom that didn't challenge them to abandon their wayward ways and the blissful distractions of peace and prosperity. Perhaps a little shame by comparison was in order. As the *New American Commentary* explains verse 5, "Isaiah exhorts his own people in Jerusalem to follow the example of the foreign nations of the future. The people's response to this choice will determine whether Isaiah's audience will enjoy the kingdom God has prepared for those who follow him, or miss out on this great privilege."[15]

The nations modeled the ways of those who will be rewarded this great privilege in three ways. The nations will be a community seeking his presence, learning his will, and walking according to his kingdom's standards. In contrast, Israel was a community seeking their own conception of God, bowing to their own wills, and walking according to their own ways, as Isaiah goes on to say in verses 7–8 of chapter 2: "Their land is filled with silver and gold, and there is no end to their treasures; their land is filled with horses, and there is no end to their chariots. Their land is filled with idols; they bow down to the work of their hands, to what their own fingers have made." They had abundant riches. They had great worldly might. And they were consumed by the distractions permitted by a god of their own making who made no burdensome demands of their time, their talents, their treasure, or their character.

Could that be us today? Like the people of Israel, is the Lord using this word from Isaiah to hold it up to the church today as a challenge for us to truly commit ourselves to his kingdom agenda? If so, then we need to walk very differently.

Walk Like We're Walking in his Kingdom Come!

And just as the nations will in the future, we can begin where they began: we can seek his presence. Don't forget that in Isaiah 2, this is modeled in community. So seek him in community.

The author of Hebrews makes essentially the same point and from a like motivation—the Day of the Lord's coming kingdom drawing near—when he writes, "And let us consider how to stir up one another to love and good works, not neglecting to meet together, as is the habit of some, but encouraging one another, and all the more as you see the Day drawing near" (Hebrews 10:24–25). A 2016 Gallup poll indicates that 40 percent of Americans attend church, but only eighteen percent attend regularly. But even that's misleading, because the standard for "regular" attendance is three out of every eight Sundays! Similarly, Barna's standard is at least once a month. Three out of eight Sundays? Once a month? Is that our standard?

In Ephesians 4:15–16, Paul describes the local church as a kingdom community which is "to grow up in every way into him who is the head, into Christ, from whom the whole body, joined and held together by every joint with which it is equipped, when each part is working properly, makes the body grow so that it builds itself up in love." As citizens of his coming kingdom, this is a picture of a community seeking our Lord Jesus together, remaining intimately and vitally connected with him so that we can remain intimately and vitally connected with one another, all so that we can grow together. I pray that you'll agree with me that this picture of kingdom community is significant enough to overcome our affections for, as the author of Hebrews puts it, "neglecting to meet together, as is the habit of some." And in our time together as his people, per Isaiah 2, we should come together to learn his ways.

In Isaiah 2 we also see that the word of God is the means by which we learn his ways. In a text likely well known to most of us, Paul teaches that all of God's word is "profitable for teaching, for reproof, for correction, and for training in righteousness, that the man of God may be complete, equipped for every good work" (2 Timothy 3:16–17). What may not be so obvious about this text is that, if you consider it carefully, it requires some form of close, relational community for it to make sense—learning in community, just as we saw in Isaiah 2. Yet in those ministries your church offers to learn in community, it wouldn't surprise me if less than half of your church takes advantage of these opportunities. If something else is competing for your time, I pray you'll weigh the competition against Paul's admonition in Ephesians 5:15–16: "Therefore be careful how you walk, not as unwise men but as wise, making the most of your time, because the days are evil."

Finally, let us reflect his character. Isaiah 2:5 is really the Lord's application to Judah of his message in verses 1–4. The Lord was hoping to spur his people to turn to him through a future account of the nations which could either spur them to jealousy, or to a sense of shame and repentance. One of the things I've learned over the course of my Christian life is that God has an interesting way of correcting his children, not unlike what we see him doing in Isaiah 2. There have been more than a couple of occasions in my life when my sinful nature burst forth in glorious fashion, in settings where unbelievers had a front-row seat to it all. Pride has always been the common denominator when I fail in this way, and justifiable rebuke from an unbeliever has often been the Lord's solution to the equation. I've already shared of one such occasion while serving on staff as an instructor at the Air Force's Air University. On the upside, the lesson is always memorable and deeply impressed when the Lord corrects in this way. On that particular occasion at Air University, something especially wonderful came of it that I didn't share previously: the Lord used the humility he swiftly brought me to in the moment to draw one unbelieving observer to Jesus Christ. He is good and gracious and merciful, even when it's unpleasant to feel his hand. I'm thankful for that.

Chapter 10

Serve Faithfully and Trust the Lord with the Results (Isaiah 49:1–7)

With any building you walk in and out of on a regular basis, there are details in your surroundings which tend to fail or cease to command your attention. The church I serve as a pastor is no exception. For example, when you enter the church through the door that leads to the staff offices, the street number for the building is on the mailbox just outside the door as you enter (1771). Continuing into the building through the foyer and into the fellowship hall, you might notice there are four decorated bulletin boards in the hall and that each of them are named. One direction you can take through the hall and beyond is the hallway that makes up part of the children's wing. Not too long ago, the walls of this hallway were repainted green. If you enter the building from the back parking lot, you'll immediately see a row of lockers on your right and a trophy case on your left.

If I were to quiz the congregation, I'd likely get a variety of answers (or shrugged shoulders) indicating a variety of degrees to which people pay attention to such details (I, personally, am notorious for being oblivious to such details). The fact of the matter is that we don't always pay full or even partial attention to things. Many times this is so because we don't necessarily need to.

But Isaiah 49:1–7 begins with two commands: listen and pay attention! And these are important commands to heed because, as we'll discover, the speaker giving these commands is our Lord Jesus and we are his target audience.

Therefore, we need to pay attention to his message for us—to walk carefully through the text. This text is actually a monologue by the Lord's Servant that concludes with the Lord's response to his Servant in verse 7. As we move through the text, I'll strive to make the case that this Servant of the Lord is none other than our Lord Jesus Christ, and that his message is a pronouncement about himself, particularly his commissioning as the Lord's Servant. As the Lord's Servant, he renders faithful service to and trust in the Lord despite his circumstances. And the Lord's vindication of his Servant's faith and trust will bring worldwide salvation through him and victory over his adversaries. This message to us that the Lord's Servant gives to teach us about himself begins in verses 1–3.

The Lord's Servant: Commissioned to Effectively Serve for the Glory of God

> Listen to me, O coastlands, and give attention, you peoples from afar. The LORD called me from the womb, from the body of my mother he named my name. He made my mouth like a sharp sword; in the shadow of his hand he hid me; he made me a polished arrow; in his quiver he hid me away. And he said to me, "You are my servant, Israel, in whom I will be glorified." (Isaiah 49:1–3)

Verse 1 begins with the Lord's Servant saying *"Listen* to me, O coastlands, and *give attention*, you peoples from afar." *"Listen"* and *"give attention"* are commands, and we are part of the group he's addressing. We know this because the "coastlands" and the "peoples from afar" are the Gentile nations near to and far from Israel that the Lord's Servant will bring salvation to as we'll see in verse 6. And his plan for this salvation was not simply an idea that suddenly came to the Lord's mind, for the Lord's Servant was commissioned before time. How do we know this?

The second part of verse 1 reads "The LORD called me from the womb, from the body of my mother he named my name." The statement

"The LORD called me from the womb" indicates that the Servant's calling preceded his birth. When combined with the language of the Servant being hidden in the Lord in verse 2, it conveys the sense that his calling is timeless. Peter makes this point clearly in 1 Peter 1:20 (NIV): "He was chosen before the creation of the world." So the Lord's Servant existed and was commissioned before time—another point which supports the conclusion this is a prophetic text about Jesus the Messiah—yet he was born into time. But not just any time, because the Lord's Servant would effectively serve at the right time.

Given this reality of the Servant's preexistence and the references of being hidden away, verse 2 suggests his service had been reserved for a particular time. This should bring to mind Paul's words in Romans 5:6 when he says of Christ, "For while we were still weak, at the right time Christ died for the ungodly." And we see his effective service in his comparison of himself to a sharp sword and a polished arrow, indicating that his mouth would be a powerful instrument to declare God's word and that, like a pointed arrow, his word would hit home with convicting precision. We see this incomparable aspect of Jesus' words throughout the Gospels, for example in John 7:46 when the temple officers, after failing to arrest Jesus as they were ordered to, told the chief priests and the Pharisees "No one ever spoke like this man!" But the Servant's timely and effective service wasn't self-serving; the Lord's Servant will serve for the glory of God.

In verse 3 the Servant affirms his commissioning source by quoting the Lord, but we run into a bit of a challenge with the Lord's statement "You are my servant, *Israel,* in whom I will be glorified." Is the Lord actually referring to the nation Israel as his servant in this passage? It's difficult to come to this conclusion, not only on the basis of some of the points in the text we've already seen but also by the fact that in verses 5–6, the Servant states that part of his purpose is to turn Israel back to the Lord. Let me offer you two interpretations that I believe are both valid and resolve the apparent inconsistency here.

One explanation is that the Servant is representative of Israel on their behalf, as the one who will be faithful whereas they were faithless.

A good example of this is Hosea 11:1–2: "When Israel was a child, I loved him, and out of Egypt I called my son. The more they were called, the more they went away; they kept sacrificing to the Baals and burning offerings to idols." This is clearly a reference to Israel's failure to heed God's calling to them as a nation, yet Matthew applies this same text to Jesus in Matthew 2:15 when Joseph and Mary brought the child Jesus out of Egypt and into the land of Israel after Herod's death: "This was to fulfill what the Lord had spoken by the prophet, 'Out of Egypt I called my son.'" Jesus here, and in a multitude of other gospel texts, clearly fulfilled, on Israel's behalf, what they failed to fulfill themselves.

Another possible explanation is this: There is a form of punctuation in the Hebrew text which introduces a pause between the words "servant" and "Israel" in verse 3, which may be intended to disconnect the word Israel from the statement "you are my Servant" and connect it instead with what follows, making an independent statement which would then be translated, "Israel, in you I will be glorified." In this case, "Israel" would refer to the place or the people where God will glorify himself through the work of his Servant.

So thus far, the Lord's Servant has given us some detail about himself concerning his commissioning for service and the nature of that service, but now we get to see something remarkable. We get to hear, firsthand, the Servant's perspective of his service.

The Lord's Servant Faithfully Served and Trusted God with the Results (Isaiah 49:4)

But we see this through some candid sentiments. Verse 4 reads, "But I said, 'I have labored in vain; I have spent my strength for nothing and vanity; yet surely my right is with the LORD, and my recompense with my God.'" You get the sense in the first part of verse 4 that the Servant sees his ministry as an abject failure. He has spent all of his strength and accomplished nothing. But as we consider the gospel accounts, isn't this just an honest evaluation of his audience's unwillingness to listen to what he had to say?

At the close of his ministry, the great crowds of Jesus' Galilean ministry were gone, Israel's religious leaders were plotting his death, and the disciples had forsaken him in the face of danger. Even in the last week of his ministry we see this pattern repeat, as the choruses of "Hosanna!" give way to "Crucify Him!" and his followers flee. Yet despite these distressing initial results, note the second half of verse 4 where the Servant's heart, mind, and will faithfully remain, particularly through the NIV's rendering: "Yet what is due me is in the LORD's hand, and my reward is with my God." The Lord's Servant met the Lord's standard for service to him. He was faithful and trusted whatever results which might come from the Lord's hand. And his reward from the Lord was no small thing.

The Lord Will Vindicate His Servant's Faith and Trust

And now the LORD says, he who formed me from the womb to be his servant, to bring Jacob back to him; and that Israel might be gathered to him—for I am honored in the eyes of the LORD, and my God has become my strength—he says: "It is too light a thing that you should be my servant to raise up the tribes of Jacob and to bring back the preserved of Israel; I will make you as a light for the nations, that my salvation may reach to the end of the earth."

Thus says the LORD, the Redeemer of Israel and his Holy One, to one deeply despised, abhorred by the nation, the servant of rulers: "Kings shall see and arise; princes, and they shall prostrate themselves; because of the LORD, who is faithful, the Holy One of Israel, who has chosen you." (Isaiah 49:5–7)

Verse 5 begins with "And now *the* LORD *says*," but the rest of the verse is the Servant's declaration of his work and purpose before sharing what the Lord says in verse 6. In verse 5, the Servant reminds us of his commissioning source, tells us his purpose of bringing about Israel's return to the Lord, and indicates the very high place he holds in his intimate relationship with the Lord. And then, in verse 6, he shares with us the Lord's statement of his Servant's matchless purpose: to bring worldwide salvation through his Servant.

Verse 6 reads "It is too light a thing that you should be my servant to raise up the tribes of Jacob and to bring back the preserved of Israel; I will make you as a light for the nations, that my salvation may reach to the end of the earth." And now we come to my purpose in selecting this text in the telling of this redemption and restoration story. Back in Genesis 3, we were introduced to a promised offspring of a woman God would bring into the world to conquer the consequences of our sin and its devastating effect on all creation. We continued through Genesis, seeing how faith in God's promise to bring this deliverer was the basis of faith for the way of the faithful, but then we saw the identity of this deliverer refined in God's promise to Abraham: he would come out of the great nation that God would raise up from Abraham's descendants to bring blessing to all the nations. We then saw the identity of this deliverer refined even further as a descendant of David who would reign over an everlasting restored kingdom of Israel and our story focused next on the blessings this would bring to Israel.

But what about God's promise to Abraham of blessing to the nations? Well, we caught a glimpse of that blessing in Isaiah 2, but now we see how: the Lord's Servant—Jesus the Messiah and descendant of David—will be the means of blessing to the nations by bringing salvation to the nations. And although this will, at first, seem like a failed effort as the Lord God acknowledges in verse 7, he does so in light of the result that the Lord will ultimately bring victory over his Servant's adversaries: "Thus says the LORD, the Redeemer of Israel and his Holy One, to one deeply despised, abhorred by the nation, the *servant* of rulers: 'Kings shall see and arise; princes, and *they shall prostrate themselves*; because of the LORD, who is faithful, the Holy One of Israel, who has chosen you.'" Or as Paul puts it in Philippians 2:5–11 (NIV):

> *Christ Jesus*: Who, *being in very nature God*, did not consider equality with God something to be used to his own advantage; rather,

he made himself nothing by taking the very nature of *a servant*, being *made in human likeness.* And being found in appearance as a man, he humbled himself by becoming *obedient to death*—even death on a cross! Therefore God *exalted* him *to the highest place* and gave him the name that is above every name, that at the name of Jesus *every knee should bow*, in heaven and on earth and under the earth, and every tongue acknowledge that *Jesus Christ is Lord*, to the glory of God the Father.

We see in this passage a Servant with a particular name, commissioned before time, coming as a man in time, seemingly to labor in vain, honored by the Lord in the highest way for his faithfulness in this seemingly vain labor, ultimately victorious as Lord over all—even over kings and princes—and all to the glory of God. Doesn't this sound like Isaiah 49?

And with respect to his being sent, Jesus considered the church's mission as an extension of his mission. In John 20:21 he told his disciples, "As the Father has sent me, I am sending you" and in Matthew 28:19 he commissions them, sending them to *"all nations."* And, with a twist that is very similar to Isaiah 49:6 where the Lord promised he will be "a light for the nations, that my salvation may reach to the end of the earth," Jesus tells his disciples in Acts 1:8, "you will be my witnesses in Jerusalem, and in all Judea and Samaria, and to the ends of the earth."

Isaiah 49:1–7 is a prophetic example of the Lord's Servant Jesus' ministry, which the Servant then clearly applies to us in the New Testament's revelation of this prophecy fulfilled. Have we paid attention to his message? If so, then there is a prominent aspect of his example for us to follow.

Serve Faithfully and Trust the Lord with the Results

The great nineteenth-century Christian missionary to China, Hudson Taylor, once said, "God's work done in God's way will never lack God's supply."[16] Jesus' earthly ministry perfectly served the Father's will, yet for a time appeared to be a vain labor that accomplished nothing, as the

Servant himself observed in verse four of Isaiah 49. But as we know, the Lord will bring great salvation and victory through our Savior's faithful service in God's plan of redemption and restoration.

American churches—I think more under the restless influence of the culture than of the Scriptures—typically measure the success of their ministries by swiftly attained results. We ought to measure our success by faithfulness to "God's work done in God's way," leaving the results in the Lord's hand where they belong.

Let me close this part of our story by making this point with a vivid illustration from the ministry of America's first missionaries, Adoniram and Ann Judson, as documented by Ruth Tucker in her book *From Jerusalem to Irian Jaya*. The Judsons set sail for south Asia in 1812, thirteen days after they were married, ultimately arriving at their mission field in the nation of Burma. Along the way, their first child was stillborn and Ann was bedridden upon their arrival. For the next twenty-six years, Adoniram would be consumed with the task of learning and translating the Burmese language from the original Hebrew and Greek biblical texts, all the while sharing the gospel and seeking to plant a church. Burma was a deeply impoverished nation and religiously consumed by the rituals and idolatry of Buddhism, and the threat the gospel represented to this religious culture routinely resulted in harsh oppression from the Burmese authorities.

In 1820, five years after their arrival in Burma, they saw the first profession of faith by a Burmese native; and by that summer, this first Burmese church had ten baptized members. But in that same year, just as the ministry was beginning to bear fruit, trial and tribulation began to dominate the Judsons' reality. Their second child died at the age of six months and Ann returned stateside for two years, gravely ill. She returned to Burma shortly before the nation fell into war with Britain in 1824, during which Adoniram was accused of being a spy and was imprisoned for a year and a half in appalling conditions, including a lengthy death march to relocate prisoners away from invading British forces—a march Judson barely survived.

In the ensuing years after his release from prison, Adoniram Judson lost his wife Ann and their third child, casting him into a deep depression which led him to dig his own grave and write "God is to me the Great Unknown. I believe in him, but I find him not."[17] Judson was eventually delivered from his depression and revived in his ministry, and married again to Sarah Boardman in 1834. They had eight children while serving in Burma, lost two, and then Sarah died as well in 1845. In 1846, having briefly returned stateside, Judson married a third time to Emily Chubbock and in 1847 they returned to ministry in Burma. Three years later, Judson died and Emily would die three years after that.

All told, Adoniram Judson served faithfully as Christ's servant in building the church in Burma. His life's work gave the Burmese people the Scriptures in their own tongue and his labor for the gospel led to a church in Burma, still very small at the time of his death. But one of his first conversions in 1820—a man named Maung Ing—led to the conversion of his daughter, and ultimately her son, who came to Christ in the very act of attempting to kill his mother on behalf of the Buddhist-influenced authorities: a dramatic conversion brought on by his witnessing the power of his mother's faith in Christ in the face of his attempt to kill her. His great-grandson Maung Tun—five generations after Adoniram Judson's ministry—founded the Burmese evangelistic movement "Witnessing for Christ," which continues Judson's work to this day.[18]

Our circumstances do not dictate our course. Faithfulness is our standard. The results are the Lord's to bring in his time. Trust in that.

Chapter 11

How Do You Save Lost Sheep?
(Isaiah 52:13–53:12)

In Isaiah 53:6, Isaiah records a profound confession: "*We all*, like sheep, have gone astray, *each of us* has turned to our own way." Phrases like "we all" and "each of us" don't leave any room for escape. As you consider this redemption and restoration story until now, we have walked purposefully to trace the thread through the Old Testament of the central message in the Bible. Now we come to both the midpoint of the story and the climax of the Bible's message.

A quick summary of the story to this point sounds something like this: There is one God who is infinitely good, powerful, and pure, and has always existed, and will always exist, as infinitely good, powerful, and pure. We know of him because he created everything—to include us—and has revealed himself to us in human history in ways that he has preserved for us to know and understand through the Bible. And although the Bible is very rich in details, one message rises to the fore amidst these details: "We all, like sheep, have gone astray, each of us has turned to our own way." We all have chosen to wander from the infinitely good, powerful, and pure God who created us to live in right relationship with him. We have all gotten ourselves . . . lost. And so, we are all in need of being found—to be saved from an existence, both now and forever, apart from our Creator. We have learned that God promised to send a deliverer into the world—a Savior—to save a humanity gone astray, but we've yet to get to the point in the story where God reveals *how* this deliverer—this Savior—will save us. Until now.

"How do you save lost sheep?" If we were the authors of this story, the answer to this question would probably involve an attractive hero with exceptional abilities who makes bold claims, saving the sheep and riding off into a sunset with cheers and applause! But that's not the picture of the hero we see in this passage from chapters 52–53 of Isaiah. What we get instead is a portrait so shocking that we need God's insight to understand it. It is an astonishing message with an astonishing result, because it turns our understanding of God and ourselves inside-out and upside-down.

How astonishing is the message? Astonishing enough that those who believe it wonder if those they share the message with could possibly believe it as well. In Isaiah 53:1, Isaiah writes, "Who has believed our message and to whom has the arm of the LORD been revealed?" And those who bear this message of a Savior have reason to be concerned over its reception.

God's Astonishing Message Defies Our Expectations

In Isaiah 53:1, the phrase "the arm of the Lord" is a way of referring to God's plan to save us. A well-known paraphrase of the Bible (MSG) states verse 1 this way: "Who believes what we've heard and seen? Who would have thought GOD's saving power would look like this?" Who indeed? It's a great question to ask, because God's saving power looked like something we would reject.

In verse 14 of chapter 52, God himself describes our reaction to the Savior he sends us: "many . . . were appalled at him." Why? The Lord explains in the rest of the verse: "his appearance was so disfigured beyond that of any human being and his form marred beyond human likeness." This was a result of this Savior being disfigured and marred at the hands of men. Beaten. A loser. Tender shoots and roots out of dry ground don't amount to anything by human terms, and Isaiah goes on to describe God's hero and Savior as a man who "had no beauty or majesty to attract us to him, nothing in his appearance that we should desire him" (53:2). The whole description is that of a "nobody." He couldn't have appeared to be any more insignificant.

Isaiah describes humanity's prevailing response to God's long-promised deliverer in verse 3: "He was despised and rejected by mankind, a man of suffering, and familiar with pain. Like one from whom people hide their faces he was despised, and we held him in low esteem." So, at least in appearance, God's plan to send a Savior to deliver the straying herd of humanity was received by a humanity thoroughly unimpressed. We were appalled. We held him in low esteem. We despised and rejected him. But not only did God's saving power look like *something* we would reject—it acted like *someone* we would reject.

I love action movies, particularly superhero movies. One of my favorite superhero movies is the first Marvel *Thor* movie. Thor was down and out and defeated by the end of the movie. In fact, he was dead: seemingly ultimately defeated by the forces of evil who killed him. But in an astonishing twist, he's restored to life with all of his former mighty powers and thrashes all of his foes, leaving them to wallow in defeat. This is how heroes act! Even if they lose, they go down with a fight and always bounce back!

But in verse 7 of Isaiah 53, the Savior is described as someone who is "oppressed and afflicted, yet he did not open his mouth; he was led like a lamb to the slaughter, and as a sheep before its shearers is silent, so he did not open his mouth." This is an image of a man who is accused by powers who seek to take his life. In verses 8–9 we see that it is a totally unjust accusation that leads to his execution, yet he doesn't utter a word or offer any other form of resistance to the judgment against him. God promised a deliverer to save the whole of humanity who had strayed from his good and perfect fold like sheep, and what he sends to us is a man who goes like a lamb to its slaughter. *God's astonishing message about a Savior defies our expectations about him because his saving power looks and acts like something and someone we would reject.* Would you believe this message, or would you join in rejecting this message about such a Savior?

This text from Isaiah was written more than seven hundred years before the time of Jesus Christ, and as God continued to reveal himself to humanity he revealed to us that the Man described in this passage is a prophetic description of Jesus Christ: a person God revealed to us to be not just a man, but the very Son of God. An eternal person who, along with God the Father and God the Holy Spirit, have each existed eternally as three persons, who are each fully God by nature, each living always in perfect relationship with one another. And Jesus Christ, the eternal Son of God, according to the will of God, took on human form and became, *by nature*, fully man as well. In other words, God's long-promised deliverer to save straying sheep . . . *became* a sheep. As we've seen in this passage from Isaiah, God himself submissively subjected himself to the great humility and suffering described here. Do you find this picture of a humble, suffering, and yet infinitely powerful God satisfying? Many do not.

A Christian minister named John Dickson once spoke on the theme of the wounds of God on a university campus in Sydney, Australia. During the question time, a Muslim man rose to explain how preposterous this claim was that the almighty Creator of the universe should subject himself to the forces of his own creation—that he would have to eat, sleep, and go to the toilet, much less die on a cross. The man went on to argue that it was illogical that God, the "cause of all causes" could have pain inflicted on him by any lesser beings. Dickson described the man's remarks as intelligent, clear, and civil. He simply responded by thanking the man for making the uniqueness of the Christian claim about Jesus Christ so clear. Then Dickson concluded, "What the Muslim denounces as blasphemy the Christian holds precious: God has wounds."[19]

What a statement! God has wounds. But why? What purpose could they possibly serve? *Perhaps it's because a true hero defeats our true enemies.* God's saving power defeats the enemy we must acknowledge.

Verses 4–6 and the first part of verse 10 in Isaiah 53, read together, state:

> Surely, he took up our pain and bore our suffering, yet we considered him punished by God, stricken by him, and afflicted. But he was pierced for our transgressions, he was crushed for our iniquities; the punishment that brought us peace was on him, and by his wounds we are healed. We all, like sheep, have gone astray, each of us has turned to our own way; and the LORD has laid on him the iniquity of us all. . . . Yet it was the LORD's will to crush him and cause him to suffer.

Consider the following three points from these verses that point us to our great need for the Savior Isaiah describes in this passage. First, we must align our understanding with God's will as to why Christ suffered. Isaiah teaches that it was God's will for Christ to suffer as he did, and reveals our tendency to miss the point as to why this is so when he writes "we considered him punished by God." Our tendency to resist finding fault in ourselves in the eyes of God is so strong that we fail to see ourselves as the reason for Christ's suffering. We'd rather attribute the cause for his suffering to something he did. But to receive God's saving power through Jesus Christ, we must see ourselves as the reason for Christ's suffering.

Second, given that we see ourselves as the reason for Christ's suffering, we must embrace specifically *why* we are the reason for Christ's suffering. The first part of verse 5 reads, "But he was pierced for our transgressions, he was crushed for our iniquities," a vivid reference to Christ's tortuous death on the cross. What Christ suffered on the cross has its root cause in our transgressions and iniquities. These two words describe the offences every human being commits against God's perfect moral law. Our nature is like that of sheep, as verse 6 teaches—to go astray, to choose our own way above God's way. This nature leaves us under God's punishment and destined for the terrible outcome of our spiritual illness: death.

Thirdly, in embracing the fact that we are the reason for Christ's suffering and we know why, we must embrace hope as well. God didn't send us a Savior to leave us to wallow in the despair and hopelessness of this terrible outcome of our straying; he sent us a Savior who saves lost sheep. To receive this rescue offer, we must trust the Savior to save the day. Notice at the end of verse 6 that, just as we've all strayed, so "the LORD has laid on him the iniquity of us all." Everything in us worthy of God's judgment and punishment was laid upon our Savior, and as the end of verse 5 teaches us, "the punishment that brought us peace was on him and by his wounds we are healed." In other words, Jesus suffered the fullness of the punishment for all of us, and for all our iniquities. He took it all in our place. He suffered what we deserve, and when we place our faith and trust in him, he forever gives us peace with God and healing from the consequences of our straying ways.

God's Astonishing Message Can Lead to an Astonishing Result!

God's work in saving lost sheep is an improbable story, but the first verse of the passage, Isaiah 52:13, begins the story in a very probable way: "my servant will act wisely; he will be raised and lifted up and highly exalted." However, as we've seen thus far, acting wisely entailed the improbable from a human perspective: deny yourself in every possible way; humbly and submissively accept God's will to shoulder the burden of untold suffering; and do all this to make salvation possible for the very people you've created, who reject your will and willfully go their own way. As the comments of the Muslim man above reveal, if this message is true, then God's way of doing things is not humanity's way of doing things. It does not appeal to a human sense of reason. But for those who embrace, by faith, this message as true, the One who suffered and died to save us has a promise for us—because he did not remain in the grave.

On the third day after his crucifixion, Jesus Christ rose from the dead to live eternally as both fully God and fully man. He is the Savior—the hero—who conquered sin and death on our behalf and made it possible for us to freely receive the eternal human life he alone possesses.

Just as Jesus unjustly suffered in our place to bear our punishment for our iniquities at the hands of God, so God will graciously grant us the eternal life in his presence that his Son Jesus alone deserves—the greatest exchange of fortune ever offered in the history of the universe, freely given by God—if we place our faith and trust in Jesus Christ.

This is essentially what Isaiah foretells in verses 10–11 of chapter 53, although in very figurative language. I'll close this chapter with the question Isaiah asks in verse 1 of chapter 53: "Who has believed our message?" Have you? In the Gospel of John, written some 750 years after Isaiah, John gives an eyewitness account of how Isaiah's prophecy was fulfilled by Jesus Christ. John records Jesus' promise, which still applies to those who hear it today: "Very truly I tell you, whoever hears my word and believes him who sent me has eternal life and will not be judged but has crossed over from death to life" (John 5:24, NIV).

Won't you accept Jesus' invitation to hear and believe the message about him, receive the eternal life he freely gives, and cross over from a destiny of death and judgment to the life he alone can give? As one appointed and called by him to bear this message to you, I invite you—I plead with you on his behalf—to trust in him today.

Chapter 12

The Great Commission, Part One: To the Jew First (Matthew 10:1–15)

In the beginning, God created everything, and it was very good. Soon thereafter, the first people he created—Adam and Eve—rebelled against his will. "The fall," as it is often called, resulted in our separation from God and the tragic consequences of death and judgement. This was followed over some length of time by the account of Noah and the worldwide flood, demonstrating that rebellion is universally inevitable in our nature and that the finality of God's judgment must be equally universally inevitable, apart from his gracious intervention on our behalf. Thankfully, as indicated very early on in the biblical story, God's gracious intervention was promised in the form of a man he would send into the world to deliver us, to save us. A gracious deliverance was demonstrated through God's intervention to save Noah and his family—and, as we saw in the previous chapter from Isaiah 53, a gracious deliverance was accomplished for us through the life, death, and resurrection of Jesus Christ.

But, as both the Old and New Testament accounts beautifully come together to portray, God's deliverance through Jesus Christ didn't just save us from consequences; it also saved us *for* something. It saved us for a restored creation God that will ultimately make completely new.

God's plan of salvation in the Old Testament seems to unfold as a particular offer, rooted first in his promise to the faithful remnant of his people Israel and then expanded to the Gentile nations of the world. Paul implies this progression in Romans 11, as he describes the Gentiles as wild olive shoots grafted into God's plan of salvation; and he explicitly indicates this progression in Romans 1:16 as he describes the gospel as "the power of God for salvation to everyone who believes, *to the Jew first* and also to the Greek." Jesus Christ has accomplished everything to obtain eternal salvation for all who believe, and with this chapter, we begin the first part of a four-part segment within our story intended to show how the Great Commission both followed this progression of salvation—Jew first and then Gentile—and entailed a gospel which remained rooted in the age-old promise to Israel of the coming kingdom of God.

Matthew 10:1–15 is chock full of ministry principles that apply well to us today. I don't want to pass up the opportunity to capitalize on this teaching, so I'm going to begin with a topical look at the text, which focuses on application; and then conclude with a second point of focus which shows, from the text, the place of Israel and the kingdom in the advance of the gospel under Christ's direction. As Christ's followers, we must always submit ourselves to his direction. We are the laborers in his harvest, and it ought to be our desire to serve him well. Even though we may stumble in our service to him, he is never faithless.

Jesus' Instruction Is Faithful, and His Ways the Highest Example

At the core of Jesus' approach to discipleship is his commitment to his people. From Matthew 10, an application the church can take by his example—particularly ministry leaders—is to purposefully invest a godly life in people, and with an eternal perspective.

In the verses immediately preceding Matthew 10—Matthew 9:35–38—Jesus models to his disciples the hard and loving work of ministry, proclaiming the gospel of the kingdom from city to city and healing people amidst the crowds who came to him, all with a deep sense of compassion for the people he was ministering to.

Back in Matthew 4, after Jesus first began calling disciples to follow him, we see this exact same pattern. Knowing the gospel writers did not include every blow-by-blow detail of Jesus' ministry, Matthew's repetition of this pattern indicates that Jesus consistently and repeatedly lived his ministry before his disciples through words, attitudes, and actions. They heard the gospel preached repeatedly, they saw his genuine compassion for the needy, and they saw him labor tirelessly. Having invested his life in his followers by fully modeling the very labors he was about to commission them into, in verses 1–5 of Matthew 10 Jesus calls them to himself, delegates his authority to them, and sends them out.

In these verses, for the first time, Matthew lists all of the twelve together and calls them apostles. The twelve aren't perfect and have a long way to go, but as his apostles Jesus knows the eternal significance of what he's preparing them for. In Luke 22:30, Jesus will tell these men that they will eat and drink at his table in his kingdom "and sit on thrones judging the twelve tribes of Israel." These men go bearing the gospel of the very kingdom that they will, in part, rule over alongside Jesus Christ. In 2 Timothy 2:12, Paul says the same of those who have placed our faith and trust in Jesus Christ: "if we endure, we will also reign with him."

If you're a leader in Christ's church, entrusted by him with a ministry, then you're entrusted with the people who serve under your leadership in ministry. Model genuine Christlike words, attitudes, and actions, with the aim of imparting those very things to the people you lead. Do this as a tireless labor of love, both for those who will follow your example in ministry and for the sake of those who will be blessed by their ministry. And do so mindful of whom you're leading: children of God who, in Christ, are more than conquerors and are joint heirs with him in his coming kingdom. *There is no greater undertaking for the believer in this life, but don't go it alone.* Pursue ministry as a team effort.

You'll notice in verses 2–4 that Matthew lists the twelve apostles in pairs; and in Mark's account Jesus sends them out in pairs. This approach accomplished two things that applies in any church ministry context. Pairing up enabled the disciples to support, protect, and empower each other better than if each went alone. In the military, they refer to this concept as *mutual support*: a conviction grounded in the tried and true experience that solo acts bring both risk to the mission and to the individual. God fashions us as a church—one body, supernaturally connected to Christ by his Holy Spirit, and through Christ, to one another. We serve him as a community working together . . . *but not as a herd*.

Notice in the text that, by not staying together as a larger group of twelve, the disciples also maximized their ability to reach large numbers of people. The body of Christ is both connected and diverse, and the nature of his ministry for the church is diverse. A timeless principle for discipleship is that we serve in community. But our works of service, by Christ's design, are as diverse as his body. As a church, we need to always labor under the direction of the Spirit to recognize how we best serve as groups within our fellowship without diminishing the unity of our fellowship. So then, *any church seeking to be faithful in its calling to discipleship must invest Christlike lives in one another, working as a team that is both unified as a community yet diverse in its ministries*. And lastly, as Christ's church serves, we serve for the sake of the gospel in a way that honors God.

In verses 8–13, Jesus essentially tells the Twelve to rely on those they will minister to for all their provisions. This is an important general principle, especially for those who are in positions where they earn their livelihood from ministry. Paul makes this point in 1 Corinthians 9, going so far as to say in verse 14 that "the Lord commanded that those who proclaim the gospel should get their living by the gospel." Although Paul presents this principle as a command, we need to look beyond Matthew 10 to fully understand the principle Jesus is impressing upon his disciples here. In Luke 22:36, Jesus reminds his disciples of the mission in Matthew 10, but with his crucifixion near, he now tells them, "But now let the one who has a moneybag take it, and likewise a knapsack." Likewise, in 1 Corinthians 9, despite the fact that Paul could claim a right to compensation on the basis of God's command, he refrains from doing so because the gospel was better served toward the Corinthians' spiritual condition by Paul laboring to meet his own needs.

In essence, the principle Jesus is calling the disciples to heed here—that the laborer is worthy of his or her wages—is true and ought to be the prevailing practice in ministry. But there are times when, for the sake of the gospel, we are called to willingly forego what God commands ought to be. Understanding when to do this is a delicate balance that the *New American Commentary* on Matthew 10 offers some great insight on:

> There are scriptural paradigms for missionary and ministry activity that recognize dependence both on others' support and on one's own resources earned through a different trade. Neither may be made absolute. What is most likely to advance the gospel in an honorable way should be adopted in any given context. A serious danger of paid ministry is that preachers will tailor their message to suit their supporters. A key problem with "tentmaking" is a lack of accountability of ministers to those with whom they work.[20]

Our service in ministry should seek, first and foremost, to advance the gospel in a God-honoring way. As the commentator points out, should we find ourselves serving and receiving the wages the laborer is worthy of, honoring God for the sake of the gospel means never tailoring the gospel to satisfy those who hear it—especially if your listeners are the ones paying those wages. But, should the ministry context lead you to become a tentmaker, honoring God for the sake of the gospel means remaining accountable to those you serve despite the independence from them that your labors may grant you.

Now, let's shift gears from points of application in ministry to points of theological understanding of God's overall plan of salvation.

Salvation to the Jew First: Rooted in the Age-Old Promise of the Coming Kingdom of God

Now this point entails two related yet distinct claims, so let me address the first: *salvation is to the Jew first.* In verses 5–6 Matthew writes "These twelve Jesus sent out, instructing them, 'Go nowhere among the Gentiles and enter no town of the Samaritans, but go rather to the lost sheep of the house of Israel.'" In the next chapter we'll look at Matthew 15, where Jesus tells a Gentile Canaanite woman who's pleading with him to heal her daughter, "I was sent only to the lost sheep of the house of Israel" (v. 24). These exclusive statements by Jesus often trouble Christians who fail to understand that Jesus' purpose was not to ultimately exclude the Gentiles but rather to honor the Father's will and purpose in his plan of salvation.

Over the course of this book, we've seen how the Old Testament Scriptures teach that the Christ would bring salvation both to Israel and to the Gentile nations, and we've also seen that God's purpose in bringing "salvation to . . . the Jew first and also to the Greek" is a plan that ultimately best serves to accomplish his desire for "all people to be saved and to come to the knowledge of the truth" (1 Timothy 2:4). For the purpose of this chapter, I want to simply let this point that salvation is to the Jew first stand; but over the course of the next three chapters, I'm going to develop it further. I hope you'll see that this point of salvation theology is worthy of at least considering how it may, and even ought, to apply to the church's approach to ministry. More to follow, but let me conclude this chapter with a similar point on the gospel.

The gospel is rooted in the age-old promise of the coming kingdom of God, yet the church today tends to present the gospel from the perspective of what Jesus Christ saved us *from,* while diminishing, or inaccurately representing, the details of what he saved us *for.* Yes, he saved us for restored relationship with God. Yes, we will go to heaven to be with Christ when we die. Yet in verses 7–8, Jesus commands the disciples to not only do the miraculous works he gave them the authority to do in verse 1, but also tells them, "And proclaim as you go, saying, 'The kingdom of heaven is at hand.'"

This idea of the kingdom is not new. God repeatedly presented salvation to the faithful in Israel as eternal life gained through their resurrection into a restored kingdom of Israel under the rule of the Messiah, the promised descendant of David who would reign from David's throne in

Jerusalem forever. Not surprisingly, the kingdom is constantly presented as part of the gospel throughout the New Testament, particularly in the Gospels. The interchangeable word and phrases "kingdom," "kingdom of God," and "kingdom of heaven" are used more than one hundred times in the New Testament. In ten instances, "the kingdom" and "the gospel" are used together in a way that makes them interchangeable as well. The gospel is a message that, when embraced by faith, saves us for a coming kingdom—what we were ultimately saved for. The message and its ultimate end are necessarily intertwined.

Is there a kingdom in your gospel? Is there a kingdom in your hope for eternity? Do we not pray "your *kingdom come*, your will be done on earth as it is in heaven?" In Acts 28:31, as Paul is living in a prison in Rome, Luke writes that Paul welcomed all who came to him, "proclaiming *the kingdom of God* and teaching about the Lord Jesus Christ with all boldness and without hindrance," not unlike how Jesus commissioned his disciples to proclaim to the lost sheep of Israel. As with the previous point, I'm going to let this point also stand for now but further develop it over the course of the next three chapters.

So, like a great cliffhanger in an old movie, I leave you for now with a couple of major assertions about the gospel without validating them! So then, read on through the next three chapters and the case for "to the Jew first," and for a kingdom in your gospel. As you consider this case, I pray you'll come to see it as an integral part of the gospel: a redemption and restoration story.

Chapter 13

The Great Commission, Part Two: Bread from the Table (Matthew 15:21–28)

Imagine arriving at your favorite restaurant on a Friday night and there's a line of folks waiting for seating. The manager takes your name, hands you a buzzer, and tells you it'll be a forty-five-minute wait. As you're waiting, a well-dressed couple whom you noticed had pulled up in a much nicer car than yours walks up to the manager, and is immediately seated . . . in a restaurant which doesn't take reservations. That would justifiably upset most folks, I think. But take the same scenario and keep everything the same with two exceptions: ditch the fancy car and replace the privileged couple with a Soldier in uniform walking on a prosthetic leg. This is far less likely to upset you, isn't it?

You see, the temptation in this story is to focus on the customers, but I'd like you to focus on the manager. It's really the motivation behind the manager's decision that affects our response in each scenario, isn't it? It helps to know that the manager has good and right intentions, doesn't it? And if we trust those intentions to be good and right, then the manager's plan for seating arrangements on a busy Friday night hopefully doesn't have to contend with our objections. Eventually, everyone waiting to get seated will be seated and served.

In John 6:48–51, Jesus says "I am the bread of life. Your fathers ate the manna in the wilderness, and they died. This is the bread that comes down from heaven, so that one may eat of it and not die. I am the living bread that came down from heaven. If anyone eats of this bread, he will live forever." There is room at the table in God's kingdom for all who place their faith in trust in Jesus Christ, the bread of eternal life, and all who partake of the bread of life will live forever. And even if the master's plan for seating arrangements might follow a particular order, a mark of saving faith in Jesus Christ is trusting that the master's plan is good and right.

Previously, we saw Jesus send his disciples on a mission exclusively to the Jewish people to proclaim God's offer of salvation, in line with God's plan to offer salvation to his people Israel first. Now we're going to see Jesus reaffirm this same order of salvation in a fascinating yet difficult story. But as I hope you see, this is a story that, when rightly understood, also shows Jesus reaffirming God's promise to Israel's forefathers that through Israel, all the Gentile peoples of the earth would be blessed with God's offer of salvation in Jesus Christ, the bread of life.

The story centers on Jesus' encounter with a Gentile woman, but there's a lot to unpack for us to rightly understand this passage. And so, with right understanding as the aim, consider this passage through the lens of *three Cs*: the *context* of this encounter; the *contact*, i.e., the encounter itself; and the *confession*—the woman's understanding of the encounter and Jesus' response to it. As we unpack this encounter, I hope you'll appreciate that this is a remarkable encounter in any context in the culture of the time, because it is an encounter with a Gentile woman—a mom, in fact, acting courageously as a mom and finding herself commended for heroic faith by none other than the Lord Jesus Christ in a way that precious few people in all of the gospels were commended by him. It's a great story in and of itself, but it's set in a very important broader *context*.

The Canaanite Woman: A Faithful Contrast to the Leaders of God's Chosen People

The text for this chapter is in the middle of a section of Matthew, beginning in 15:1 and ending in 16:12. Thematically, this large section of text begins and ends with a conflict between Jesus and different groups of

Jewish leaders; and like bookends, these conflicts end with Jesus harshly rejecting the teaching of these Jewish leaders. But in between these contentious encounters, Jesus departs from the land of Israel into two different Gentile territories—where, in striking contrast with the Jewish leaders, both this Gentile woman as well as a large, predominantly Gentile crowd respond faithfully and enthusiastically to his message.

To get a sense of the contrast, let's look at the conflict that precedes Matthew 15:21–28, beginning with verse 1 of chapter 15. Jesus is in the region of the northwest shore of the Sea of Galilee, and Pharisees and scribes came to him there from Jerusalem. What follows in verse 2 is an accusation against Jesus by these leaders that Jesus' disciples "break the tradition of the elders[.] For they do not wash their hands when they eat." Jesus then counters in verses 3–6 by pointing out that these leaders also have a tradition that effectively nullifies God's commandment to honor your mother and father, culminating in his condemnation of them as "hypocrites!" in verses 7–9. They worship God in vain, because they are "teaching as doctrines the commandments of men."

As if that wasn't enough, Jesus then publicly humiliates these leaders by pointing out to the surrounding crowd the stupidity of the elders' tradition of handwashing before meals in verses 10–11. It's the kind of straightforward, no-nonsense tongue lashing that might make one uncomfortable if you were a follower of Jesus raised to respect the authority of these religious leaders. You see this in verse 12, where Matthew writes "Then the disciples came and said to him, 'Do you know that the Pharisees were offended when they heard this saying?'" They are most concerned about offending these leaders, but Jesus' response to them in the verses that follow—as well as in his response to them in a very similar encounter in Matthew 16 (the other bookend conflict in this larger section of text)—is most concerned with his disciples' lingering desire to align their hearts and minds with the teaching of religious leaders who have rejected their Lord, King, and Messiah.

There are two masters here: one who brings the commandments of God and another who brings the commandments of men. You can't serve two masters. And so, as we move into our text, Jesus is concerned about the ambivalence of his disciples. We need to read this encounter with the understanding that Jesus is addressing two audiences: disciples who are still somewhat stuck in an allegiance to Israel's leaders, whom Jesus calls "blind guides" in verse 14 of chapter 15; and a Gentile Canaanite woman who is just what the doctor ordered as a model of great faith. Assuming that Jesus came to always do the Father's will, our text begins in verse 21 with a deliberate and purposeful movement out of the land of Israel and into Gentile territory. We've considered the broader *context*. Now it's time to consider "C" number two: the *contact*.

An Unlikely Contact in an Unlikely Place for a Profound Purpose

Jesus makes this contact in verses 21–23, as Matthew writes:

And Jesus went away from there and withdrew to the district of Tyre and Sidon. And behold, a Canaanite woman from that region came out and was crying, "Have mercy on me, O Lord, Son of David; my daughter is severely oppressed by a demon." But he did not answer her a word. And his disciples came and begged him, saying, "Send her away, for she is crying out after us."

Jesus is on the move in Matthew 15–16, and in our text he's on the move to the district of Tyre and Sidon, some fifty miles away from Jesus' previous location. This is a long distance to go for seemingly no reason. Matthew begins verse 22: "and behold"—communicating that what follows is highly unusual. You can imagine how unusual, perhaps surreal, it must have seemed to the disciples to see and hear a Gentile woman calling Jesus "Lord" and "Son of David" and Matthew refers to her as a Canaanite.

This reference would have conjured up images in the mind of a faithful Jew of the wicked Gentile nations that God drove out from the land in order to bring his people into it. Matthew may be using this term to convey to the reader that the disciples held the spectacle of this Gentile woman calling on the Jewish Messiah somewhat in revulsion. You get a sense of this in verse 23, where they are begging Jesus to "send her away," as if it couldn't happen fast enough. But Jesus has remained silent—probably adding to the disciples' level of agitation. What's going on? I'd like to contend that Jesus' journey to this region wasn't random or pointless, but rather, for a profound purpose.

Think again about the deep-seated concerns Jesus has about his disciples and the degree to which the Jewish religious leaders' traditions and commands had lingered with the disciples. Think about how Jesus verbally scourged these leaders for nullifying God's word in the process. What might the disciples be thinking as this annoying and unclean woman is hounding them like a dog? Perhaps they're thinking something like, "If only the religious leaders saw us in Gentile territory—not only tolerating the presence of a Gentile woman, but also our master remaining silent and refusing to send her away. What would they think? What would they say?" Perhaps they would say something like what Jesus says in verse 24: "I was sent only to the lost sheep of the house of Israel."

Think about how amazing this statement is in a variety of ways. First, it's true. This is Jesus' mission. As we'll see in the next two chapters, Jesus commissions his disciples to be the ones to take the gospel to the Gentiles; but his mission *as a man in his earthly ministry* is, according to the Father's plan, to offer salvation to the lost sheep of Israel.

Second, it's exactly what the disciples would expect and want to hear. "Yes, Jesus, way to tell her! The religious leaders clearly wouldn't be offended by that!" Third, it indicates that the disciples were expecting him to heal her and then send her away. Jesus' objection in verse 24 only makes sense if the disciples were asking him to respond to her request so that she would go away—especially in light of the woman's immediate reaction to fall before him in verse 25. Jesus' silence, followed by this ingenious response, is deliberate and dramatic, intended to prompt a *confession* ("C" number three) from this woman that would serve as a matchless object lesson of God's salvation plan to those men who would ultimately play a leading part to carry out God's plan in the early church.

The Confession of the Canaanite Woman Confirmed God's Plan of Salvation

Note that this woman already demonstrated knowledge of God's plan in verse 22, referring to Jesus as "Lord, Son of David"—a title that conveyed an understanding of God's promise to bring the Messiah into the world as a descendant of David. She is appealing to Jesus for mercy on the basis of God's promises. But there needed to be more. At least in the eyes of his disciples, this could be nothing more than an appeal to one of many gods by a desperate mother and a knowledgeable pagan. But as we'll see, the interaction in verses 25–28 illustrates something genuine and extraordinary about this desperate mother. The Canaanite woman's confession proves faithful in a multidimensional way, beginning with her posture.

The woman assumed the posture of worship (verse 25): "But she came and knelt before him, saying, 'Lord, help me.'" Still referring to him as Lord, she knelt before him. The verb translated "knelt" means "to express in attitude or gesture one's complete dependence on or submission to a high authority figure."[21] It is used when a person assumes an attitude and posture of worship; thus the NLT translates verse 25, "But she came and *worshiped* him." So now we have a desperate Gentile mom, pleading for her daughter's healing, calling Jesus Lord and Son of David, and proving herself at a whole new level in the eyes of everyone by worshipping Jesus! So, what would Jesus do? What would the woman do next?

The woman's faith rose to the challenge of a great test. Jesus' earlier statement "I was sent only to the lost sheep of the house of Israel" had spurred the woman to action, and his response to the desperate worshipping woman in verse 26 seems equally unkind as he replies to her cry for help: "It is not right to take the children's bread and throw it to the dogs." Ladies and moms, is this making you feel the love for the Lord right about now?

Let's unpack this statement for a moment. First, "dogs" isn't derogatory here. It's the word used for small dogs who were kept as household pets—a point that's made more evident in verse 27 when the woman notes these dogs eat the crumbs from the master's table. The dogs are part of the household in Jesus' illustration, *but they're not the children*. When taken literally, it makes the obvious point that no good master would feed his children's bread to the household pets. In this illustration, Jesus is portraying the Father as a master of a household with his children, the people of Israel. The bread is, as Jesus himself referred to himself, representative of God's salvation through Jesus Christ, the Son of God. Finally, the dogs are the Gentiles, who will not be the first to partake of this salvation for the Jew first, a point Jesus demonstrated in Matthew 10 and here again in Matthew 15. Jesus has just *fed* this woman God's plan of salvation in a masterful way that can only be rightly responded to—if she gets it.

And her response? "Yes, Lord, yet even the dogs eat the crumbs that fall from their masters' table." The good-hearted manager may choose to give the amputee veteran a seat before you, but you'll both end up enjoying your meal in good order. Because the bread of life came into the world to the Jew first doesn't mean all the nations of the earth will be deprived. The woman's response is a profound expression of humble faith, precious in the sight of God. Notice she begins by saying "Yes, Lord, yet even . . ." Those two words, "yet even," reveal immense wisdom and faith. She doesn't phrase her answer like some profound counterpunch or "gotcha" moment with the Lord; rather, she submits to her place as the dog in the illustration and then affirms to the Lord the very exalted place among the redeemed that he himself promises to bring to the Gentiles in the Scriptures. She knows God's plan, understands her place in it, and embraces it rather than dispute the mysterious ways of God's divine choice and purpose as unfair. Her faith and understanding proves to outstrip the faith and understanding of Jesus' disciples, likely to both their shame and ultimate learning, and it mocks the empty faith of Israel's religious leaders whom, as Jesus says in verse 13, will ultimately be uprooted by his heavenly Father.

So where does Jesus' heart truly stand toward this faithful, Gentile, desperate mother? Not as the insensitive cad as many uninformed readers have often concluded from this passage. Rather, Jesus exalts the Canaanite woman's faith to a high place. In verse 28, he responds with emotion and respect: "'O woman, great is your faith! Be it done for you as you desire.' And her daughter was healed instantly." The term "woman" here is a term of respect, and Jesus puts her on a plane of his commendation for her faith that only one other person in the Gospels receives: the Roman centurion in Matthew 8—who was also a Gentile.

And so, it bears repeating: there is room at the table in God's kingdom for all who place their faith in trust in Jesus Christ, the bread of life—even if that bread is presented "to the Jew first." In the mystery of his will in bringing salvation to every tribe, tongue, and nation, the Master's plan for seating arrangements follows a particular order, and a mark of a mature faith in Jesus Christ is trusting that the Master's plan is good and right. But let me take one more stab at, perhaps, helping make more sense of his plan with a concluding illustration.

Imagine you're part of a group of spelunkers—folks who like to explore caves. During one of your expeditions, the group becomes trapped because of an unexpected flood of water that leaves you with only a single, narrow, flooded passage to escape. As you evaluate this option, you come to realize that only one person in the group—a petite young woman—has any chance of even getting out to the surface. Therefore, as a group, you choose to send her to safety through this passage. The point of the choice is not so that she alone gets saved, but that she is able to bring help and equipment to ensure the rest get rescued. The choice in this case is a purposeful choice in a particular order for the sake of many.

I think God's plan of bringing salvation through and to the Jews first is similar to this in concept, although the analogy falls short in the sense our *full* understanding of the "how" in "to the Jew first" will always elude us. As Paul writes of it in Romans 11:33–34, "Oh, the depth of the riches and wisdom and knowledge of God! How unsearchable are his judgments and how inscrutable his ways! For who has known the mind of the Lord, or who has been his counselor?" He is a good Father with a good plan. Like the Canaanite woman, faith trusts in that and embraces it.

Chapter 14

The Great Commission, Part Three: To the Nations! (Matthew 28:16–20)

A few chapters back when we considered the beginning of Isaiah 49, we actually previewed our present chapter, as the Isaiah passage prophesied a movement of God's plan of salvation from Israel to the ends of the earth. Isaiah 49:6 states "It is too light a thing that you should be my servant to raise up the tribes of Jacob and to bring back the preserved of Israel; I will make you as a light for the nations, that my salvation may reach to the end of the earth." As you may recall, God is the one speaking in this passage and the Messiah is the one he is referring to, who will bring salvation both to Israel and the nations.

In the previous two chapters, we have seen how this prophecy began to unfold in Matthew's gospel more than seven hundred years after Isaiah prophesied it. We learned how Jesus, the Messiah, sent his disciples to the lost sheep of Israel with the message of salvation; and then learned how Jesus deliberately went to Gentile regions to foreshadow the great work of God in bringing salvation to them as well. Jesus' disciples have been trained in their gospel mission, going to the Jews first, and Jesus has demonstrated this mission in action to an expanded Gentile audience. And although it will take these Jewish disciples quite some time to connect the dots to their worldwide *Jew and Gentile* mission field, in Matthew 28 Jesus gives them their next set of marching orders in carrying out God's plan of salvation: "Go therefore and make disciples of all nations."

Jesus Commands His Church to Be His Agents of Salvation

Let's begin our look at this passage with what's plain. First, there's a two-part command in this passage: "Go . . . and make disciples." Second, we know from verse 18 that Jesus is giving the command and from verse 16 that he's commanding at least the eleven disciples; there may be others present. Third, we know from verse 19 that all the nations are the object of this disciple-making mission.

There are also three assertions made in this passage that need to be explained. First, there is a timeframe for this mission: to the end of the age. Second, those tasked with the mission has been expanded from Jesus' disciples to the church. And third, disciple-making has been equated with salvation blessing. Let's tackle the first two now in this point and the third—why equate disciple-making with salvation blessing?—in the next main point.

First, why is Jesus' command in effect to the end of the age? The simple answer to the question is in the second half of verse 20, where Jesus tells the disciples, "And behold, I am with you always, to the end of the age." Jesus' statement is meant to convey that he will be present with them as they carry out his command, and "the end of the age" refers to the current segment of human history which will continue until Christ physically returns to judge the earth and establish his kingdom.

You might ask, "How can this be so, since Jesus ascended back to heaven soon after giving this command?" But we also know from the Scriptures that he promised to send the Holy Spirit to dwell in his followers. We see this in John 14, as Jesus taught them, "If anyone loves me, he will keep my word, and my Father will love him, and we will come to him and make our home with him. . . . But the Helper, the Holy Spirit, whom the Father will send in my name . . . will teach you all things and bring to your remembrance all that I have said to you" (John 14:23, 26). Jesus will be with his followers until the end of the age, through the Holy

Spirit whom the Father will send to dwell in us as Jesus promised. And until the end of the age, there is a mission to accomplish, so let's get busy and complete *our* mission!

But why does Jesus' command apply to the church? Wasn't Jesus addressing his disciples? One answer is the common-sense reality that these eleven disciples have all died but the end of the age hasn't come yet, as well as the fact that it's virtually impossible for eleven guys to make disciples from every nation on the earth. Furthermore, the Holy Spirit did come, as we see in Acts 2, giving birth to the church. Throughout the rest of the Scriptures and human history to the present, it has been the church which has carried out Jesus' disciple-making mission.

Finally, this work of the church finds its place in God's overall story of redemption and restoration. Take a look at Genesis 22:17–18. God repeats an earlier promise he made to Abraham: "I will surely bless you, and I will surely multiply your offspring as the stars of heaven and as the sand that is on the seashore. And your offspring shall possess the gate of his enemies, and in your offspring shall all the nations of the earth be blessed." As we've seen in our story thus far, God's blessing of salvation will come to all the nations through Abraham's descendants. But here, in the second half of verse 17, the word "offspring" is singular, because the pronoun "his" in the phrase "his enemies" is singular. This blessing will come through a single offspring of Abraham.

Furthermore, Matthew begins his genealogy of Jesus in Matthew 1 with Abraham, and in Matthew 16:18, Jesus, the single offspring of Abraham in whom all the nations of the earth will be blessed, says this about his church: "I will build my church, and the gates of hell shall not prevail against it." Compare "The gates of hell shall not prevail against it" to "Your offspring shall possess the gate of his enemies." The church is God's chosen instrument to bring the blessing of salvation to all the nations of the earth, just as Christ commands in Matthew 28. But Christ is commanding disciple-making here. How does disciple-making equate to salvation blessing?

Jesus Commands His Church to Make Disciples as the Means of Salvation

But before we get to where we find salvation in disciple-making, let's tackle the obvious: that disciple-making entails some aspects plainly found in our text. First, as the second part of verse 19 teaches, disciple-making entails "baptizing them in the name of the Father and of the Son and of the Holy Spirit." When something is done in the name of someone, this means it is being done according to the nature and character of the one being named. Therefore, Jesus is commanding these eleven disciples that part of disciple-making entails baptizing, with their willing confession that the nature and character of God is a Trinity—that he exists as three persons: Father, the Son, and Holy Spirit.

If you're a follower of Jesus Christ and you have not been baptized, the question you must ask yourself—knowing Christ is present by the Holy Spirit who dwells in you—is, why do you insist on disobeying his very first command to a disciple? I'll leave that between you and him, but please see your pastor if this applies to you and your Lord and Savior has managed to convince you to heed his command.

A second clear dimension of disciple-making is in the first part of verse 20: it entails "teaching them to observe all that I have commanded you." The word "observe" here means "to persist in obedience."[22] Notice that Jesus never foresees a time when any part of his teaching will be needless, outmoded, superseded, or untrue. Also, notice that the disciple is measured not merely by knowledge, but by true learning; a follower both knows and obeys God's word.

If I were to stop here, you might think that one earns their status as a disciple through baptism and obedience, but not so. This is where coming to salvation enters as a component of disciple-making. The mission of disciple-making *begins* with coming to salvation: hearing and believing the gospel.

The command "make disciples" in verse 19 is actually a single verb in the Greek text. It's only used one other time in the New Testament in the sense that it's used here, in Acts 14:21. Let's look at that verse in its context: "But when the disciples gathered about him, he rose up and entered the city, and on the next day he went on with Barnabas to Derbe. When they had *preached the gospel* to that city and had *made many disciples*, they returned to Lystra and to Iconium and to Antioch" (Acts 14:20–21).

The first step of becoming a disciple is to place your faith and trust in Jesus Christ according to his gospel; the first step in *making* disciples is to go and share the gospel. To go to the nations. To go to places like Derbe, Lystra, Iconium, and Antioch. To go across the street. To go to the place where you work or work out. To go to the place where you eat or compete. To go to your own home or to a soul who's lost and alone. And when you go, bear the message of God's salvation through faith in Jesus Christ as we've been commanded. Don't save people; that's not your place. Rather, be obedient to his command. Do what he says. Tell people the good news about what he did to save them and trust God with the results. Jesus' disciples were commanded to take this message to the Gentile world, of whom they had been taught through the centuries to live in separation from, just as you would an unclean animal. If you're intimidated by the mission, imagine how they felt. And we are still a people who live in separation, yet are called to bridge those differences with a message of salvation.

Disciple-Making Requires Bridging Divides That Separate Us

Back in 2013 I traveled as a part of an evangelizing team to the Amazon jungle and the communities of the Shuar people, who lived along the Morona River in southern Ecuador. The team was a blend of Ecuadorans and Americans, and our journey into the villages was pretty arduous despite months of physical training leading up to it—a flight to Quito, a harrowing drive through the mountains to the Amazon plains of southern Ecuador, and a six-hour ride in a long-boat canoe with an outboard motor to our trailhead on the river. From there, although it was only a couple miles to the village, the hike took several hours as we were carrying in all of our gear and supplies, often walking in knee-deep mud. (I learned later from some Shuar men that you solve the sinking problem by running on the mud rather than trying to walk through it!).

The Shuar people are only five decades or so separated from the practice of headhunting, and during our first full day in the village our presence upset enough of the native men that we received a threat of death unless we leaved immediately. Given their past, it should have been a cause for great fear, but something amazing happened. To a person, none of us expressed (or, honestly, felt) fear. We quickly concluded the Lord had sent us this far to share the gospel and we were not about to leave. "Behold, I am with you always."

Only the overcoming grace of the Lord's presence can explain our reaction. All in all, the Lord arranged a series of circumstances that led to even the most hostile of the villagers to allow us to share the gospel. One such villager was their "Syndico," essentially the village's chief. We were in the midst of nearly one hundred men who had gathered for a workday on common areas, and when I asked the Syndico through an interpreter if I could share the gospel with the men, with eyes that looked as if he'd rather kill me he told the interpreter, "You've got five minutes."

When it was all said and done, by the end of the week, and after showing the Jesus Film in the Shuar's mother tongue, dozens of people had responded to the gospel. And on our last night there, we exchanged gifts with the Syndico, who was now smiling and clutching a Bible we had given to him. It's an amazing story of danger and duress and death threats . . . and amazing grace. In truth, all the team did was "go" and share the gospel. From our perspective, the cultural divides were insurmountable. Grace eats those divides for breakfast!

To be a follower of Jesus Christ is to join yourself to God's great story of redemption and restoration—to join in the promised salvation through the offspring of a woman in Genesis 3. To join in the promised salvation through the offspring of Abraham in Genesis 12 and 22. To join in the promised salvation through the descendant of David in 2 Samuel 7. To join in the promised salvation that comes through and to the Jew first. To join in the Great Commission to his church to make disciples of all the nations unto the end of the age when he returns to gather his church to himself. After all, "It is too light a thing that you should be my servant to raise up the tribes of Jacob and to bring back the preserved of Israel; I will make you as a light for the nations, that my salvation may reach to the end of the earth." It's a daunting task, but the company we keep turns "mission impossible" to mission possible!

Jesus Promises to Always Be with His Church in Its Disciple-Making Mission

We've already addressed the sense of time: of how Jesus' mission for the church continues to the end of the age. But what I'd like to do with this last point is reemphasize *who* it is that will always be with us.

Let's trace a thread through Matthew for a moment. Until the middle of Matthew 11, Jesus is on his mission to the lost sheep of Israel; but after that point, Jesus' ministry takes on a different tone. It's evident at this point that the Jewish religious leaders and most of the people have rejected him as their Messiah. And so, as we saw in the previous chapter, Jesus' interaction with the leaders becomes confrontational; pronouncements of judgment toward the Jewish crowds and cities become frequent. This goes hand in hand with a ministry focused more on his small circle of followers, as well as several favorable and intentional encounters with Gentiles, foreshadowing to these disciples the work of the very mission given in Matthew 28. And as Matthew moves to the Great Commission in his gospel, he records a growing awareness of who Jesus is as well.

In Matthew 16:16, in response to Jesus' question to his disciples "Who do you say that I am?" Peter replies, "You are the Christ, the Son of the living God." The disciples' understanding of who Jesus is grew imperfectly, but it grew. So much so that in Matthew 28:17, Matthew writes of these disciples that "when they saw him they worshiped him"—an act they would not have engaged in had they believed Jesus to be anyone but God himself in the flesh. I know Matthew goes on to write "but some doubted," but the Greek text here indicates that the "some" who doubted were a different group than the eleven disciples who were also present. Additionally, the word "doubted" here can also mean "hesitant,"[23] indicating the "some" were hesitant to worship. Their hesitation just reinforces, by contrast, the conviction the disciples had that their master was none other than God in the flesh.

When Jesus says to his church—including us—"And behold, I am with you always, to the end of the age," it is the promise that God himself labors with us as we obey his command to build his church in our disciple-making mission. And so, Matthew closes his gospel not unlike how he began it when he spoke of the miraculous circumstances of Jesus' birth in Matthew 1:22–23: "All this took place to fulfill what the Lord had spoken by the prophet: 'Behold, the virgin shall conceive and bear a son, and they shall call his name Immanuel' (which means, God with us)." We are not lacking in provision for the task. God is with us! If that's true, who can stand against us? Not death threats. Not even the gates of hell. So go . . . and make disciples.

Chapter 15

The Great Commission, Part Four: The Power to Witness (Acts 1:1–11)

Revelation 5:9 says of Jesus, "for you were slain, and by your blood you ransomed people for God from every tribe and language and people and nation." Christ's work in and through his church will not only result in salvation to the end of the earth, but salvation for individual people groups uniquely set apart by very distinct marks of language and culture. So, if the gospel is going to effectively reach and win people from every people group into the kingdom, then what is a people group?

A leading Christian research organization on people groups is The Joshua Project, which defines a people group as an individual culture, often defined by a shared language and perspective on the world. According to The Joshua Project, there are 16,584 people groups in the world. Of these, 6,733 of these people groups are unreached, representing a little more than three billion people or 40 percent of the world's population. And when I say unreached, it essentially means that there is either absolutely no Christian presence among that group— no one is actively reaching them—or there are so few Christians that they are unable to substantially spread the gospel among that people group.[24] The question that any church burdened by a desire to serve Christ faithfully needs to ask is, "Should our ministry play some part in reaching all the unreached space on the world's map?" The text from

Acts 1:11 essentially throws the gauntlet down to us to respond to this question with an unwavering "yes!"

This chapter concludes the Great Commission "mini-series" in our story, and picks right up from Matthew 28. Jesus promises to be with his church until the end of the age as it carries out his mission; and as the church does so, the Holy Spirit's ministry comes to the fore as the means for Jesus to reproduce his work in and through his church unto the end of the age. Through the Holy Spirit's ministry, Jesus will prepare his disciples for their mission, empower them for their mission, and keep them motivated for the mission by the promise of his return.

The Disciples Were Prepared for Their Mission by Jesus, through the Holy Spirit

Empowerment and motivation are wonderful things that point to success in any endeavor, but I've never seen success in any meaningful endeavor without preparation. A careful study of the prominence of the Holy Spirit in Luke's gospel would leave us fully expecting Jesus to undertake this preparation through the Holy Spirit, because the work of the Holy Spirit is to reproduce the character and the works of the man Jesus Christ in Christ's church. We know this is true from a multitude of passages elsewhere in the New Testament as well.

A great example is Ephesians 4:13. After teaching that the purpose of the church's ministry is to build up the body of Christ, Paul explains that the aim of this work is for the church to continue in it "until we all attain to the unity of the faith and of the knowledge of the Son of God, to mature manhood, to the measure of the stature of the fullness of Christ." In other words, Jesus *sets the standard* by which our character and works are measured. One of the central themes in Luke's gospel is Jesus, the Son of Man, *living out this standard* by perfectly doing the Father's will *through his full reliance upon the power of the Holy Spirit.*

At the very outset of Jesus' public ministry, Luke writes in 4:1–2, "And Jesus, *full of the Holy Spirit*, returned from the Jordan and was *led by the Spirit* in the wilderness for forty days, being tempted by the devil." After Jesus' forty-day preparation for ministry through testing was complete, Luke writes in verse 14, "And Jesus returned *in the power of the Spirit* to Galilee." This pattern of Jesus being filled with the Spirit in power and led by the Spirit occurs throughout Luke's gospel. It was God's chosen method for empowering Christ's mission in his ministry, and it was a method conducted for the purpose of reproducing, by the Holy Spirit, the power of Christ's life in his followers.

Now move forward to Acts 1, and notice in verses 1–2 that Luke refers to his first or former book—his gospel—and how it dealt with the topic of "all that Jesus began to do and teach, until the day when he was taken up." In other words, Jesus' earthly ministry, all the way up to his ascension back to heaven, was just the beginning of his work. As the rest of verse 2 shows, even the final commands he gives before his ascension were through the Holy Spirit, just as we see throughout Luke. And so, through the Holy Spirit, Jesus prepared the disciples for their kingdom mission during a forty-day period.

In Acts 1:3, Luke writes, "He presented himself alive to them after his suffering by many proofs, appearing to them during forty days and speaking about the kingdom of God." Jesus confirmed the truth of his physical resurrection to his disciples by "many proofs," but his time with them wasn't spent only to confirm his resurrection. The forty-day period clues us in that it was a time of preparation for God's work which lay ahead, just as the people of Israel were prepared to conquer the Promised Land through forty years in the wilderness. Likewise, Moses was prepared to lead them through forty days on Sinai, and Jesus himself was prepared through forty days in the wilderness.

As we know from the end of verse 3, the content of Jesus' teaching was "the kingdom of God." A thought to tuck away for now, which we'll come back to shortly, is that the disciples must have had a thorough immersion into the topic of the kingdom if it was Jesus' focus during the forty days between his resurrection and ascension. I'd love to have the full transcripts of those conversations. Although we don't, early church history has some indirect accounts of them in the writings of the second-century church leader Irenaeus, who was a disciple of one of the elders who had served with the apostle John in Ephesus.

According to Irenaeus, this elder who served with John (Polycarp) wrote and taught that Jesus described the kingdom as a time of supernatural abundance and peace on earth. In his book *Against Heresies*, Irenaeus describes the future kingdom as a time on earth when the righteous will rule with Christ following their resurrection from the dead and "the creation, having been renovated and set free,"[25] will become incredibly abundant and fruitful. He cites as his source the elders who were with John toward the end of his life. Specifically, these elders related what John had shared to them about Jesus' teaching on the kingdom.

According to this account, Jesus told John and the others, "The days will come, in which vines shall grow, each having ten thousand branches, and in each branch ten thousand twigs, and in each true twig ten thousand shoots, and in each one of the shoots ten thousand clusters, and on every one of the clusters ten thousand grapes, and every grape when pressed will give five-and-twenty metretes of wine."[26] These men also related John describing how Jesus taught the disciples that all the animals of the earth would "become peaceful and harmonious among each other, and be in perfect subjection to man."[27] A real kingdom, with real blessing, on a real earth that God's faithful people of all ages will be resurrected into to live in, rule in, and enjoy, beginning in his kingdom and into eternity. This kingdom will come—but there's a mission that precedes it.

The Disciples Would Soon Undertake Their Mission by the Power of the Holy Spirit

And the Spirit's power and presence are essential to the mission, so much so that Jesus puts the mission on hold until the Spirit comes. One of the hardest things to do in our Christian lives is to both know that the Lord has given clear direction to go but has also given you equally clear direction to wait until an appointed time. We're not good at waiting—and as we'll see in a moment, neither were the apostles.

In verses 4–5, they're ordered to wait specifically in Jerusalem (another important point we'll get to in a bit), because the Father's promise that they will be baptized with the Holy Spirit will come to pass very soon—a baptism that we know from Acts 1 and other New Testament passages connects us to Christ and to one another, transforming us into his likeness and empowering us for his worldwide kingdom work of seeking and saving the lost, which he will do in and through his church until he returns at the end of this age. It's an astounding undertaking, but one Jesus necessarily puts on hold because the Spirit must bring the power to witness.

The Apostles are clearly excited about the kingdom, for God's great promise to the faithful remnant of Israel throughout history has been to live under the reign of their Messiah in a gloriously restored kingdom of Israel. They have this promise overflowing to them in the Scriptures, and Jesus has just spent his time with them over the past forty days talking about it, In verse 6, Luke writes "So when they had come together, they asked him, 'Lord, will you at this time *restore the kingdom to Israel?*'" Given what we've learned of this kingdom in our story thus far, wouldn't you ask that too? "Lord, can we have it now?"

But in a verse we've encountered a few times already—Isaiah 49:6— Isaiah writes ,"I will make you as a light for the nations, that my salvation may reach to the end of the earth." And if the Messiah is the light to the nations to bring them salvation, and his church is the means through which he brings them this light, then a worldwide mission must precede the Messiah's kingdom. And so, Jesus responds to their question by telling them, in verses 7–8, "It is not for you to know times or seasons that the Father has fixed by his own authority. But you will receive power when the Holy Spirit has come upon you, and you will be my witnesses in Jerusalem and in all Judea and Samaria, and to the end of the earth."

Let's follow Jesus' train of thought as he corrects his disciples' perspective here. 1) *Certain things* will happen at a time or season the Father has determined, and we will be kept ignorant of the timing of those things. 2) By inference, Jesus isn't disputing the promise of the kingdom;

he's just making the point that the kingdom is one of those *certain things*. 3) Our focus should not be on when those certain things will happen, but on the mission of witnessing—the testifying of the gospel of Jesus Christ which precedes it. (By the way, if the church in America today took this point seriously, a great many of the church's most popular authors and TV personalities would go out of business and find themselves with the opportunity to be more fruitfully occupied!) 4) The mission follows a particular progression from Jerusalem to Judea and Samaria, and to the end of the earth. In other words, once again, *to the Jew first, and then to the Gentiles*. This progression, by the way, is exactly how the growth of the church progresses through the book of Acts. And finally, 5) the power to do this witnessing mission comes only through the Holy Spirit. No Spirit, no mission, and any church which goes down the road of concluding he is unknowable, inactive, or not present will find itself going its own direction, producing its own results, and walking in its own power.

As the church undertakes this mission, Jesus essentially commands us to stay focused on the mission, follow his lead through the ministry of the Holy Spirit, and to not get distracted by things to come. This doesn't entail ignoring things to come, but rather, keeping those things in their God-ordained perspective.

The Disciples Were to Focus on Their Mission in Light of the Promise of Jesus' Return

In verses 9–11, Luke succinctly records Jesus' ascension back to heaven, but he spends most of the time focusing on the disciples' reaction to it. They were struck by the sight of it. Luke stressed this by referring to their seeing and looking intently no fewer than five times in verses 9–11. Not unlike their earlier fixation on the kingdom instead of the mission, they're now gazing so intently that, even after he's gone, they're still looking up.

In verse 11, the heavenly messengers standing by snap them out of it: "Men of Galilee, why do you stand looking into heaven? This Jesus, who was taken up from you into heaven, will come in the same way as you saw him go into heaven." This statement suggests the disciples may have been very understandably concerned about Christ's departure and what would come next, and equally suggests that the disciples don't need to worry about what comes next—they have a mission to do. But by the same token, "Jesus . . . will come in the same way as you saw him go" is very clearly a purposeful promise. In his commentary on this passage, Richard Longenecker writes:

> In Acts 1:9–11 Luke insists that Christian mission must be based on the ascended and living Lord, who directs his church from heaven and who will return to consummate what he has begun. Missions are an essential element in [God's ultimate] plan of salvation. The missionary work of the Church is the . . . foretaste of the Kingdom of God, and the Biblical hope of the 'end' constitutes the keenest incentive to action.[28]

As we undertake Christ's mission for his church, the mission and God's promise of Christ's return to establish his kingdom should go hand in hand, with the latter serving as our joy-filled, hope-filled incentive to do his kingdom work. It should be incentive to *do* the work, not a distraction *from* the work by becoming obsessed with "times or seasons that the Father has fixed by his own authority." Thanks be to God that through the ministry of his Holy Spirit, we have the power to witness unto the end of the earth and to the end of the age.

Before we conclude, let's tie some things together from Acts 1 as it relates to this four-part miniseries on the Great Commission as a whole.

A Kingdom of People Groups and a Church on a Mission

How can all of this talk of kingdom and people groups apply to us today? Let's start with people groups. Simply put, more than 40 percent of the world's people groups are effectively unreached, yet Revelation 5:9 teaches that Christ's redeeming work will effectively ransom people from every one of them. Whether your church is big, small, or somewhere in between, reaching these groups singlehandedly is impossible.

However, reaching some small part the Lord may point you to is not. Should not a church's ministry be invested in this work, as we see in the New Testament? A work of planting and strengthening churches where Christ isn't known and the gospel isn't proclaimed?

And while we're on the topic of people groups, what about a particularly notable people group? What about "to the Jew first?" We've already unpacked this point pretty well, but notice in verse 8 of Acts 1 that even the ministry of the church followed this order: Jerusalem and Judea first. And not only that, but Paul followed this order as well. In Acts 13, he takes the gospel to the synagogue in Antioch of Pisidia first. Some Jews embrace Christ but many others harshly reject him, at which point Paul tells them in Acts 13:46, "*It was necessary that the word of God be spoken first to you.* Since you thrust it aside and judge yourselves unworthy of eternal life, behold, we are turning to the Gentiles." This same pattern plays out in Corinth in Acts 18, Ephesus in Acts 19, and Rome in Acts 28. Is it possible that Paul took "to the Jew first" as a model for evangelism?

Theologian Craig Blomberg, commenting on this pattern, writes, "it is at least possible that God intended Israel to be the first mission field in every era of Christian history. Even if this is not the case, it certainly does not justify relegating the Jews to the relatively low position in Christian missionary strategy they have usually been assigned."[29] If "to the Jew first" is reflected repeatedly in practice within the Scriptures, should not our own approach to ministry consider including God's people Israel as part of our outreach?

Finally: Is there a kingdom in our gospel? I asked this question in part one of this miniseries, given that the Gospels overwhelmingly frame the gospel message in light of the kingdom of God. In Acts 1, Jesus spent the forty days after his resurrection speaking of it to his disciples, and they had high expectations of its immediate coming—not lived in as a spirit on a cloud in heaven or as some vague picture of the reality of the believer but as a real, concrete existence as miraculously resurrected people on a miraculously renewed earth under the blessed rule of Jesus Christ. Did Christ die to save us for a mundane or a vague, ill-defined existence, or did he save us for a kingdom in a universe united in him and made forever new by God?

In John 10:10, Jesus declared "I came that they may have life and have it abundantly." This is the eternal life Jesus gives to those who place their faith and trust in him, and if our eternal life is abundant, then our life in eternity will clearly be abundant. Whatever that ultimately looks like in detail, it is clearly a glorious kingdom life that will be anything but mundane.

Chapter 16

The Case for Jesus as Christ and Lord (Acts 2:22–36)

When I was a young Air Force captain and a brand-new Christian, I was at the bar in the officer's club at Osan Air Base, Korea. A buddy of mine and I were having *more than one too many,* as we were arguing with a colonel from higher headquarters who was making his disagreeable case to us to redefine the mission of the airplane we flew, the A-10. Evidently, our comments ultimately went beyond argument to outright disrespect and unbecoming conduct.

You can imagine my surprise the next night when I got to meet this colonel again . . . as the guest speaker at a formal function for the group my wife Lucia was working for as that group commander's secretary. But the emotion was far more than surprise. Shame and humiliation were much more involved, as he shook my hand on the receiving line and wryly told me, "You drank yourself pretty smart last night." God used that shame and humiliation to drive me from the drunken lifestyle I had brought into my Christian life and was still living—therefore, shaming his name and grieving his Holy Spirit who dwells in me.

It's humbling to discover that your actions disgraced an honorable occasion and the guest of honor. But imagine one's reaction when you discover that your sin led to the crucifixion of the Lord Jesus Christ, the Son of God himself. It's a reaction some three thousand souls had after Peter's sermon on the day of Pentecost.

Pentecost Sunday is the day the church celebrates God's creation of the church, and Acts 2 covers the heart of the message in the very first sermon preached by the church on that day some two thousand years ago. The twelve apostles, along with more than one hundred other disciples of Jesus, had been waiting in Jerusalem for the coming of the Holy Spirit as Jesus promised, and the Spirit filled them in magnificent fashion, accompanied by a sound like a mighty rushing wind and the sight of divided fiery tongues resting on each of them.

And with the Spirit in them as promised, they proclaimed the wonders of God's mighty works in a diversity of languages unfamiliar to themselves, but understood by a crowd of devout Jews who spoke a diversity of native languages because they had come from around the Roman empire to attend the festival of Pentecost. These Jews were drawn to the sound of the wind, amazed by a message each heard in their own native language—as if God were announcing the reversing of the curse of Babel by the inauguration of his church—and then were drawn to Peter as he addressed them with the good-news explanation for what they were seeing and hearing.

In this chapter, we're going to study the heart of Peter's Pentecost sermon that commences God's new direction in his plan of salvation: bringing salvation to the world in and through his church. And how does he choose to begin? Through his servant Peter, and with a logical and compelling case: the case for Jesus as Christ and Lord—which begins with God's own endorsement.

Jesus Is the Man God Miraculously Endorsed in the Midst of Israel

In Acts 2:22, Peter begins the heart of his sermon: "Men of Israel, hear these words: Jesus of Nazareth, a man *attested* to you by God with mighty works and wonders and signs that God did through him in your midst, as you yourselves know." Christ, or Messiah, is not part of Jesus' name, but rather is a title Jesus takes on as One who fulfills and accomplishes the works of the Messiah according to the Old Testament Scriptures. Knowing his Israelite audience, Peter knew that for these men to embrace Jesus as their Messiah he would have to make the case that Jesus had the right to the title Messiah because he accomplished the works of the Messiah.

The key word in this verse is "attested," a technical word used in the culture of the day to describe the endorsement of public office holders[30] which is why the NLT translates here that "God publicly endorsed Jesus." Peter's point to his Jewish audience is that the miraculous works, wonders, and signs of the Messiah were done in their midst in accordance with the Scriptures, and they knew it. In other words, "God has not failed to make the case for Jesus as Messiah; you have failed to perceive and receive it."

Having established this fact, Peter now puts his audience under conviction by driving home the point of their guilt and shame, with the added fact of the consequence of their guilt.

Jesus Is the Man We Crucified—According to God's Will

In verse 23, Peter pulls no punches in telling these men of Israel, "this Jesus, delivered up according to the definite plan and foreknowledge of God, you crucified and killed by the hands of lawless men." Remember, this is a crowd of devout Jews from across the Roman Empire who were likely also present in Jerusalem during the week leading up to Christ's crucifixion. They're not the religious leaders. They're not the people who gave orders or drove the nails. Yet Peter ascribes their guilt in the matter to them, along with the "lawless men" who did the dirty work—a reference to the Gentile Romans who carried out the act.

Christ's death on the cross, Peter says here, was not an accident; it was the purposeful work of God according to his will to die for the sake of sinful man because of our sinful nature. It was God's will for the Messiah to suffer on our behalf because he loves us and desires that we be saved from his justifiable wrath against us because of our sin. Jesus isn't just the man these Jews and lawless men crucified. Jesus is the man *we too* crucified according to God's will. But if Jesus is the Messiah, the Christ, promised through the Old Testament Scriptures, then his death could not have been the end of his works because, as Peter says in verse 24, "it was not possible for him to be held by it."

Jesus Is the Christ God Resurrected in Power

In *The Message*, Eugene Petersen puts verse 24 in a wonderful way: "God untied the death ropes and raised him up. Death was no match for him." In verse 24, Peter gives the first hint in his sermon about the true identity of the Christ. You can imagine his audience beginning to think, "Who has the power to overcome death? Can a mere man do this?" But Peter couldn't just declare that Jesus was resurrected and was therefore the Christ; he had to make the case that the Old Testament Scriptures taught that resurrection was a work of the Christ—in part because it is a vital part of the Christ's work, but also because it was not well understood among the Jews.

We see Jesus dealing with this lack of faith and understanding after his resurrection in Luke 24. On the day of his resurrection, Jesus joins two disciples on their lengthy walk from Jerusalem to a village called Emmaus, and he sees that they're distraught because they believed Jesus was the Christ but now he—in their minds—is crucified, dead, and buried. In response to this, the risen Jesus tells these two men, "O foolish ones, and slow of heart to believe all that the prophets have spoken! Was it not necessary that the Christ should suffer these things and *enter into his glory*?" (Luke 24:25–26). That phrase "enter into his glory" refers to Jesus' resurrection and subsequent ascension back to heaven. Jesus gently chastises these men for not understanding what the Scriptures taught about the Christ, and so Jesus makes the case for himself as the Christ as Luke goes on to write: "And beginning with Moses and all the Prophets, he interpreted to them in all the Scriptures the things concerning himself" (Luke 24:27).

Here in Acts 2, Peter more concisely makes his case through a logical argument from Psalm 16, a psalm written by David. Peter quotes from it in verses 25–27, with the key verse being verse 27: "For you will not *abandon my soul* to Hades, or let your Holy One *see corruption."* In verses 29–31, Peter then applied the psalm to the Christ. His reasoning was straightforward. In verse 29 he makes the logical point that it is well known that David died, so the psalm could not apply to him. And so, Peter concludes in verses 30–31, the psalm is a prophecy of David intended for his descendant who would rule on David's throne as the Christ, as God promised David in 2 Samuel 7. But not just any descendant—God promised David this descendant would sit upon his throne and rule forever over his kingdom. Therefore, the Christ would have to have been the descendant who fulfilled the words of David in verse 27 by not being abandoned in the grave or suffering the decay of death— the one who conquered the grave through resurrection to eternal life. That is Peter's case that the Christ must be resurrected; now all that remained was the proof.

Peter had to provide the proof that Jesus was resurrected, and he does in verse 32: "This Jesus God raised up, and of that we all are witnesses." The Apostles met all the Old Testament requirements for a reliable testimony as witnesses; they had more than the required numbers and prerequisite character. Notice back in Acts 1:21–22 that Peter, in acting to replace Judas among the ranks of the Apostles, sets the requirement for the replacement: "So one of the men who have accompanied us during all the time that the Lord Jesus went in and out among us, beginning from the baptism of John until the day when he was taken up from us—one of these men must become with us *a witness to his resurrection."*

From the Scriptures, Peter made the case to these men of Israel that the Christ had to be resurrected and that Jesus was the Christ—not only on the basis of God's endorsement in their midst through his mighty works, wonders, and signs, but because of the mightiest of these works: his resurrection that overcame the power of death. But again, what kind of man must the Christ be if he possesses such power? Peter has one more point to make.

Jesus Is the Lord God, Exalted to the Father's Right Hand

In verse 36 Peter says, "Let all the house of Israel therefore know for certain that God has made him both Lord and Christ, this Jesus whom you crucified." Jesus is Lord as well as Christ. Notice how Peter once again makes the case from the Scriptures before he makes this assertion. He uses another psalm of David—Psalm 110—to make the case that the Christ is not merely a man, just as Jesus used this psalm for the same purpose in Mark 12:35–37. Both Peter and Jesus make the point from Psalm 110 that the Christ isn't just a man—he is Lord. And they use the same verse Peter quotes in verse 34: "The Lord said to my Lord, sit at my right hand."

This is an exalted position at the right hand of God that Jesus ascended to as Peter points out in verse 33. But now, instead of appealing to himself and the other apostles as witnesses, Peter appeals to everyone who saw and heard the miraculous outpouring of the Spirit as witnesses to his assertion that Jesus is Lord. Look back in verses 17–18, where Peter is quoting from the prophet Joel to explain the outpouring of the Spirit the crowd is witnessing: "And in the last days it shall be, God declares, that I will pour out my Spirit on all flesh, and your sons and your daughters shall prophesy, and your young men shall see visions, and your old men shall dream dreams; even on my male servants and female servants in those days I will pour out my Spirit, and they shall prophesy." In Joel's prophecy, it is God who pours out the Holy Spirit; and in verse 33 Peter declares it is the ascended and exalted Jesus who has poured out the Spirit—Jesus, the Christ, the Lord, as Peter says in verse 36. And having made his case for Jesus as Christ and Lord, Peter comes back to where he started at the end of verse 36: "this Jesus whom you crucified." Can you imagine the effect of that? "You crucified the Christ! You crucified the Lord!" Can you imagine the horror of being an unjust executioner?

In early 2013, a sixteen-year-old Florida teenager believed that a burglar had entered his house and, knowing his parents owned a firearm, located it and shot the person he thought was an intruder. It turned out to be his twelve-year-old brother. Their parents were out when the incident occurred, and when the older brother heard strange noises coming from another part of the house, he called out for his younger brother but didn't get a response, leading him to believe something was amiss. The younger brother then approached and startled his older brother, prompting the shot. The older brother immediately called 9-1-1, but his brother was dead before paramedics could get him to the hospital.[31]

Can you imagine the horror, guilt, and shame this older brother must have felt? For those men of Israel who were convicted over their role and place in the death of their Messiah, do you suspect the feeling may have been similar? Like this older brother, I suspect these men would embrace deliverance from their guilt, shame, and the consequences of their action if such a deliverance were possible. But then again, maybe that deliverance was the good news Peter had in mind all along.

Everyone Who Calls on the Name of the Lord Will Be Saved

These were Peter's words in this sermon (Acts 2:21) before he made his case for Christ. Peter made this elaborate case for Jesus as the Christ and the Lord because he was seeking to convince them. Although their sins against God brought this terrible and necessary tragedy of Jesus' crucifixion to pass, even so, everyone who calls upon the name of the Lord Jesus who was crucified for our sakes will be saved.

If you continue to read verses 37–41, you'll see the response of many to Peter's sermon. The message cut them to the heart. Does it cut to your heart? Three thousand of the crowd embraced the salvation God freely gives to those who call upon Jesus to save them from the consequences of their sin—consequences so grave that they led to God having to sacrifice his one and only Son in a cruel crucifixion to save us from them.

Are you a name and a face in a crowd like this who needs to call on the name of the Lord Jesus? This is your invitation. Call on him today.

Chapter 17

Be Impartial and Proclaim the Full Gospel (Acts 10:30–45)

From time to time in our tracing of this redemption and restoration story, we've revisited the big picture of God's story to remind us to find our current place in it. Time for another recap.

God creates everything and it is all very good, but his adversary Satan corrupts everything by successfully tempting humanity to rebel against God's will. God immediately begins to reveal his plan to overcome Satan with his promise that he will bring a man into the world who will reverse the curse of corruption brought on by our rebellion. He will redeem the created universe held in bondage to this corruption, and he will redeem created humanity held in bondage to the corrupting power of sin.

As we saw through the Old Testament portion of this story, this deliverer was progressively revealed to be the Messiah: the descendant of Abraham and David who would ultimately accomplish every necessary and mighty work to bring this redemption to pass for all eternity—not only for God's people Israel but for all the nations of the earth. And at the climax of this story, the Messiah's mighty works were fulfilled in very short historical order: his miraculous birth, sinless life, powerful ministry, atoning death, death-conquering resurrection, glorifying ascension, and Holy Spirit-powered creation of a new humanity—his church, his first wave of an invasion from heaven which will ultimately destroy every power opposed to God's will to restore his creation forever to a very good state.

With the previous chapter and now this one, we are actually in the "falling action" of the story. We are now in the present; God's work in and through his church in the final age before Christ returns to usher in the age to come. And so, as a preview to the rest of the story, beginning with the next chapter and its focus on the depiction in 1 Thessalonians 4 of Christ's return to resurrect the church, the remainder of this story will focus on how God brings his redemption and restoration story to its forever new and forever good eternal conclusion.

In Acts 10:30–45, we see a pattern thoroughly repeated in Scripture. In the previous chapter, God effectively brought the gospel through Peter to the Jew first, and in accordance with his practice and prophetic promise God now effectively brings his gospel through Peter to the Gentiles, paving the way for the church to become the new humanity Paul writes of in Ephesians 2. Through Peter's faithful response to God's leading, the mystery of salvation through faith in Jesus Christ is revealed to be an impartial salvation to all who believe: both Jew and Gentile in the new community of God's people, at peace with God and one another through faith in Christ.

Sometimes referred to as the "Gentile Pentecost," Acts 10 records Peter's mission to the Roman centurion Cornelius—all at the very intentional direction of God, who uses Peter to answer Cornelius' prayer, provide for Cornelius' need, and confirm Cornelius' faith. And in a way that should apply to and instruct each of us, God worked not through a perfect messenger, but through a *faithful messenger*.

God Answers Cornelius' Prayer

As with the previous chapter, Acts 10:30–45 is actually part of a much longer narrative that runs from Acts 10:1–11:18. In fact, this narrative about the Gentile Pentecost is the longest narrative in Acts, which gives us a sense of the importance of the occasion to God not only by its length but also through the vivid way in which it reveals God moving in every detail to bring Gentile inclusion into the church to pass.

In verse 2 of Acts 10, Luke describes Cornelius as "a devout man who feared God with all his household, gave alms generously to the people, and prayed continually to God." Cornelius was a man who had come to know the God of Israel, sought to honor him with his life, and did so to the point of a notable testimony amongst the Jews, as Luke records in verse 22 of chapter 10. If God's people rightly regarded Cornelius well, then we should not be surprised by the fact that God faithfully responds to those who sincerely seek him.

Cornelius prayed continually to God, and in verses 30–31 he recalls to Peter that God revealed himself during his prayer time through a heavenly messenger, telling Cornelius that his prayers were heard by God and his gifts to God's work remembered. In a marvelous insight into the work of God's grace and a person's response to it, Cornelius was responding to his knowledge of God in a meaningful way that reflects sincere faith, while God is taking the initiative to bring the substance of Cornelius' faith to its full fruition. To accomplish this work in Cornelius' life, God faithfully moved in those who sincerely served him. Sincerity is important, but it can often be accompanied by flaws, as was the case with Peter, whom God commanded Cornelius to send for in verse 32. We all have our flaws and Peter was no exception, and so God moved in his servant to overcome his *inhibitions*.

In verse 33 Peter responded to Cornelius' request to come. Cornelius says to Peter "So I sent for you at once, and you have been kind enough to come. Now therefore we are all here in the presence of God *to hear all that you have been commanded* by the Lord." Whatever Cornelius had been specifically praying for, it's evident that he and the household full of guests he had invited were expecting a particular message the Lord commanded Peter to bring—and although Cornelius commended Peter as being "kind enough to come," Peter's coming had to overcome the obstacle of his inhibitions.

In verses 28–29, after he had entered Cornelius' home, Peter expressed a concern about how forbidden it had always been in his Jewish culture to associate with a Gentile but that God had overcome Peter's cultural objections. If you go back and read verses 9–21 of chapter 10, you'll see that God did this by commanding Peter, through a vision and in the midst of his hunger, to take and eat unclean animals. God did this with Peter three times, and in each instance Peter objected to the command, leading God to admonish Peter by saying "What God has made clean, do not call common" (v. 15). This was *immediately* followed by the arrival of the Gentile soldiers Cornelius had sent to bring Peter to see him, prompting the Holy Spirit to command Peter in verse 20 to "Rise and go down and accompany them without hesitation, for I have sent them."

Peter gets the point of the vision and the Spirit's command. God has made clean the Gentiles whom Peter and his fellow Jews construed to be unclean. "Get with the program. Get up and go—it's OK to associate with Gentiles." Peter's inhibitions are overcome, but his misconceptions about God's intentions toward the Gentiles are still fully in place; therefore, God moved in his servant to overcome his *misconceptions*.

It's pretty telling in verse 29 when, after entering Cornelius' house and explaining to Cornelius how God had changed his convictions about associating with Gentiles, Peter then tells Cornelius "So when I was sent for, I came without objection. I ask then why you sent for me." Peter's now cool with being in a Gentile's house, but he still has no idea why God would want Cornelius to send for him! But after Cornelius explains that he and his household are there to hear Peter share with them all the Lord had commanded Peter, the light bulb comes on. Luke writes in verse 34, "So Peter opened his mouth and said: 'Truly I understand that God shows no partiality.'" Peter then concludes that God truly accepts all people who fear him and do what is acceptable to him.

At Pentecost, God worked through Peter to proclaim the gospel to God's people Israel in Jerusalem, giving birth to the church. Here in Acts 10, God enlightens Peter and leads him to once again proclaim the gospel, this time to a Gentile audience—opening the door for every family, tribe, tongue, and nation to join faithful Jews in God's family, God's church. And so, with Peter's inhibitions and misconceptions overcome, the door to the gospel was opened, through his faithfulness to the task of being a witness.

God Provided for Cornelius' Need through his Faithful Messenger

And Peter was faithful. Not perfect, but faithful. Throughout the Scriptures, *God calls his people to be faithful by doing things that we are both able and commanded to do, so that he can do in and through us things which are impossible for us to do.* As James so thoroughly teaches in his epistle, genuine faith is accompanied by the actions which reflect genuine faith. And so, with Peter, we see that God's faithful messenger heeded God's command to preach and testify about Jesus.

Remember, in verse 33, Cornelius expected Peter to share what God had commanded him to share. In verse 42, in the midst of preaching his message to Cornelius' household, Peter confirms that obedience is what is driving him: "he commanded us to preach to the people and to testify that he is the one appointed by God to be judge of the living and the dead." We're going to see some remarkable results in the response to Peter's message in a moment—results Peter can't possibly produce. But Peter is simply doing what he was commanded to do: proclaim a message both he and we are more than able to proclaim. But how Peter goes about proclaiming the message offers much for us to learn from, particularly that *a faithful message about Jesus is a complete message about Jesus.*

I can't tell you how many times I've heard someone seeking to share the gospel do so with so few details that the message becomes almost meaningless. Perhaps my "favorite" is the simple invitation to "invite Jesus into your heart" without any other kind of detail—most notably, any detail on who Jesus is in the first place. But that's not the approach Peter takes with Cornelius and his household; Peter brings a very full gospel message.

So let's briefly walk through the elements of it, beginning in verse 36 where Peter tells Cornelius that Jesus Christ is Lord of all. He is Lord of the Jews. Lord of the Gentiles. Lord of every created being in the universe and Lord over the universe. As Paul says in Colossians 1:16, "For by him all things were created, in heaven and on earth, visible and invisible, whether thrones or dominions or rulers or authorities—all things were created through him and for him." As the Scriptures teach, Jesus Christ is fully God and fully man. And as the man Jesus Christ, Jesus lived a life filled with God's presence and power.

Peter describes this in verses 37–38, and as discussed in the previous chapter, as the Christ, Jesus accomplished all of the mighty works foretold of the Christ in the Old Testament. These works, in their entirety, testified to his status as the Christ and accomplished every necessary act to bring salvation to the world to include the fact that Jesus suffered the curse of death.

In verse 39, Peter says of Jesus, "They put him to death by hanging him on a tree." Referring to Jesus' crucifixion in this way communicated that Jesus was accursed in his death, reflecting the truth that Christ made himself the object of God's wrath in our stead. He became the object of God's judgment for our sin, taking our death and judgment upon himself—a necessary work of the Christ for our salvation. But because he is both Christ and Lord, death did not have the power to hold him.

As Peter declares in verses 40–41, Jesus was resurrected according to the testimony of faithful witnesses. Peter testifies to Cornelius in these verses that Christ was raised on the third day after his crucifixion and that ample faithful witnesses attest to his bodily resurrection; he "ate and drank," as Peter says in verse 41. And so, just as Jesus suffered our death and judgment in our place, through his resurrection we will also be raised into the likeness of Jesus' eternal resurrected human life—a future promise of God we enter into the moment we place our faith and trust in Jesus.

And we are invited by God to do so because, as Peter shares in verse 42, Jesus will exercise the final judgment over all humanity. As John 3:16 and 18 teach, whoever believes in Jesus will "not perish but have eternal life. . . . Whoever believes in him is not condemned, but whoever does not believe is condemned already, because he has not believed in the name of the only Son of God." To place your faith and trust in Jesus is to be delivered from the finality of death and judgment, but the sobering thought in John 3:16 and 18 is that rejecting him places us in a position of being condemned already. This message was likely very clearly sinking in for Cornelius and his household, but the point that moved his audience to faith may well have been the last point Peter made in his message: the judgment of Jesus will be forgiveness for all who believe in him.

In verse 43, Peter says to Cornelius, his household, and everyone reading this chapter today that "everyone who believes in him receives forgiveness of sins through his name." This point may have been the clincher that moved Peter's audience to respond, because verse 44 states that their response began, "While Peter was still saying these things." Imagine a service on a Sunday where, as the gospel is being proclaimed (like it is right now), in mid-message people begin publicly responding to the gospel. This happened to Peter in an unmistakable way.

God Confirmed Cornelius' Faith through His Mighty Presence

Verses 44–45 show that the Gentile response to Peter's message was very much like the response on Pentecost: "the Holy Spirit fell on all who heard the word. And the believers from among the circumcised who had come with Peter were amazed, because the gift of the Holy Spirit was poured out even on the Gentiles." This outpouring of the Spirit into the life of the believer, as the Scripture teaches, gives us rebirth as new creations of God in Christ and serves as God's guarantee that our future resurrection to eternal life is as good as done.

So, with our study of both of Peter's "Pentecost" sermons complete, let's conclude by briefly considering one more time how this applies to the church today.

Be Impartial and Proclaim the Full Gospel

What does it mean to be impartial? For Peter, it meant losing his inhibitions toward associating with non-Jews. For us it could be the same, or perhaps may entail abandoning our prejudices. As mentioned earlier, Peter's sermon in Acts 10 sits within a larger passage which ends at Acts 11:18. Interestingly, immediately after Peter opens the door of the church to non-Jews, Luke describes the church at Antioch, which was the first church to put Jew-Gentile integration into practice: "And in Antioch the disciples were first called *Christians*" (11:26). According to Christ's design for the church, we merit the title "Christian" when his church reflects the God-given ways he created us differently, serving him together in unity and peace as a testimony to the world. The world can't pull this off without hostilities present. And we draw the diversity of his created humanity to the church through the faithful proclamation of the gospel that is the "power of God for salvation to everyone who believes." And a true gospel is a full gospel. Therefore, proclaim the full gospel.

Peter gives us a great model to follow. Who is Jesus? Fully God and fully man. He is Lord of all and he is the Christ; the man who accomplished every necessary work for our salvation as foretold in the Old Testament. The most notable of these are the death he suffered on our behalf, making himself the object of God's wrath and judgment for our sin; and his resurrection which makes God's future promise that we will also be raised into the likeness of Jesus' eternal resurrected human life a reality the moment we place our faith and trust in Jesus. Jesus will exercise the final judgment over all humanity. But the good news for those who, by faith, embrace his good news message of salvation is that the judgment of Jesus will be forgiveness for all who believe in him, rather than the eternity of torment and ruin under his judgment that those who go to the grave rejecting him are condemned to suffer.

A watered-down gospel will result in a watered-down church. As witnesses to the world of God's message of salvation through faith in Jesus Christ, God calls every church that faithfully confesses and follows Jesus Christ to know the full gospel message and to proclaim the full gospel message.

Chapter 18

Grieve Like You Believe
(1 Thessalonians 4:13–18)

First Thessalonians 4:13-18 is the central passage in all of the Scriptures portraying the event often referred to as "the rapture," but the church today often packages this portrayal within a particular narrative that sounds something like this: "The world's falling apart! The rapture is near! Don't miss it or you'll be left behind!" In other words, they use "the rapture" to terrify people into the kingdom. What's troubling about this approach to this text is that it is completely contrary to the very explicit purpose Paul gives for writing it, as we'll see.

Undoubtedly, this passage always provokes deep interest over when the rapture will occur, in light of all the end-times events. Mindful of that deep interest and the depth of convictions that accompany it, for the record, I believe the Scriptures teach the rapture is the next major event in God's plan of redemption and restoration. Furthermore, I believe the rapture will be followed soon thereafter by the great tribulation and Christ's return at the end of that tribulation, to judge the earth and establish his kingdom on earth in a thousand-year reign leading to eternity.

As we move through this future-looking part of the story of redemption and restoration, I'll do my best to humbly validate this end-times timeline, but that's not my focus in this chapter with this text. My focus will be on Paul's purpose for teaching this passage; a purpose he clearly expresses.

I titled this chapter "Grieve Like You Believe" because Paul's purpose in writing about the rapture isn't to terrorize, but rather to encourage and comfort believers who are grieving. The main event in the text is Jesus' future return to resurrect his church to eternal life, but it has been popularly referred to as "the rapture" for ages because "rapture" transliterates the verb used in the Latin (a language widely used to translate the Scriptures for many centuries in the history of the church) to describe in verse 17 how Jesus will "snatch up" his church as he resurrects us. So then, "rapture" was coined as a description of the event.

But in 1 Thessalonians 4 Paul describes the rapture in order to bring hope. Hope to the grieving. Hope grounded in the promise of the resurrection of the church, and therefore, a hope that can be realized in the life of the grieving believer because of this promise. It's an elusive hope if our understanding of essential matters of our Christian faith is lacking, but a more confident hope can come through a better understanding.

An Informed Faith in God Should Lead Us to Grieve with Hope

Paul writes in verse 13, "But we do not want you to be uninformed, brothers, about those who are asleep, that you may not grieve as others do who have no hope." This verse is vitally important in understanding Paul's purpose in writing this passage. Paul has a threefold purpose, beginning with the Thessalonians' understanding: "we do not want you to be uninformed." Paul is indicating that the words which follow in this passage are either intended to introduce or correct an area of teaching where the Thessalonians are presently lacking in understanding, and that area where they are lacking in pertains to "those who are asleep."

It was common both within the culture of the day and within the early church to refer to those who were dead as being asleep, just as a dead body appears to be asleep. Paul wants the Thessalonians to have a right understanding of those who have died, because his heart for them in those times of tragic loss or reflecting upon that loss is so that they "may not grieve as others do who have no hope."

If we approach this passage as we often do, expecting Paul to write a detailed theological survey of the end times, we will get frustrated because we'll see Paul failing to more fully provide the details we want. But if we understand the passage as an essential teaching that serves to comfort the grieving, we'll discover that the passage is complete. The pagans in the Thessalonian culture grieved the loss of their dead with a flawed understanding of the fate of the dead—very much like we see in the worldly culture of our day, marked by ignorance, hopelessness, or the vain hope of wishful thinking. But the follower of Jesus Christ need not be ignorant, hopeless, or vain in their hope as they grieve the loss of a brother or sister in Christ.

We Can Grieve with Hope Because of the Promise of the Resurrection of the Dead

Our faith in Jesus' resurrection is the basis for our hope. Just as verse 13 is important for us to understand because we learn Paul's purpose in writing this passage (to grieve the loss of fellow believers with hope), so verse 14 is equally important, because Paul explains the particular aspect of our faith in Christ which makes this grieving with hope possible. So let's unpack verse 14 as we did verse 13.

The Greek text of verse 14 is difficult to translate, but the New Living Translation does a nice job of giving us the clear sense of the verse: "For since we believe that Jesus died and was raised to life again, we also believe that when Jesus returns, God will bring back with him the believers who have died." So then, Paul begins with a point of common understanding with the Thessalonians. Faith in Jesus' resurrection from the dead and his future return are things the Thessalonians have already been taught and believed, but they seem to have lacked an understanding of how Jesus' resurrection and future return affects them; particularly those who have died. So, Paul gives them a general understanding of the implications of Christ's resurrection and future return: when that return happens, "God will bring back with *him* [that is, Jesus] the believers who have died." In other words, the resurrected Jesus will return, and when he does, he will gather all who have died as Christians and will somehow bring these who have died back with him, with the implication that he is bringing them back to where he came from. All of this is possible because of Christ's resurrection; it becomes reality for believers through faith in Christ because they believe he died and rose again.

But will Christ come to gather decayed bodies or bags of dust? What hope is there in that? No, Christ will come to do far more. His resurrection and return is a hope we can hang our hats on forever—a hope that will not disappoint because our hope in the resurrection is a living hope.

Paul declares this to be the very word of the Lord, as he says in verse 15. He then proceeds to describe Jesus' return in verses 15–16 as one which has joyful implications for the living and the dead, but he emphatically gives the dead in Christ—those whom the Thessalonians and Christians of all ages *rightly grieve* when they die—preeminence in the occasion of Jesus' return. In verse 15, Paul says, "we who are alive, who are left until the coming of the Lord, will not precede those who have fallen asleep." The language in the Greek text is highly emphatic to Paul's point that when Christ returns, the living will be blessed by the outcome, but that the living in Christ will absolutely not precede the dead in Christ. Those who have passed through the crucible of death will have first place on that day, just as Paul describes so majestically in verse 16: "For the Lord himself will descend from heaven with a cry of command, with the voice of an archangel, and with the sound of the trumpet of God. And the dead in Christ will rise first."

There will be no mistaking the day as the Lord commands the "sleepers" to arise accompanied by trumpets and the voice of an archangel. There is a great and glorious hope for the dead in Christ's return, but this is a hope for the living as well. Notice that Paul lumps himself in with the believers who will be alive when Christ returns in verse 15: "*we* who are alive, who are left." The promise of Christ's coming to resurrect the church has always been regarded as imminent by the church—as an event that could happen at any moment. This is the next "big step" in God's plan of redemption and restoration. It has always been the living hope of the believer to be present when Christ returns, to forego death and enter directly into the joy of our resurrected life upon his command.

You get the sense this was Paul's desire when he writes "we" in this passage, and you see this excitement and passion in Paul's hope as he writes of this resurrection day in 1 Corinthians 15:

> Behold! I tell you a mystery. *We shall not all sleep*, but we shall all be changed, in a moment, in the twinkling of an eye, at the last trumpet. For the trumpet will sound, and the dead will be raised imperishable, and we shall be changed. For this perishable body must put on the imperishable, and this mortal body must put on immortality. When the perishable puts on the imperishable, and the mortal puts on immortality, then shall come to pass the saying that is written:
>
> "Death is swallowed up in victory."
>
> "O death, where is your victory?
>
> O death, where is your sting?" (1 Corinthians 15:51–55)

"We shall not all sleep [that is, die], but we shall all be changed"—in a moment . . . in the twinkling of an eye . . . at the last trumpet. It is our living hope that through the resurrection of Jesus Christ, we too shall be changed, even if we have decayed to dust. For if he formed us from the dust, can he not restore us to eternal life from the very same dust? So then, whether we are alive or dead when he returns, we shall all be forever changed into his resurrected likeness—a point in and of itself which should give great hope and comfort to the grieving. But there's one more aspect of this resurrection Paul teaches as a source of hope and comfort.

Our hope in the resurrection is a healing hope. We've probably all been to some form of a reunion. Family reunions, military unit reunions, high school and college reunions. You get t-shirts, mugs, or some other commemorative mementos; you gather for a time, have fun, and then you disperse. Reunions are a joyful time of coming together. Death is a tragic time of tearing apart. It creates a heartbreaking void in a relationship. It is the ever-present and inevitable reminder of the devastation brought on by the consequences of our sin. *The right response to it among the living is weeping and sorrow and grieving and mourning.*

Paul doesn't teach here that Christians don't grieve but that they can and ought to grieve as those who have a sure and reliable basis for hope. Don't be the Christian who comes alongside a grieving brother or sister and says, "God works all things for the good of those who love him." True text (Romans 8:28), wrong occasion. Rather, "weep with those who weep" (Romans 12:15). Join others in their grief and, without dismissing the fact and deep pain of their grief, share the healing truth of a coming reunion.

Paul writes in verse 17, "Then we who are alive, who are left, will be caught up together with them in the clouds to meet the Lord in the air, and so we will always be with the Lord." As we grieve because sin and death have torn us from our beloved sisters and brothers in Christ, Paul teaches us here that our grief can lead to healing when we are reminded of the fact that the resurrection of the church will be the greatest reunion in all of history. Once again, Paul emphasizes to "we who are alive, who are left" that we will come together with our dearly departed to forever be with one another and the Lord. No more death. No more grief from death. No more separation brought on by death. No more sting. We will all rise together by the resurrection power present in the very life of the resurrected Jesus who will come to gather us, perhaps like a hen gathers her chicks. And if we believe these words are true, then real hope reigns in any setting.

We Must Grieve Like We Believe

In verse 18, Paul closes the loop in his train of thought in this passage: "Therefore *encourage* one another with these words." The New American Standard Bible translates it, "Therefore *comfort* one another with these words." Both "comfort" and "encouragement" get to the point of the passage. "These words" refer to Paul's teaching in verses 14–17. Through our faith in Jesus' death and resurrection, both the living and the dead in Christ will experience together the joy of our transformation from perishable mortal people into imperishable, immortal, finished new creations in Christ. It's a message Paul teaches will enable us to grieve with hope, and it's not a suggestion.

The verb "encourage" or "comfort" is not only a command, but it is the first command Paul gives in the entire book of 1 Thessalonians. Christians are commanded to share this message of hope with our sisters and brothers who are grieving, for their sakes in the midst of their grieving. But we minister in these moments and with this message in a way that enters into the grief of a friend rather than dismissing it or running roughshod over it with an ill-selected thought or biblical text. Let's conclude with an illustration that hopefully helps us to learn how to better put Paul's command into practice.

In her book, *Holding onto Hope: Drawn by Suffering to the Heart of God*, Nancy Guthrie writes of her grief over the loss of her six-month-old daughter Hope, who was born with a fatal condition which caused her to have constant seizures: "We had Hope for 199 days. We loved her. We enjoyed her richly and shared her with everyone we could. We held her during her seizures. Then we let her go." The day after they buried Hope, Nancy's husband reflected on how their faith influenced how they responded to their loss. While acknowledging that their faith sustained them greatly in the midst of this loss, he placed these blessings within the reality of their suffering: "Faith keeps us from being swallowed by despair. But I don't think it makes our loss hurt any less."[32]

Our faith in Christ makes the pain and hurt of loss no less real and no less deep. What our faith does give us is a comfort and hope which is not imagined or well-wishing, but very real—as real as an empty tomb and a risen Savior who is coming back to swallow up every sorrow of death into everlasting life. As we seek to minister to those who suffer from loss, such grief must run its course. We must not commit the grave error of "fixing" the grieving by trying to lead them from grieving rather than walking with them through it. When we walk with them through it, weeping with those who weep and grieving with those who grieve on their schedule and not ours, we speak our love and compassion and care for the grieving in ways far louder than words.

If we are to grieve like we believe, then we must respect the door of the broken and grieving heart the Scriptures teach we must empathetically walk through—in order to have the latitude, before God and the grieving, to share the comforting and encouraging hope of the resurrection Paul commands us to share in 1 Thessalonians 4. "We do not want you to be uninformed, brothers, about those who are asleep, that you may not grieve as others do who have no hope. Therefore encourage one another with these words."

Chapter 19

Live Like We'll Be Delivered
(1 Thessalonians 5:1–11)

C. S. Lewis once wrote, "Christianity . . . if false, is of no importance, and, if true, of infinite importance. The one thing it cannot be is moderately important."[33] When compared to the standard of infinite importance, what does moderately important look like? Hard to say. In 1 Thessalonians 5, Paul describes a state of spiritual *indifference* that believers must avoid, which may give us a clue to what *moderately important* looks like.

In his speech "The Perils of Indifference," Elie Wiesel, a Romanian Jew who survived the Holocaust concentration camps, defines indifference as "'no difference': a strange and unnatural state in which the lines blur between light and darkness, dusk and dawn, crime and punishment, cruelty and compassion, good and evil." In words that touch on the second greatest commandment, Wiesel goes on to assert that such indifference ultimately renders neighbors to be of no consequence, and so renders their lives meaningless to the indifferent. So then, "Indifference elicits no response. . . . And, therefore, indifference is always the friend of the enemy, for it benefits the aggressor—never his victim, whose pain is magnified when he or she feels forgotten."[34]

When Christ returns, how do we think he'll respond to a church that considered his work and purpose *moderately important*? Would he see that church any differently than one that is indifferent? "The friend of the enemy?"

The message in First Thessalonians 5:1–11 serves both as a challenge to serve Christ with the sense of infinite importance he calls us to, and so serves as a prescription against the deadly disease of spiritual indifference I pray we would all wish to avoid being found afflicted by when he returns. And his day will come.

The Day of the Lord Will Come to the Children of Darkness and the Children of Light

As we move through this passage, we're going to see Paul present a contrast over the nature and ultimate fate of two groups of people: the children of darkness and children of light. And as he does this, Paul will exhort the children of light to live in a manner consistent with their nature and ultimate fate. To draw this contrast, Paul uses the drastically different outcomes these two groups will experience in the coming day of the Lord, beginning with the fate of the children of darkness in verses 1–3.

The children of darkness will be shocked from their perceptions to endure an inevitable destruction. Although this experience will be sudden as Paul says in verse 3, an understanding of how the day of the Lord is described and fulfilled throughout the Scriptures, as well as how Paul describes it here, leads to the conclusion that Paul is describing *an extended period of judgment which will begin suddenly.* Consider the following and see if you find any basis for this assertion about the day of the Lord.

Paul begins in verse 1 by reminding the Thessalonians that they fully possess an understanding of "times and . . . seasons," a phrase meant to communicate an extended yet definite period of time. In the New Testament, it is used to describe the future definite period of time in which the events of the end times will occur. Furthermore, Paul equates these "times and . . . seasons" to "the day of the Lord," which the Thessalonians are "fully aware" of in verse 2. And this is appropriate because the "day of the Lord" in the Old Testament is consistently presented as a period of time where God brings his wrath as a judgment upon the wicked while at the same time bringing deliverance to his faithful people. The New Testament continues this theme with the added detail that Jesus is the Lord who brings both this judgment and deliverance. In short, *the day of the Lord is an extended yet definite period of time where God brings judgment and wrath upon the wicked—the children of darkness—while bringing deliverance to his people: the children of light.* If you look carefully at how Paul describes the fate of the children of darkness, this conclusion about the nature of the judgment to come is both confirmed and further described by the analogy of a thief and labor pains.

The day of the Lord will come like a thief and continue like labor pains. Like a thief, it will come by surprise and with hostile intent. Like those in the days of Jeremiah who arrogantly defied God's word, claiming that Jerusalem would know peace and security rather than the judgment he would inevitably bring through the Babylonian invasion, the day of the Lord will assault the perceptions of the children of darkness. Like labor pains, this destruction will begin suddenly but will continue for a time until their inevitable end. And as they continue, just like labor pains, God's wrath will increase in intensity over time. In Matthew 24:4–8, Jesus describes the beginning of these birth pains as false Messiahs coming in the midst of wars and rumors of wars as nations and kingdoms rise against each other, while famines and earthquakes become widespread. Jesus then explains that the intensity of these birth pains will increase until the end comes, when he returns in judgment. This is the extended period of time that will come like a thief and as labor pains: the day of the Lord that will both shock and destroy the children of darkness. But the children of light are not of the stock who will be shocked.

In verse 4, Paul shifts focus from the "people [who] are saying 'there is peace and security'" in verse 3 to "brothers," and he does so to show the contrast in nature between the children of darkness and the children of light. Paul writes in verses 4–5, "But you are not in darkness, brothers, for that day to surprise you like a thief. For you are all children of light, children of the day. We are not of the night or of the darkness." It's important to understand the distinction Paul is making here between night and day, between darkness and light. Paul makes this distinction and later describes it, as we'll see, as distinctions in behavior.

In verse 5, he describes it first and foremost as a distinction in being, in nature. "You *are* all children of light, children of the day." This is who you are! In John 3, the scripture makes the same distinction between darkness and light and the basis for the difference in being and nature is in Christ himself, the light of the world. John writes, "the light has come into the world, and people loved the darkness rather than the light because their works were evil. . . . But whoever does what is true comes to the light" (John 3:19, 21).

The children of light are the ones who have come to Christ. The children of darkness are the ones who have loved the life of darkness, and so have rejected Christ. Therefore, if the thief comes at night, not only will this not surprise us as Paul says in verse 4, but it can't surprise us *because we don't live in the night,* in the darkness. We don't live in the domain where the thief's hostile intentions will be directed because, we are not of the night nor of the darkness. And if this is true—if this is who we are, if this is our nature—then what ought to be true of us?

"So Then," the Children of Light Ought to Live Like the Children of Light

In 1 Thessalonians 4:13–18, you may recall that Paul described the dead in Christ as those who are asleep, and he comes back to the topic of sleepers again in this passage. But this time he uses a different verb for "sleep"—one which can either mean to actually sleep or to describe a state of spiritual indifference or blindness—and he uses it in both its literal and figurative ways in this passage, beginning with the figurative sense in verse 6.

Paul writes, "So then let us not sleep, as others do, but let us keep awake and be sober." The "others" are the children of darkness. In their rejection of Christ, they are spiritually blind and indifferent, and so they won't see the day of the Lord coming. But Paul begins verse 6 with "so then." Because believers in Christ are children of the light, they must not live like children of darkness, but rather, "keep awake and be sober." In other words, although it is impossible for the day of the Lord to catch Christians unprepared, it is possible for them to adopt the same lifestyle as those who will be caught unawares. Paul is saying "don't do that!" Instead, be diligent to remain alert and stay self-controlled. If you're a child of light, be careful and determined to stay in the light because a life in the darkness will lead to the deeds of darkness.

This is Paul's point in verse 7: "For those who sleep, sleep at night, and those who get drunk, are drunk at night." Paul now shifts to the literal sense of the word for "sleep," to appeal to everyday experience to make the point that sleep and drunkenness are most often associated with the night. Thus, Paul creatively illustrates his figurative use of "sleep" in verse 6 by referring to the nighttime practices of sleep and drunkenness in order to contrast the deeds of the children of darkness—like drunkenness—with the sober self-control which ought to be the character of the believer. This should be the testimony of the child of light because of who they are in Christ, but this should also be their testimony—because their testimony should reflect their hope for salvation.

In verses 8–10, Paul continues to develop the quality of a sober, self-controlled life more specifically in light of who we are in Christ: destined not for the coming wrath but for salvation. As we saw in Paul's teaching on the rapture, both the dead and the living will experience together the great outcome of our salvation: Christ's return to resurrect his church to eternal life. This is our great hope, and this hope should be demonstrated in our Christlike character.

In verse 8, Paul reminds the Thessalonians once more who they are: "we belong to the day." We are owned by the day, and if the day is representative of Christ then no power in heaven and earth can take us from him. But if that's so, then "let us be sober." Paul then elaborates on what he means, through a reference to the alert and sober warrior clothed with Christ's character: clothed with faith, love, and hope. And Paul purposefully concludes verse 8 with "hope"—not just any hope, but the "hope of salvation" which is assured through Christ's work on our behalf.

Paul writes in verses 9–10, "For God has not destined us for wrath, but to obtain salvation through our Lord Jesus Christ, who died for us so that whether we are awake or asleep we might live with him." In verse 3 we saw that the children of darkness will face "sudden destruction . . . they will not escape." But this is not the destiny of the children of light. God has destined us for salvation because our "Lord Jesus Christ . . . died for us so that whether we are awake or asleep we might live with him."

And here is amazing grace. Remember, Paul is using a different verb for "sleep" in this passage. In the earlier rapture passage, we would have taken Paul's point here to mean: alive or dead, we will live with Christ—and that's true. But that's not the point Paul is making here. This verb for "sleep," as we've already seen, can be used figuratively to mean spiritually indifferent or sluggish. Paul charges a young Thessalonian congregation here to live like the children of light Christ has made them, but comforts them with grace should they stumble into sleep. As the *New American Commentary* so beautifully puts it, "Paul was assuring his readers here of the security of those for whom Christ died. Human vigilance may flag, but Christ's sacrifice will not fail to deliver the believer from wrath, even believers who have fallen asleep at their post."[35]

Nevertheless, this is grace to comfort us in our weakness, not a license to wander into the darkness on the crutch of that weakness. Jesus commands in Matthew 24:42, "Therefore, *stay awake*, for you do not know on what day your Lord is coming." Why? Because when he comes, he will come to deliver God's children: a promise packaged with an exhortation.

Live Like We'll Be Delivered!

Paul has a command for us as well. Just as he closed the preceding passage on the rapture with the command to "encourage one another" with the hope of Christ's return to resurrect the church, here again he closes this teaching on the day of the Lord and our right response to it with the commands to "encourage one another and build one another up."

So how do we apply these commands? How do we live like we'll be delivered?

To begin with, let's encourage one another with the hope of our deliverance. Maybe it's time for a brief excursion into a timeline. As I mentioned previously, I do believe the rapture will precede the period of the great tribulation where, as John indicates in Revelation 6:15–17, those on the earth during this time will plead "to the mountains and rocks, 'Fall on us and hide us from the face of him who is seated on the throne, and from the wrath of the Lamb, for the great day of their wrath has come, and who can stand?'" (vv. 16–17). But in 1 Thessalonians 5, Paul comforts the Thessalonians that God has not destined us for this wrath. In Revelation 3:10 Jesus himself tells the church at Philadelphia, "I will keep you from the hour of trial that is coming on the whole world, to try those who dwell on the earth." Yet a great debate among theologians is whether this deliverance is "from" wrath or "through" wrath.

In my reading of 1 Thessalonians 5, Paul seems to strongly suggest that the children of light, of the day, will not experience this destruction which will come upon those of the night, of the darkness. Still, this does not dispel the argument that we could be preserved *from* the experience *while in the midst of it*, not unlike Noah and his family through the flood. But once again, I come back closer to the context in 1 Thessalonians 5. Paul commends the Thessalonians for their testimony in chapter 1, verses 9–10: "For they themselves report concerning us the kind of reception we had among you, and how you turned to God from idols to serve the living and true God, and to wait for his Son from heaven, whom he raised from the dead, Jesus who delivers us *from* the wrath to come." Paul's teaching on the day of the Lord's wrath in 1 Thessalonians 5 immediately follows his teaching on Christ's return to resurrect his church, and here in chapter 1 he clearly refers to this return as a deliverance "from" the wrath to come.

I strongly believe the rapture will precede the tribulation and, hopefully, I've begun to make a reasonably compelling case for you in this chapter. Regardless, I always counsel believers to hold fast to God's promise that we will not experience his wrath, whether "through" or "from." And whether "through" or "from," the act of preparation for the believer for these coming "times and . . . seasons" is as Paul commanded: build one another up as we await our deliverance.

Building one another up is one of Paul's favorite ways to describe the corporate work of the church in helping one another to grow spiritually. The verb *building up* means "to help improve ability to function in living responsibly and effectively."[36] Paul uses the related noun in Ephesians 4:12–13 to describe the church's responsibility "to equip the saints for the work of ministry, for *building up* the body of Christ, until we all attain to the unity of the faith and of the knowledge of the Son of God, to mature manhood, to the measure of the stature of the fullness of Christ." If our great hope is that Christ is going to return to transform the living and the dead in Christ into eternally new human beings; in so doing, he's going to deliver us "from the hour of trial that is coming on the whole world"; and that while we wait, he commands us to "stay awake, for you do not know on what day your Lord is coming," then our compelling and consuming passion ought to be to build one another up until that day comes.

In his command to build one another up, Paul commands a local church in Thessalonica, and your local church, and mine, to unconditionally commit—each and every one of us—to the works of service that can build even the weakest in faith to a spiritual maturity that equals "the measure of the stature of the fullness of Christ." The challenge for each faithful church in Christ is a challenge that asks introspectively "are we awake or asleep?" Let's live like we'll be delivered!

Chapter 20

Reject the Intrusions of Strong Delusions (2 Thessalonians 2:1–12)

"The check is in the mail." "It's only going to be a ten-minute meeting." "I'm from the government, and I'm here to help you." I would venture that most, if not all of us, have fallen for at least one of these. We were all deluded by an expectation we chose to embrace while, deep down inside, we knew the promises that fed these expectations were false.

Sometimes our expectations can be driven by good intentions. One of my sisters once nearly fell for an email from a person stuck at Heathrow Airport who needed $5,000 to get home to Nigeria (doesn't everybody get those?). In fairness to sis, I've opened more than my fair share of phishing emails, even when I knew it was a scam before I did so.

Sometimes our expectations can be quite pessimistic. In the military, bad news travels fast, and in a culture where the cynical counterpart of "it's too good to be true" is "it's too bad to be false" often thrives, I remember well the rumor mill running wild in my first combat deployment to Saudi Arabia for Operation Desert Shield in August of 1990. By November of 1990, me and the guys in my A-10 squadron were on a veritable bungee cord of changing news as then-President Bush had not yet decided to go to war to drive the Iraqis out of Kuwait. We were now in our third month at a barren desert base when the rumor hit the street that we were going to remain in place until the next fall. Another year at a barren desert base to include an all-expenses-paid summer of 120-degree heat. . . . It was "too bad to be false," but it turned out to be false nonetheless. We were deluded into assuming the worst, despite the fact that the worst made very little sense.

So many things about our nature and the cultures we live in leave us ripe for delusion and deception. As we come to our next stop in our short journey through Paul's letters to the Thessalonians, we'll see that Paul addresses a problem with a young Thessalonian congregation that was deceived by a false teaching about the day of the Lord that was contrary to what they had been clearly taught—and therefore, should have been contrary to their expectations.

Were we not aware of our own susceptibility to be deceived, we might be deceived into being unkind toward a bunch of Christians so easily duped, but since we can humbly acknowledge we are spiritually kindred to the Thessalonians (and therefore also susceptible), the message and challenge to reject the intrusions of strong delusions is for us as well as them. And just like the Thessalonians, the messages which may lead to our delusions can leave us shaken and alarmed. Therefore, we need to stand fast in the truth because the wicked mighty powers that seek to delude men and women prove their power to be most effective in the lives of those unarmed with the truth. For the Christian, being unarmed in this way is inexcusable and leads to unfortunate and unnecessary consequences. We see this in a distressing way with the Thessalonians.

The Thessalonians Were Unnecessarily Alarmed by Deceptive Teaching

Now you may ask why they were *unnecessarily* alarmed. We'll see why Paul considered it unnecessary as we move through the text, but some background on what Paul had previously taught the Thessalonians helps reinforce this point. In the first three chapters of 1 Thessalonians and in the first chapter of 2 Thessalonians, Paul speaks often of their afflictions under persecution, in one instance telling them, "For you yourselves know that we are destined for this" (1 Thessalonians 3:3). Yet, in teaching them in 1 Thessalonians 5 about the coming wrath which God would bring upon the world in that extended period that the day of the Lord entails, Paul told them, "For you yourselves are fully aware" of this aspect of the day of the Lord but "God has not destined us for wrath." To sum up a point Paul had made to the Thessalonians in his prior inter-actions with them: as Christians, they were destined to be afflicted by persecutions; but also as Christians, they were not destined for the wrath that would come in the day of the Lord. There was a distinction between these two experiences, and Paul was very confident that they knew this. Nevertheless, they were shaken and alarmed, and the cause for their con-cern pertained to a deceptive teaching about the rapture with respect to the day of the Lord.

In verses 1–2 of the second chapter of his second letter, Paul writes, "Now concerning the coming of our Lord Jesus Christ and our being gathered together to him, we ask you, brothers, not to be quickly shaken in mind or alarmed, either by a spirit or a spoken word, or a letter seem-ing to be from us, to the effect that the day of the Lord has come." If you look carefully at these two verses you'll see that what was disturbing the Thessalonians was a teaching they had received by some means from a person or group claiming to be Paul and those ministering with him, further claiming "that the day of the Lord has come." The tense of the verb "has come" indicates that the claim was that the day of the Lord had arrived and was presently ongoing. In other words, if this claim was from Paul and was true, then the Thessalonians were presently living in the midst of the wrath of the great tribulation and had either missed "the coming of our Lord Jesus Christ and our being gathered together to him"—the rapture of the church, which Paul had taught them about in 1 Thessalonians 4—or had misunderstood Paul entirely. In either case, they likely construed that their present afflictions were evidence that they were in the great tribulation. You can imagine then why they were shaken and alarmed.

But Paul makes the point that they have been misled in the first part of verse 3: "Let no one deceive you in any way," He then proceeds to demonstrate to them why they cannot be in the midst of a time of God's wrath in the coming day of the Lord, providing the proof to the Thessalonians that the day of the Lord has not come.

Continuing in verse 3 and through verse 4, Paul writes, "For that day will not come, unless the rebellion comes first, and the man of lawlessness is revealed, the son of destruction, who opposes and exalts himself against every so-called god or object of worship, so that he takes his seat in the temple of God, proclaiming himself to be God." Verses 3–4 are often misunderstood (I believe) as teaching that this rebellion and the revealing of this man of lawlessness are prerequisite indicators to the coming day of the Lord, but if Paul was making this point, he would be contradicting both his own teaching and the widespread teaching in the NT that both God's deliverance and God's judgment in the coming day of the Lord are imminent. Coming like a thief. Could happen at any time. No forewarning.

Remember, the Thessalonians are convinced they're in the midst of the day of the Lord, not in the timeframe leading up to it. Paul essentially tells them that's impossible, for two reasons: 1) there will first be a great rebellion against God *in this time*, and then 2) this man of lawlessness will be revealed to take leadership of this rebellion in flamboyant fashion. He will ultimately claim to be the supreme god of gods and publicly proclaim himself to be God in the temple of God—most likely in the Jewish temple in Jerusalem, either restored or newly constructed during the tribulation period.

Paul's point is this: these things clearly aren't happening; therefore, the day of the Lord clearly hasn't arrived, and by implication the Thessalonians haven't missed the rapture. Paul gives them sufficient proof to this point, but then chastises them for not knowing better.

Paul challenges the Thessalonians to stand firm in what they've been taught, beginning with the fact that they've been taught about the day of the Lord: "Do you not remember that when I was still with you I told you these things?" (v. 5). Paul is telling them, "C'mon guys, this is nothing new!" Remember his words to them in 1 Thessalonians 5:1–2: "you have no need to have anything written to you. For you yourselves are *fully aware* that the day of the Lord will come like a thief in the night." You get a hint of Paul's frustration back in verse 2 when Paul told them "not to be *quickly* shaken." In saying "quickly," Paul was telling them that they had far too easily abandoned what they knew to be true. But Paul isn't done with reminding them of what they know, because they've also been taught about the Holy Spirit's role in the day of the Lord.

Paul continues in verse 6, "And you know . . . ." The Thessalonians already possess even further understanding, which should reassure them. Paul reminds them in verses 6–8 that this man of lawlessness will ultimately be brought to nothing by the Lord Jesus but that he won't be revealed until God removes the force that is now restraining him. We'll see in a moment that this man of lawlessness will be supernaturally empowered by Satan, but that in a mysterious way, this lawless power is already at work in the world. In Ephesians 2:2 Paul calls it "the spirit that is *now at work* in the sons of disobedience," and 1 John 4:3 describes this power as "the spirit of the antichrist, which you heard was coming and *now is in the world already*." The fact that this power is already at work explains to the Thessalonians why they're presently suffering affliction, but this restraining force and the one who now restrains also offers another explanation as to why the day of the Lord hasn't come.

The restrainer is most likely a reference to the Holy Spirit, because such a force has to have the power to restrain a satanic power. Furthermore, there are grammatical features used here to describe the restrainer that are otherwise unique to how the Holy Spirit is described by Jesus in John's gospel. And so, if the restrainer is the Holy Spirit who will one day move "out of the way," consider what Robert Thomas offers in his commentary as an explanation for what that actually means: "The special presence of the Spirit as the indweller of saints will terminate abruptly at the [rapture] just as it began abruptly at Pentecost. Once the body of Christ has been caught away to heaven, the Spirit's ministry will revert back to what he did . . . during the OT period."[37]

I think Thomas's explanation is very plausible on a number of levels, but most importantly within the immediate context. Paul is reminding the Thessalonians of things they've already been taught in order to reassure them the day of the Lord could not have possibly come yet. All told, Paul is telling them there has been no great rebellion, no man of lawlessness, and no removal of the restrainer, and that the only "day of the Lord" event that could explain that removal would be the rapture—"the coming of our Lord Jesus Christ and our being gathered together to him" was the principal aspect of the day of the Lord that had shaken and alarmed the Thessalonians in the first place (presumably having missed it). But they are not destined for wrath—another point Paul has already made to them and makes once again, but now in a way that draws attention to how easily deceived they were. Christians should not stumble over the deceptions of the wicked because of who they are in Christ.

The Antichrist Will Delude Those Who Are Perishing

The Antichrist's power to delude the perishing will be supernatural. In verse 9 Paul says, "The coming of the lawless one is by the activity of Satan." It will be by the very power of Satan that this man of lawlessness comes, and Satan will seek to mimic the coming of Christ in the process, hence the name Antichrist. Power, signs, and wonders were all means that God used to validate Jesus as the genuine article, as the promised Christ who would come into the world to save it. In the same manner the Antichrist will be validated by his lord, Satan, but his objective will be to destroy rather than save. Paul teaches the Thessalonians in verse 10 that the sum of the Antichrist's work will be directed "at those who are perishing, because they refused to love the truth and so be saved." This too is a subtle rebuke of the Thessalonians, who were deceived by a power *that should only be able to mislead those who refuse to love the truth.* And although the Thessalonians are suffering persecution at the hands of those under Satan's sway, they can rest assured that God is in control in all these matters, for even the Antichrist serves God's sovereign purpose to judge the perishing.

In verses 11–12, Paul writes, "Therefore God sends them a strong delusion, so that they may believe what is false, in order that all may be condemned who did not believe the truth but had pleasure in unrighteousness." Ultimately the schemes of Satan, played out through the lives of wicked people today and a lawless man tomorrow, serve God's purposes to bring condemnation upon those who reject him. As the verses immediately following 2 Thessalonians 2 show, Paul ultimately sought to comfort the Thessalonians with his teaching in this passage, to include this point that God sends a strong delusion to enhance Satan's aims, at least toward a particular audience. For many today, the thought of God permitting or even capitalizing on the performance of evil is, on the surface, disturbing. But if we look more deeply than a surface understanding, we should see that this is consistent with the absolute sovereignty of God. A sovereign God must be sovereign over evil as well as good, otherwise he is not really sovereign at all.

God's great story of redemption and restoration, unlike most pagan religions, isn't a story of a struggle between good and evil gods. Rather, it is a story where the will of the one true God is brought to pass, so that even those who exercise their freedom to do evil will ultimately discover that their actions have paradoxically served the eternal purposes of the one true God. Paul tells the Thessalonians that the one true God sends a strong delusion on those who are perishing, but he tells the Thessalonians directly, "Let no one deceive you in any way."

Reject the Intrusions of Strong Delusions

Verses 13–15 close out this section of Paul's teaching to this church. The Thessalonians had been thoroughly taught on matters of the day of the Lord which, by the time of the writing of this letter, included a right understanding of how the rapture fit into the overall scheme of this future period of God's deliverance and wrath. Yet they were deceived. They fell for a lie. And so, Paul wraps up these concerns in verse 15, commanding them to "*stand firm and hold* to the traditions that you were taught by us, either by our spoken word or by our letter." So, how do we stand firm and hold? Let's start with the foundation of God's word; a sure place to stand.

Strive to accurately handle God's Word. In 2 Timothy 2:15, Paul charges Timothy to *"Do your best* to present yourself to God as one approved, a worker who has no need to be ashamed, *rightly handling* the word of truth." If God's Word can be rightly handled, then it can be wrongly handled as well. In the preceding verse, Paul gives us a sense of what he means here by "rightly handling" when he tells Timothy, speaking of his flock, to "charge them before God not to quarrel about words, which does no good, but only ruins the hearers" (v. 14).

The Thessalonians, afflicted by persecutions, were likely given over to a false message which played on their fears aroused by their circumstances. Their handling of God's Word was swayed by unhealthy emotions. I have seen people in church, very knowledgeable of the content of the Scriptures and very accurate in their theology, still wrongly handle the Scriptures by expressing their convictions through the unhealthy emotion of a quarrelsome spirit. And as Paul writes in 2 Timothy, that has no edifying effect but "only ruins the hearers," ultimately leaving all concerned under the sway of a spirit which ought to have no power over us. But led by the Spirit of truth, we can hold to convictions in a manner which is pleasing rather than grieving to him.

We also stand firm when we hold to sound convictions with a sound spirit. A woman was coming home from work and stopped by a butcher to buy a chicken for supper. The butcher reached into a barrel, grabbed the last chicken he had, flung it on the scales behind the counter, and told the woman its weight. She thought for a moment. "I really need a bit more chicken than that," she said. "Do you have any larger ones?"

Without a word, the butcher put the chicken back into the barrel, groped around as though finding another, pulled the same chicken out, and placed it on the scales. "This chicken weighs one pound more," he announced. The woman pondered her options and then said, "Okay. I'll take them both."[38]

I love this story because it touches on the message of 2 Thessalonians 2 in several ways. First of all, the woman wasn't driven by a rash response to her circumstance. She was steady and thoughtful, and so was unshaken by an attempt to deceive her. Her response reflected the wisdom of a woman who walked in this fallen world on solid ground. But also notice her attitude toward the deceiver. She didn't condemn him, but rather showed the kind of grace which offered the possibility, as grace does, to allow the man to fall under the conviction of his own conscience.

In 2 Thessalonians 2, the Thessalonians were comforted by the truth that many of those who afflicted them would know the finality of God's judgment in due time. But in a fallen world, some of those who afflict us come to Christ through our witness—even someone like Paul, who once was Saul. God alone knows who is truly perishing and must receive strong delusion. For us to assume we can take his place in bringing condemnation is a strong delusion we can sometimes bring upon ourselves. So, whether from the mystery of lawlessness already at work in the world, or from the innate delusions of our fallen nature, let us reject the intrusions of strong delusions.

Chapter 21

Live Like a Conqueror
(Revelation 13:1–10)

In Ephesians 6:12, Paul puts our entire Christian lives in proper context: "we do not wrestle against flesh and blood, but against the rulers, against the authorities, against the cosmic powers over this present darkness, against the spiritual forces of evil in the heavenly places." If you know Jesus Christ as your Lord and Savior and God's Holy Spirit dwells within you, then you live every moment of every day on a cosmic battlefield in which evil cosmic powers seek to devour you. But Paul continues to say in Ephesians 6:13 that God has given us what we need to conquer evil cosmic powers, telling us to "take up the whole armor of God, that you may be able to withstand in the evil day, and having done all, to stand firm." Do you feel like you're in that kind of a battle today? Do you feel like it's one you can win?

The message from Revelation 13:1–10 is that we are to live like conquerors—all the more when the cost of living in this cosmic battlefield comes at a terrible and terrifying price. Previously, we saw Paul describe the coming Antichrist as a man of lawlessness who will be empowered by Satan for the purpose of exalting Satan and his Antichrist as the object of worldwide worship in place of God. But what comes next is the terrible cost of going against the grain of Satan's program during this time of terror for those on the earth who reject him: a time which Jesus describes in Matthew 24:21 (NET): "For then there will be great suffering unlike anything that has happened from the beginning of the world until now, or ever will happen."

In Revelation 12:12, John gives us some insight as to why this will be so: "But woe to you, O earth and sea, for the devil has come down to you in great wrath, because he knows that his time is short!" His time is limited, but in that limited time we'll see that Satan will empower the Antichrist to bring him worldwide worship, and gain for him a worldwide victory over God's people that God will temporarily allow. Through all that, God will command his people to faithfully endure the suffering Satan's wrath will bring. In the midst of this cosmic battle, God himself is ultimately Satan's diabolical objective.

From what we know of the time of Satan's first act of rebellion against God, the Scriptures give us a picture of a mighty and glorious angel who ultimately bristled at the commandment "You shall have no other gods before me." Satan clearly saw himself as God's equal, and so equally worthy of worship. Therefore, it should not surprise us to learn that, when he knows his time is short, at the end of the age, Satan will pull out all the stops.

Satan Will Empower the Antichrist, to Bring Him Worldwide Worship

Satan's actions at the end of the age, although occurring within a God-ordained limited timeframe, need to be understood in an age-old context—for his actions are rooted in an age-old conflict.

In Revelation 12, John gives a behind-the-scenes summary of the great and age-old cosmic battle between good and evil. There is a great deal of symbolic imagery in Revelation 12 that's very difficult to interpret, so in the interest of time, let me sum up what I believe John tells us.

At some point in the distant past, and at least prior to the fall of humanity in Genesis 3, Satan led a rebellion against God, in which he enticed one third of the angelic host to follow him. Ultimately, Satan and his angels were consigned to the earth. And as we discovered in Genesis 3, Satan was given power and authority over the earth. This dominion of Satan is well attested in the Scriptures, as even Jesus refers to Satan as "the ruler of this world" three separate times in John's gospel. And through this dominion over the earth, Satan has endlessly waged war against God and God's people, especially seeking to destroy Christ and seemingly succeeding in doing so. Yet in Revelation 12:5, John points out Satan's great failure in his aims, as Christ was raised from the dead, exalted to heaven and God's throne, and that despite Satan's dominion on earth, the day will come when Christ will "rule all the nations with a rod of iron."

Presently, Satan has not been denied access to God's presence. The Scriptures teach, and John affirms in Revelation 12:10, that Satan accuses God's people "day and night before our God." But John describes a future day when war will break out in earnest in heaven, and led by the angel Michael, Satan and his angels will be defeated by a host of heavenly angels and be irreversibly cast to the earth. Satan will know he has little time; he will be filled with wrath, and will direct that wrath at God's people Israel—those Jews who will turn to Christ in unprecedented numbers during this time of great tribulation. But God will provide refuge for these Jewish saints in the last half of this seven-year tribulation, and so Satan, the great dragon of old, will redirect his war against those Gentiles who will come to Christ in this time: "those who keep the commandments of God and hold to the testimony of Jesus" as John writes in 12:17.

Having given us the cosmic setting for Satan's hostile ambitions, John then transitions to how those ambitions will be brought to pass in Revelation 13 by building on the readers' expectations. He closes 12:17 by saying of Satan, "And he stood on the sand of *the sea*." And as he stood, as Revelation 13:1–2 states, "I [John] saw a beast rising out of *the sea*, with ten horns and seven heads, with ten diadems on its horns and blasphemous names on its heads. And the beast that I saw was like a leopard; its feet were like a bear's, and its mouth was like a lion's mouth. And to it the dragon gave his power and his throne and great authority."

Although the language here is very symbolic, Satan is essentially bringing to pass in these verses what he attempted to do when he tempted Jesus in the wilderness, when "the devil took him to a very high mountain and showed him all the kingdoms of the world and their glory. And he said to him, 'All these I will give you, if you will fall down and worship me'" (Matthew 4:8–9). Jesus rejected Satan's offer, but the Antichrist will willingly embrace Satan's offer.

We see this in the way the Antichrist, referred to as "a beast" in verse 1, is described "with ten horns and seven heads, with ten diadems on its horns"—nearly identical to the description of Satan in Revelation 12:3 "with seven heads and ten horns, and on his heads seven diadems." John reverses the order of where the diadems (or crowns) are on Satan and the beast because the heads are the main feature with Satan—very likely indicative of Satan's age-old authority as the ruler of this world—while the horns are the main feature with the beast. This is very possibly indicative of the worldwide power structure Satan will engineer at the time of the end to enact his diabolical will, just as parallel texts in Daniel 7 and Revelation 17 indicate.

As verse 2 states, Satan will grant the Antichrist the power, throne, and authority to rule over this end-time worldwide power structure; and as verse 1 indicates, this power structure will serve the purpose of bringing great blasphemies against God to pass. This blasphemous character of worldly kingdoms is not new to human history. But as verse 2 indicates with its comparison to the leopard, bear, and lion, John is recalling Daniel's use of different beasts to symbolize worldly kingdoms over the ages to teach us that the kingdom of the Antichrist will be like the sum of the worst of these kingdoms combined.

And the greatest blasphemy Satan will perpetrate through the Antichrist will be to mock and counterfeit the death and resurrection of Christ. Satan will mimic the redeeming work of Christ with the apparent death and resurrection of his Antichrist. Very simply, in verses 3–4 John teaches that the beast will suffer what appears to be a mortal wound (most likely a deception), but will be healed from this mortal wound. And we know this will be a very public and widely known event because John says in verse 3, "the whole earth *marveled* as they followed the beast."

The verb translated "marveled" here is used more than twenty times in the Gospels to describe people's reaction to Jesus and his miracles. Yet unlike Jesus, whose miraculous works did not keep him from scorn and crucifixion, and whose death and resurrection has never led to a dominant worldwide following, God will reveal the depth and breadth of fallen humanity's depravity. The work of this demonic counterfeit will win a widespread worldwide community of believers who will not only marvel at him, but as verse 4 indicates, will worship the beast and his Lord Satan with awe and wonder saying, "Who is like the beast, and who can fight against it?" The world will finally find the messiah it has been looking for and will fall head over heels in admiration of him. He will create the universal impression he is unbeatable, as Paul mentioned in 2 Thessalonians 2, a strong delusion God will enhance rather than refute . . . at least for a time.

God Will Temporarily Allow the Antichrist Worldwide Victory over His People

Not only will God allow this but he will enable it. Three times in verses 5–8, John uses the passive form of the verb "to give," which the ESV translates in two of these instances "to allow." This is what's known as a divine passive, indicating that a certain activity finds its source—by permission, authority, power, etc.—from God himself. And in verse 5, we see first that God will give the Antichrist the authority and the means to blaspheme for three-and-one-half years. Ironically, although Satan is the one who will seemingly grant the beast his authority as we saw in verse 2, in truth it will be the sovereign God who does so. And in so doing, God will open the door, as we see in verse 6, for this vile creature to blaspheme God, his heavenly dwelling place, and all who dwell there. The word "blaspheme" means to speak in a way that denigrates or defames someone in a reviling and slanderous way.[39] But this won't simply be a war of words.

God will permit the Antichrist to successfully wage war against his people. The first part of verse seven states "Also it was *allowed* to make war on the saints and to conquer them" or as Jesus may have been describing in Matthew 24:9, "Then they will deliver you up to tribulation and put you to death, and you will be hated by all nations for my name's sake." And all the nations will be moved to hate those who come to Christ in the tribulation because God will give the Antichrist authority over all the nations—"every tribe and people and language and nation," as John writes at the end of verse 7.

Like his master Satan, the Antichrist will hate God's people, and the vast majority of the earth who worship him will, as Jesus said, join the beast in this hatred. But we can infer from John's words in verse 8 that those who have trusted in Christ in this time—whose names are "written . . . in the book of life of the Lamb who was slain"—will be the exception to this hatefest. Yet in a world where, for a time, God allows Satan and his Antichrist to wage world war against God's people unfettered, refusing to worship the beast will come at a terrifying cost. In Revelation 6:9–11, John once again gives us a heavenly behind-the-scenes look at that cost:

> I saw under the altar the souls of those who had been slain for the word of God and for the witness they had borne. They cried out with a loud voice, "O Sovereign Lord, holy and true, how long before you will judge and avenge our blood on those who dwell on the earth?" Then they were each given a white robe and told to rest a little longer, until the number of their fellow servants and their brothers should be complete, who were to be killed as they themselves had been.

This time of suffering for tribulation believers will be so severe that the distress of it will remain palpable even in heaven—yet on earth, his people are to follow the example of their Savior.

God Commands His People to Faithfully Endure Suffering

Having painted this ominous and terrifying future picture of hell unleashed on earth, John then abruptly shifts to a command in verse 9, using the very same preamble and command that Jesus used earlier in Revelation to each of the seven churches: "If anyone has an ear, let him hear"—or as the NET puts it, "If anyone has an ear, *he had better listen!*" And what is the command believers had better heed in this unprecedented time of tribulation for God's people?

John tells us in verse 10, in a way that the New Living Translation communicates in a very understandable fashion: "Anyone who is destined for prison will be taken to prison. Anyone destined to die by the sword will die by the sword. *This means that God's holy people must endure persecution patiently and remain faithful.*" Prison and death will be the fate of the faithful who refuse to worship the beast. All authority over the nations will have been given to the beast. No earthly authority, therefore, will respond to appeals for clemency or mercy. It will be a world war on God's people and the Antichrist will seem, by every account, to conquer them, as we saw in verse 7. What are believers to do in so hopeless a state?

Oddly enough, in verses 9–10 John gives believers a snapshot of this command in action during his preview to this time of tribulation in chapter 12: "And they have conquered him by the blood of the Lamb and by the word of their testimony, for they loved not their lives even unto death" (v. 11). In other words, John's command to tribulation believers is to live in a very particular way.

Live Like a Conqueror!

"They loved not their lives even unto death." Jesus makes a very similar statement in John 12:25: "Whoever loves his life loses it, and whoever hates his life in this world will keep it for eternal life." For tribulation saints to be conquerors, they will need to forego any right or claim on their own lives while holding fast to the faithful testimony of the gospel of Jesus Christ, even if death is the cost of doing so. But if, as I've hopefully humbly contended, the church will be delivered from this time of wrath, why should we at all be concerned about applying this text to ourselves?

Well, for starters, remember that Paul taught the Thessalonians that the church was destined for persecution—which, both in the Scriptures and in church history to the present, has many times led to great suffering and even death. Furthermore, Jesus uses this enduring and faithful work of his conquerors as the basis for his promised rewards to the seven churches in Revelation 2–3, telling each "to the one who conquers" he will give many things—being granted to eat of the tree of life; to not be hurt by the second death; to be given authority over the nations; and as Jesus promises the church at Laodicea, "to sit with me on my throne, as I also conquered and sat down with my Father on his throne" (3:21). The fact of the matter is that believers of every age are called by God to hold fast to a faithful testimony under every circumstance; even in the face of the loss of our well-being, our liberty, or even our lives. As John says in Revelation 13:10 (NLT), "God's holy people must endure persecution patiently and remain faithful." To do so is to live like a conqueror.

I'd like to conclude with an illustration of what this can entail with a striking example from early church history—the martyrdom of Polycarp, a disciple of the apostle John. In the third chapter of the early church work *The Martyrdom of Polycarp*, an elder believer named Germanicus is regarded as an inspiration to the church in the way that he died:

> For the most noble Germanicus strengthened the timidity of others by his own patience, and fought heroically with the wild beasts. For, when the proconsul sought to persuade him, and urged him to take pity upon his age, he attracted the wild beast towards himself, and provoked it, being desirous to escape all the more quickly from an unrighteous and impious world.[40]

The Romans actually regarded Christians as atheists because they rejected worship of the multitude of Roman gods, yet having witnessed Germanicus's faith and courage in the face of death, the Roman crowd is recorded in chapter 3 as responding this way:

But upon this the whole multitude, marvelling at the nobility of mind displayed by the devout and godly race of Christians, cried out, Away with the "Atheists; let Polycarp be sought out!"[41]

And having found the "atheist" Polycarp, chapters 9 and 11 capture how Polycarp followed Germanicus's "conquering" example:

> And as he was brought forward, the tumult became great when they heard that Polycarp was taken. And when he came near, the proconsul asked him whether he was Polycarp. On his confessing that he was, [the proconsul] sought to persuade him to deny [Christ], saying, Have respect to your old age, and other similar things, according to their custom, [such as], Swear by the fortune of Cesar; repent, and say, Away with the Atheists. But Polycarp, gazing with a stern countenance on all the multitude of the wicked heathen then in the stadium, and waving his hand towards them, while with groans he looked up to heaven, said, Away with the Atheists. Then, the proconsul urging him, and saying, Swear, and I will set you at liberty, reproach Christ; Polycarp declared, Eighty and six years have I served him, and he never did me any injury: how then can I blaspheme my King and my Saviour?
>
> The proconsul then said to him, I have wild beasts at hand; to these will I cast you, unless you repent. But he answered, Call them then, for we are not accustomed to repent of what is good in order to adopt that which is evil; and it is well for me to be changed from what is evil to what is righteous. But again the proconsul said to him, I will cause you to be consumed by fire, seeing you despise the wild beasts, if you will not repent. But Polycarp said, You threaten me with fire which burns for an hour, and after a little is extinguished, but are ignorant of the fire of the coming judgment and of eternal punishment, reserved for the ungodly. But why do you tarry? Bring forth what you will.[42]

Chapter 22

The Uneasy Prelude to the Sure Conclusion (Revelation 13)

reat stories that endure long enough to become classics tend to have a message that resonates with our souls. They also tend to follow a particular pattern which the Bible also follows. Given the lordship of God over all time, creation, history, powers, principalities, etc., I'm prone to think that the Bible—God's revelation to us through his Word—*sets* the pattern for great stories rather than follows a pattern. In other words, great stories tend to have a message that resonates with our souls because they follow the pattern of the greatest story ever told.

By way of a reminder, the pattern looks something like this: The story begins in a setting where the hero and the hero's desired conditions are prevailing. The hero is good and so are his/her conditions, but then a villain appears on the scene with an agenda: to disrupt or destroy the hero and the hero's conditions so that the prevailing conditions conform to the villain's will. "Did God actually say, 'You shall not eat of any tree in the garden'?" (Genesis 3:1). This intrusion of the villain onto the scene introduces conflict into the story, and the rest of the story entails how the conflict will play out. Will the hero recover his or her footing and prevail? Or will the villain rise victorious over everything that is good so that his or her dastardly will and wishes become the new reality? To the latter outcome, as Paul was fond of writing in his letters, "may it never be!"

Since childhood, I have been a hopeless lover of Marvel Comics, their characters and stories. And now, with the advent of filmmaking technology to bring those stories to life, I am a hopeless lover of the slew of movies which have been made over the past decade or so. In April 2018, the film *Avengers: Infinity War* was released *but not the sequel*. If you're a fan, you know that the film ended with the villain, Thanos, standing victorious over everything that is good so that his dastardly will and wishes had become the new reality . . . in the entire universe! May it never be! Frenzied Marvel fans desperately searched for clues in the movie to see how this outcome would be reversed. Why the desperation? Because *this can't be*!

Unless people are themselves truly evil, something in our souls is deeply provoked when evil prevails. Something unbeknownst to us has to be in the works to undo this great injustice. But why do we feel this way? Perhaps because we are made in the image of the Author of the greatest story ever told. Even though that image has been marred by our sin, in most of us there is enough of a spark to still sense what is "good" on the basis of what the Author of the greatest story ever told declares to be "good." Fans of the Marvel complex of films were confident that the conflict was still playing out—that their heroes would prevail. And that confidence in a better ending was ultimately sustained in Marvel fans by the sequel to *Infinity War*.

We also see an example of this in another fairly contemporary action film. In the film adaptation of Tolkien's classic story *The Lord of the Rings: The Two Towers*, the king and people of the good kingdom of Rohan have fled to their traditional place of refuge called Helm's Deep, because the powerful and overwhelming army (evil, of course) of the wizard Saruman is on the move and headed their way to destroy them. Days before the battle even commences, a conversation happens between Gandalf and Aragorn, two of the main heroes. As Aragorn prepares to accompany the king and people of Rohan to Helm's Deep to aid in their defense, Gandalf tells Aragorn, "Look to my coming at first light on the fifth day. At dawn, look to the east."

The battle later commences and by the early hours before dawn on the fifth day, things look hopeless for the people of Rohan. Their defensive positions have been nearly completely overrun and their complete slaughter at the hands of Saruman's army seems all but inevitable. In a last, desperate act of bravery and glory, Aragorn, Théoden the king of Rohan, and others decide to ride out from their last defensive position straight into the marauding onslaught of their seemingly victorious enemy—on the fifth day, at dawn. And as they do, they look to the east. There, on a high ridge above the battlefield, they see Gandalf on his horse, and with him a large cavalry force ready to descend from the ridge to fall upon Saruman's army. And as they do, just before the opposing forces of good and evil collide, the brilliant shaft of light from the sun crests the ridge, illuminating the path of the cavalry and blinding the evil hordes. And the good guys win . . . and as they do, something down to the very core of our souls rejoices as we watch it unfold.

You see, before the battle had even begun, before the darkest hour hit when all hope seemed lost, when the forces of evil clearly seemed to have brought to pass that which must never be—the ultimate triumph of evil over good—Gandalf had already set in motion what was necessary to ensure the victory for the forces of good. In the classic pattern of great stories, this is known as the climax: the point where the hero has done what is necessary to ensure the villain will ultimately come to ruin. The conflict has played out through the rising action of the story, but now, at the climax, although the villain may not yet be aware of it, his or her end is as good as done.

In John 19:28–30, as Jesus is hanging upon the cross, John records, "After this, Jesus, knowing that all was now finished, said (to fulfill the Scripture), 'I thirst.' A jar full of sour wine stood there, so they put a sponge full of the sour wine on a hyssop branch and held it to his mouth. When Jesus had received the sour wine, he said, '*It is finished*,' and he bowed his head and gave up his spirit." On the third day after his crucifixion, as we know, the grave did not have the power to keep him there. He rose victorious over sin and death, but to most of the watching world (and his followers), defeat and hopelessness hung heavy in the air. On this very same day of Jesus' resurrection, two of Jesus' followers described their feelings this way: "our chief priests and rulers delivered him up to be condemned to death, and crucified him. But we had hoped that he was the one to redeem Israel" (Luke 24:20–21). We "had" hoped!

Do you look at the state of the world today with a sense of despair and hopelessness? Is evil on an inevitable trajectory of victory in all things? If you feel this way, reconsider that we've already hit the climax of the greatest story ever told. The hero has done everything necessary to ensure the villain will ultimately come to ruin. "It is finished" regardless of what Satan, his world, and his followers believe, and regardless of how much they seem to be prevailing.

Remember Revelation 13:1–10. Satan and his Antichrist will be worshipped. An adoring world will say of his Antichrist, "Who is like the beast, and who can fight against it?" (v. 4). John goes on to write in 13:5–7, "And the beast was given a mouth uttering haughty and blasphemous words, and it was allowed to exercise authority for forty-two months. It opened its mouth to utter blasphemies against God, blaspheming his name and his dwelling, that is, those who dwell in heaven. Also it was allowed to make war on the saints *and to conquer them*. And authority was given it over every tribe and people and language and nation." That's a pretty bleak picture. In the rest of Revelation 13, John goes on to describe how the Antichrist will be perceived as he works miracles, even seemingly mimicking the resurrection of Christ. He'll be a worldwide rock star with unlimited power and authority over the earth . . . for a time. Remember what Gandalf said: "Look to my coming . . ." And so we should.

Chapter 23

The Return of the King, Part One
(Revelation 19:1–10)

In 1717, King Louis XIV of France died. Preferring to be called "Louis the Great," he was the monarch who declared, "I am . . . the State!" His court was the most magnificent in Europe, and his funeral was the most spectacular. In the church where the ceremony was performed, his body lay in a golden coffin. To dramatize his greatness, orders had been given that the cathedral would be very dimly lit with only one special candle set above the coffin. The thousands of people in attendance waited in silence. Then the presiding bishop began to speak. Slowly reaching down, he snuffed out the candle and said, "Only God is great."[43]

As followers of Jesus Christ, we know this to be true as well. Yet we also know that Louis XIV wasn't alone in his aspirations. In Isaiah 14:13–14, Isaiah prophecies the cause of the fall of Babylon when he says of their king, "You said in your heart, 'I will ascend to heaven; above the stars of God I will set my throne on high . . . I will ascend above the heights of the clouds; I will make myself like the Most High.'" As we know from the Scriptures, this inclination to seek such glory, honor, and worship for ourselves is satanic at its root. Whereas God created us in his image to exercise worldwide dominion as his image-bearers, Satan's deceptive temptation of Eve was to lead her to claim her own dominion apart from God with the twisted promise to her that when she did, "your eyes will be opened, and you will be like God" (Genesis 3:5). And so it has been Satan's aim throughout human history to usurp and exercise dominion over creation in a way that is completely antithetical to God's will.

As we also know from the Scriptures, Satan has been divinely restrained in his efforts. Yet a time is coming when God will remove his restraint and permit Satan to pursue his will unfettered. As Jesus describes in Matthew 24:21, "then there will be great tribulation, such as has not been from the beginning of the world until now, no, and never will be." But only for a time.

As we'll see in this chapter and the next, Christ's return will bring a sudden and swift end to Satan's age-old effort to challenge God's dominion over his creation. In 2 Thessalonians 1:10, Paul describes this return as a time "when he comes on that day to be glorified in his saints, and to be marveled at among all who have believed." He will be glorified among us and we will marvel at him. In Revelation 19, John depicts this time of marveling as both a sight and sound phenomenon. We will be in awe and wonder as we marvel at what we *hear* and what we *see*. John records the auditory dimension of the response to the return of the King first: his return will be greatly anticipated and will be cause for our highest praise. Anticipation is born of suspense and suspense is fed by the clues within our circumstances. And as the time approaches for God to climactically intervene to thwart the god of this age through the return of the King, the intervention will be evident.

God's Preparations for the King's Return Will Be Evident to the Faithful (Revelation 13-18)

Why? Because the efforts of his adversary will compel his preparations. In Matthew 24:22, Jesus says of this time of tribulation, "if those days had not been cut short, no human being would be saved. But for the sake of the elect those days will be cut short." Such days will be possible because Satan will be allowed to wield his power unfettered, but he will not do so for long or unopposed. Revelation 13 reveals that Satan will

be permitted to exercise his dominion as the ruler of this world uncon-
strained for the limited time of the great tribulation. His power, throne,
and great authority will be unleashed, and in so doing he will strive to
replicate the nature of God with his false trinity. And through that false
trinity, he will strive to mock the works of God—and his striving won't
(initially) be fruitless.

Chapters 13–18 of Revelation show how Satan will finally see the full
fruits of his labors, as his Antichrist and false prophet bring him worldwide worship as well as complete control over a worldwide institution of
government and its economy. Mimicking God's creation mandate, Satan
will bring to pass—through the institutions of religion, government, and
economy that he will create—a world ruled by *his image-bearers* who will
subdue and seek to rid the earth of those who faithfully follow God.
This comprehensive, demonic worldwide system, variably referred to as
the great prostitute and Babylon the great in chapters 14–19 (the latter
also referring to the seat of power for this demonic worldwide system),
will inspire much of the earth to mirror the darkest of satanic immorality, blaspheme God with the greatest of determination, and prolifically
shed the blood of those who hold to a faithful testimony of Jesus Christ
in this time. Without even a close competitor in human history, this will
be the darkest time the earth will ever see. Yet in this darkest of time,
God's hand will intervene on behalf of his people.

Summarizing the chapters leading up to Revelation 19, here are
the major movements of God's intervention that follows the terrible
implications of Satan's work we saw in chapter 13: In Revelation 14,
John continues to record for us what he heard and saw in this time of
divine revelation to him. Despite Satan's efforts to the contrary, an angel
will proclaim the gospel to every person on earth with the command to
worship God alone; people will respond, finding redemption in Christ.
Another angelic messenger will proclaim the inevitable downfall and
eternal judgment of Satan, his Antichrist, and all who worship them. In
the midst of the great suffering that the faithful will experience at their
hands in this time, the Spirit himself will give comfort to the faithful,

according to 14:13: "Blessed are the dead who die in the Lord from now on. Blessed indeed . . . that they may rest from their labors, for their deeds follow them!"

And then, in chapters 15–18, in a way very reminiscent of the judgments God brought upon Egypt to prepare for the deliverance of his people Israel from bondage, John records the plagues and actions God will bring and take upon this world fully under Satan's dominion, along with their consequent effects. A stunning indication of this and the parallels to the Exodus account is in Revelation 16:10–11: "The fifth angel poured out his bowl on the throne of the beast, and its kingdom was plunged into darkness. People gnawed their tongues in anguish and cursed the God of heaven for their pain and sores. They did not repent of their deeds."

Like Pharaoh and the Egyptians of old, the defeat of the Antichrist and his intransigent worldwide following at the hands of God will be inevitable. The way will have been prepared. The course of events pointing to victory will be clear, even before the final battle makes it so. And so, John records the declaration of another angel in Revelation 18. With the fall of Babylon the great—that great prostitute whose "sins are heaped high as heaven" (18:5)—as good as done, the angel commands those who dwell in heaven saying "Rejoice over her, O heaven, and you saints and apostles and prophets, for God has given judgment for you against her!" (18:20).

And so, with the stage set "for battle on the great day of God the Almighty" as John records in 16:12–14, the anticipation of the consummation of the age-old cosmic battle between good and evil builds to a pitch in a way that has always moved God's people to respond to his mighty works on their behalf with a particular word: Hallelujah!

The Return of the King Will be Cause for the Highest Praise (Revelation 19:1–10)

In verses 1–5 of Revelation 19, John records what he had *heard*—and the dominant theme in what he was hearing was praise for the Lord. The word "hallelujah" is a transliteration, both in the Greek text and in English, of the Old Testament Hebrew phrase, "praise Yahweh!" or "praise the Lord!" The only time it is used in all of the New Testament is right here in this passage.

"A great multitude in heaven" cry it out with a loud voice in verse 1 and once again in verse 3, and the heavenly residents whose constant place is in the presence of God and his throne—the twenty-four elders and the four living creatures—proclaim it in verse 4. All of heaven will be joined together praising God with thunderous hallelujahs. And then in verse 5, the audience shifts and likely includes those on earth as well with the command from God's throne to "Praise our God." Every voice in heaven and earth will be moved to praise God, and they will do so because the King's return will bring true, just, and lasting *judgment*.

John gives us the basis for this creation-wide praise in verses 2–3: "for his judgments are true and just; for he has judged the great prostitute who corrupted the earth with her immorality, and has avenged on her the blood of his servants. Once more they cried out, 'Hallelujah! The smoke from her goes up forever and ever.'" It's the great paradox of fallen humanity that we rejoice when justice is done on human terms, yet we challenge and often condemn God in every possible way in matters of justice. On human terms, when the serial killer meets his end, we are pleased. The murderous dictator is overthrown and we rejoice. Yet when it comes to God acting (or not acting) in judgment on his terms, there may be no greater stumbling block to the gospel. In our eyes, he either has no standing to judge or he is criminally negligent because he fails to judge. This attitude toward him, sadly, even finds its way into the church. But in Revelation 19, his judgment is cause for celebration and praise by his kingdom citizens because "his judgments are true and just."

God's justice is "true" because it is based on his own covenant faithfulness, and it is "just" because it is based on his holy character. In other words, his judgments are always both morally true and legally just, which means his restraint from judgment is also always both morally true and legally just. Here, Satan's worldwide system is being destroyed because its evil deeds demand the most extreme punishment. As one sees in a study of chapters 14–18, the deceitful corrupting force of this evil empire will make all the nations, their inhabitants, and their rulers embrace the deepest of immoralities Satan can inspire. Now this empire must pay the price for its evil folly, and every creature faithful to God in heaven and earth will resoundingly praise him for it. But they will also praise him because he hears the cry of his people and acts on their behalf with a mighty hand.

In Exodus 2:23–24, Moses records that Israel cried out to God in the midst of their hard bondage: "Their cry for rescue from slavery came up to God. And God heard their groaning, and God remembered his covenant with Abraham, with Isaac, and with Jacob." In a very similar way, in the midst of this great tribulation, John records in Revelation 6:10 that those who will have been slain for their faithfulness in this tribulation cried out from their place in heaven "with a loud voice, 'O Sovereign Lord, holy and true, how long before you will judge and avenge our blood on those who dwell on the earth?'" And in verse 3 of chapter 19, it is once again with a loud voice that the multitudes in heaven now proclaim that our God "has avenged on her the blood of his servants." He has heard his people. Salvation and glory and power belong to him. And his people cry out "hallelujah!" because he has not failed to be true and just in his judgments, both for his name's sake and for the sake of his people.

But though it is true that God will deal justly and eternally with the past injustices committed against him and his people will praise him for it, his judgment also points to a future glory that once again prompts praise—because the King's return will bring his true, just, and lasting *reign*.

Once again John records the voice of the great multitude in verses 6–7, crying out, "Hallelujah! For the Lord our God the Almighty reigns. Let us rejoice and exult and give him the glory." The great battle of all times still remains to be fought but the reign of God and his ultimate aim that his "will be done on earth as it is in heaven" is without doubt, because his kingdom will come in the person of the King of kings and Lord of lords. And so, the multitude looks beyond the battle to the celebration: "the marriage supper of the lamb." This event will usher in the beginning of the earthly kingdom of God over which Christ will reign: a celebration of the great victory of our God through Jesus Christ in the cosmic battle between good and evil. Christ's bride, his church in all her purity, along with the invited guests—both the bride and redeemed of all ages—will celebrate with him as they inherit the kingdom prepared for them from the foundation of the world.

This will include a Roman centurion whom Jesus marveled at in Matthew's gospel, telling his disciples "Truly, I tell you, with no one in Israel have I found such faith." And it will include many others, some of whom you may recognize as Jesus then immediately says "I tell you, many will come from east and west and recline at table with Abraham, Isaac, and Jacob in the kingdom of heaven" (Matthew 8:10–11). It will include the apostles, as Jesus indicates when he told them on the night he was betrayed: "You are those who have stayed with me in my trials, and I assign to you, as my Father assigned to me, a kingdom, that you may eat and drink at my table in my kingdom and sit on thrones judging the twelve tribes of Israel" (Luke 22:28–30). And as the faithful body of Christ at your local church, it will include us, as Paul teaches in 2 Timothy 2:11–12: "The saying is trustworthy, for: If we have died with him, we will also live with him; if we endure, we will also *reign with him*."

The anticipation of Christ's coming kingdom is worthy of praise, as we anticipate the celebration of it and as we anticipate the just and lasting nature of it. For then will come to pass what Isaiah foretold in Isaiah 2:2–4:

> It shall come to pass in the latter days that the mountain of the house of the LORD shall be established as the highest of the mountains, and shall be lifted up above the hills; and all the nations shall flow to it, and many peoples shall come, and say: "Come, let us go up to the mountain of the LORD, to the house of the God of Jacob, that he may teach us his ways and that we may walk in his paths." For out of Zion shall go forth the

law, and the word of the LORD from Jerusalem. He shall judge between the nations, and shall decide disputes for many peoples; and they shall beat their swords into plowshares, and their spears into pruning hooks; nation shall not lift up sword against nation, neither shall they learn war anymore.

Soon but not yet. There is still a dark lining in this silver cloud. As John writes in Revelation 16:12–14, war is brewing:

The sixth angel poured out his bowl on the great river Euphrates, and its water was dried up, to prepare the way for the kings from the east. And I saw, coming out of the mouth of the dragon and out of the mouth of the beast and out of the mouth of the false prophet, three unclean spirits like frogs. For they are demonic spirits, performing signs, who go abroad to the kings of the whole world, to assemble them for battle on the great day of God the Almighty.

John goes on to say in Revelation 17:13–14 that these kings "are of one mind, and they hand over their power and authority to the beast. They will make war on the Lamb." And that is where we'll leave the story for now. Cliffhanger time! But if you want to forego reaching for the bookmark and press on, then turn or scroll the page to see how this great battle turns out in part two of "The Return of the King!"

Chapter 24

The Return of the King, Part Two
(Revelation 19:11–21)

In the first part of Revelation 19, the creation-wide praise of "hallelujah" in anticipation of the very imminent return of the King of kings and Lord of lords has an ominous accompaniment. War is brewing. The false trinity of Satan, the Antichrist, and the False Prophet is moving "the kings of the whole world, to assemble them for battle on the great day of God the Almighty." These kings and their vast armies will assemble with demonic unity to "make war on the Lamb," as John records in Revelation 16–17.

In his magnificent story reflecting key themes of the biblical story, J. R. R. Tolkien portrays this great and final battle, with the evil forces of King Sauron arrayed in overwhelming might against the city of the coming king, the city of Minas Tirith. If you're familiar with the film version of the story, things are grim for the people of this city. Sauron's forces have begun to breach the city's defenses and terrible and final defeat seems inevitable, yet that all changes swiftly and suddenly when the king returns.

But as you read through the latter half of Revelation 19, the nature of the battle described in the scripture seems anticlimactic—a very one-sided battle. Was Tolkien creatively dramatizing things to make a better story, or did John have a different purpose in mind in his account of the return of the King? More on that question in a few moments.

In the first half of Revelation 19, John focused on what he had heard: the creation-wide praise in anticipation of the return of the King and his everlasting reign. But in the second half of chapter 19, John shifts from what he heard to what he *saw*. Three times John repeats the phrase "then I saw . . ." and each repetition traces the flow of John's account nicely. John *saw* the return of the King bring Satan's demise: the demise of his counterfeit *claims*, *promises*, and *dominion*. And of these three, Satan's claims are of foremost in importance. As we've seen, Satan's great, proud, and rebellious desire is to be like God, and his diabolical creation of his false trinity consisting of himself, the Antichrist, and the False Prophet will be his means to bring the glory and worship he seeks for himself—but not if the King has a say in the matter.

The King's Return Will Proclaim the Glory of God over Satan's Claims (Revelation 19:11–16)

This passage depicts this final battle between the forces of heaven and the forces of Satan as anticlimactic, yet Tolkien's story portrays the forces of evil knocking on the door with victory in their grasp. Is there more to the battle than what John records here? Let's take a moment to consider this battle from a different perspective, through the lens of Zechariah 14. Zechariah gives us the details of this battle from the perspective of the battle's focal point: Jerusalem and its inhabitants (just as Tolkien showed the fictional city Minas Tirith and its residents to be the focal point):

> Behold, a day is coming for the LORD, when *the spoil taken from you will be divided in your midst.* For I will gather all the nations against Jerusalem to battle, and *the city shall be taken and the houses plundered and the women raped. Half of the city shall go out into exile, but the rest of the people shall not be cut off from the city.* Then the LORD will go out and fight against those nations as when he fights on a day of battle. On that day his feet shall stand on the Mount of Olives that lies before Jerusalem on the east,

and the Mount of Olives shall be split in two from east to west by a very wide valley, so that one half of the Mount shall move northward, and the other half southward. And you shall flee to the valley of my mountains, for the valley of the mountains shall reach to Azal. And you shall flee as you fled from the earthquake in the days of Uzziah king of Judah. Then the Lord my God will come, and all the holy ones with him.

On that day there shall be no light, cold, or frost. And there shall be a unique day, which is known to the Lord, neither day nor night, but at evening time there shall be light.

On that day living waters shall flow out from Jerusalem, half of them to the eastern sea and half of them to the western sea. It shall continue in summer as in winter.

And the Lord will be king over all the earth. On that day the Lord will be one and his name one.

The whole land shall be turned into a plain from Geba to Rimmon south of Jerusalem. But Jerusalem shall remain aloft on its site from the Gate of Benjamin to the place of the former gate, to the Corner Gate, and from the Tower of Hananel to the king's winepresses. And it shall be inhabited, for there shall never again be a decree of utter destruction. Jerusalem shall dwell in security.

And this shall be the plague with which the Lord will strike all the peoples that wage war against Jerusalem: their flesh will rot while they are still standing on their feet, their eyes will rot in their sockets, and their tongues will rot in their mouths.

And on that day a great panic from the Lord shall fall on them, so that each will seize the hand of another, and the hand of the one will be raised against the hand of the other. (Zechariah 14:1–13)

Notice the detail of Zechariah's prophecy. All the gathered nations will seem to have accomplished Satan's aims. Jerusalem, the city from which the promised Messiah will reign, will have fallen in defeat, but God will make a way for some to escape. Rather than an anticlimactic battle, Christ's appearance, and the host of heaven with him, to make war against the nations will come at a desperate time when all hope seems lost. And when he makes war, his enemies will know the mighty and terrible power of the Lamb of God, and on that day, the end of it will be very unlike its beginning: with the Lord Jesus Christ as king over all the earth and the very creation transformed to glorify his name.

And it is in the matter of Christ's glory that John focuses on, which explains the difference between John's and Zechariah's account of this battle. The King's return will proclaim the glory of God over Satan's claims to authority.

In actuality, all of this passage in the latter half of Revelation 19 is written to demonstrate the stark contrast between the real thing and the counterfeit, between the truth of God and the false substitute Satan seeks to offer in himself. Notice in verse 11 that Christ returns on a white horse, a symbol of victory. Back in Revelation 6:2, John describes what he saw as a result of the first seal judgment: "And I looked, and behold, a white horse! And its rider had a bow, and a crown was given to him, and he came out conquering, and to conquer." This rider of a white horse is the Antichrist and the power, throne, and great authority Satan is permitted to grant him will enable him to be a victorious conqueror. Remember in Revelation 13:4, the Antichrist's adoring worldwide worshippers will say of him "Who is like the beast, and who can fight against it?" As we'll see in the rest of Revelation 19, John answers this question resoundingly in his description of the King's return. But also notice that unlike the Antichrist's army, *all* of Christ's army ride upon a white horse of victory, in verse 14.

Also notice in verse 12 that Christ has many diadems on his head. Diadem crowns were a type of crown used as a symbol of the highest ruling authority. We find them in only three instances in all the New

Testament: *many* on Jesus' head here, and the more limited numbers of seven and ten respectively associated with Satan and the Antichrist in Revelation 12–13. All of these subtle cues combine in John's point that he builds to at the end of this account of what he saw: this King who has come from heaven has no equal or remotely close competitor, regardless of the competitors' claims. He possesses the infinite and matchless authority of the King of kings and Lord of lords, as John writes in verse 16. He has matchless authority, and contrary to Satan's desires and claims he has a matchless name. The text from the previous chapter ended with John being rebuked by an angel with the command "Worship God" (Revelation 19:10). There is only one "name that is above every name . . . the name of Jesus," which alone will bring every knee in creation to bow before him in worship, as Paul teaches in Philippians 2. The King's return will proclaim the glory of God over Satan's claims to worship.

In Revelation 13–19, John frequently refers to the mark of the beast that the whole world will be commanded to take, and always associates taking the mark with worshipping the beast. But in Revelation 13:17, John describes this mark as "the name of the beast or the number of its name" and then says in verse 18, "let the one who has understanding calculate the number of the beast, for it is the number of a man, and his number is 666." The name and number are synonymous here and speak to the nature and character of the Antichrist. His nature and character can be fully discerned by people of understanding: he is merely a man, and the 666 may well indicate that he falls completely short of the perfection of God's nature and character in every way. In other words, his name is perfectly unworthy of worship.

Likewise, Christ's name refers to his nature and character, and in verse 12, in contrast to the Antichrist, the fullness of who he truly is remains unknowable to all but God. And in verse 13, in contrast to the Antichrist, Christ's nature and character perfectly conforms to the word of God. Once more, in verse 16, in contrast to the Antichrist, his nature and character rises above every power and authority in heaven and earth, for his name is "King of kings and Lord of lords." And as such, he is able to fully and perfectly bring to pass his will, in great contrast to whatever *promises* Satan and his Antichrist deceptively offered to the multitudes in our fallen world. Just as the King's return will refute all of Satan's counterfeit claims, it will also make a mockery of Satan's promises.

The King's Return Will Mock the Counterfeit Promises of Satan (vv. 17–18)

Verses 17–18 read, "Then I saw an angel standing in the sun, and with a loud voice he called to all the birds that fly directly overhead, 'Come, gather for the great supper of God, to eat the flesh of kings, the flesh of captains, the flesh of mighty men, the flesh of horses and their riders, and the flesh of all men, both free and slave, both small and great.'" Recall that the false trinity of Satan, the Antichrist, and the False Prophet will collude to bring supernatural demonic forces to bear on the kings of the earth to inspire them to "hand over their power and authority to the beast" in order to corporately "make war on the Lamb" as John writes in Revelation 17. One can only imagine what false promises were made to them in return, but with a divine irony that is very likely intended, they get invited to . . . *be* the supper!

In verses 7 and 9 of chapter 19, John mentions the invitation to the redeemed of all ages to the marriage supper of the Lamb: a great celebration of the long-promised victory of God and his people in the age-old cosmic battle of good versus evil. But whatever the false trinity may have promised to the mass of humanity coming together in battle against the Lamb, in what might best be construed as mocking those promises, their end will be an invitation to a supper where they are the main course! In other words, the saints will partake of the great banquet, and the wicked will be that great banquet. Whatever dominion they may have been promised will, ironically, be carried off in the bellies of gorged birds of prey. Diabolical claims and promises have been undone. Only a diabolical *dominion* remains.

The King's Return Will Destroy the Counterfeit Dominion of Satan (vv. 19–21)

We've already seen a very graphic picture of Christ's victory in Zechariah 14, but in verses 19–21, John doesn't give us the graphic details of the battle; he gives us the graphic outcome. In verses 19 and 21, we see that all the kings of the earth and their armies "were slain by the sword that came from the mouth of him who was sitting on the horse, and all the birds were gorged with their flesh" (v. 21). Whatever power and authority Satan will have won to his dominion by gaining the power and authority of the kings of the earth will be lost to him now. All that might be left to him now would be the power and authority of his own dominion—but in chapter 13, as you may recall, Satan had given all of that over to the Antichrist and his False Prophet; and as we see in verse 20, both the Antichrist and the False Prophet will be captured and "thrown alive into the lake of fire that burns with sulfur," a punishment John describes in Revelation 20:10 as an experience where "they will be tormented day and night forever and ever." Refuting and defeating the counterfeits of Satan—his claims, promises and dominion—will all come to pass with the return of the King. But before we leave Revelation 19 . . .

A Couple of Parting Thoughts on the Return of the King

The first of these parting thoughts is from verse 10 of chapter 19. After receiving the breathtaking insight of the great number of visions through the mediation of a heavenly angel, John "fell down at his feet to worship him"—earning a sharp rebuke and command from the angel who said "You must not do that! I am a fellow servant with you and your brothers who hold to the testimony of Jesus. Worship God." John records his own failure in this regard a second time in chapter 22, which may have been a second failure rather than a retelling of his failure here.

Remember Paul taught in 2 Thessalonians 2:10–11 that the coming of the Antichrist will be a strong delusion God permits, so that those who "refused to love the truth and so be saved . . . may believe what is false" and give worship to the Antichrist. Jesus likewise warned believers in Matthew 24:24: "For false christs and false prophets will arise and perform great signs and wonders, so as to lead astray, if possible, even the elect." The power of miraculous things is a strong lure, and Jesus warns that the faithful can succumb to it. Although it was from a faithful servant of God, John may have succumbed to such power and sinfully rendered worship twice. Satan is capable of the miraculous, and we must never be swayed by the miraculous that does not hold to a proven testimony of Jesus Christ. This is a point I think John was making in his own editorial comment on his failure in 19:10: "For the testimony of Jesus is the spirit of prophecy."

A second point worth emphasizing is our role in this future event. I hope you noticed that in verses 7–8, the bride of Christ—the church—is described as being clothed "with fine linen, bright and pure" (verse eight), and that in verse 14, the armies of heaven are "arrayed in fine linen, white and pure." The Scriptures teach in a multitude of places that the angels will accompany Christ in this return, but this seems to indicate that the church may at least make up part of this number as well. This is further reinforced by John's statement in 17:14 where he describes this battle: "they will make war on the Lamb, and the Lamb will conquer them, for he is Lord of lords and King of kings, and those with him are called and *chosen and faithful*." It is extremely unlikely that the angels would be described as "chosen and faithful," whereas God's people of every age are often described this way.

By the way, this is one of the points I use to make a case for a pretribu-lation rapture because, as verse 11 indicates, *heaven* opens for this return of the King and these armies follow him *from* there, as verse 14 states. If the rapture described in 1 Thessalonians 4 and the return of Christ here in Revelation 19 were one and the same event, it would be very difficult to explain how this is so, since Christ's descent is from heaven in both instances. The difficulty comes from the fact that in 1 Thessalonians 4, the church is resurrected and gathered up to him, whereas in Revelation 19, the church, along with a host of others, accompanies him *from* heaven.

That doctrinal point aside, don't miss that John describes these fine linen garments in verse 8 as "the righteous deeds of the saints." Later on, in Revelation 22:12, Jesus states, "Behold, I am coming soon, bringing my recompense with me, to repay each one for what he has done." How we live our Christian lives matter. We will ride into battle in the armies of the King of kings and Lord of lords to bring victory over Satan and his dominion. We ought to live now as worthy soldiers of our King.

Chapter 25

Victory and Vindication (Revelation 20:1–15)

When it comes to our beliefs regarding the end times, for those in the church who believe Christ's return to resurrect his church (the rapture) is a separate event from the return described in Revelation 19, many are divided over when this separate event will occur. Will it be before the tribulation? In the middle of it? At the end? Arguments from the Scripture can be made for each, but they all typically have one point of agreement in common: there will be a millennium, a literal, thousand-year reign of Christ upon earth after his return—a final age of human history that will usher in the age of eternity. In the early centuries of church history, it was a very prominent view within the church that the end times would be a literal sequence of events consisting of the resurrection and Christ's return, Christ's thousand-year reign, the final judgment, and the age of eternity.

But by the fourth century AD or so, the prominent teaching within the church viewed the events of Revelation 20 as symbolic. The binding of Satan in verses 1–3 was understood to be the restraint placed on Satan in the church age. The resurrection spoken of in Revelation 20:4–6 was understood to be a spiritual resurrection at the moment of salvation. The thousand-year reign of the saints with Christ in verses 4 and 6 symbolized the present role of the church and its rulers. The time of rebellion coincident with the unbinding of Satan in verses 7–10 symbolized the great tribulation and Christ's return to bring Satan's final defeat. And the events in verses 11–15 were understood as the resurrection and judgment of the just and the unjust at Christ's coming. Simply put, this view taught that Revelation 20 was a symbolic depiction of Christ's work and reign through his church in the present age and all the events associated with his future return—i.e., there will be no literal thousand-reign of Christ, no millennium (which is why this view is called amillennial). It was the dominant view within the church from the fourth century up to at least the nineteenth century.

I say all this both to make you aware of this diversity of views within the church universal (which divides us in our interpretation but not in our fellowship) and to inform you that I will be approaching Revelation 20 through the early church's interpretive lens for this text: that there will be a literal thousand-year reign of Christ on earth. And as the title of this chapter indicates, Christ's thousand-year reign will bring victory and vindication, both for God and his people. My approach to Revelation 20 will thematically follow this title because I believe victory and vindication are the primary purposes for Christ's thousand-year reign.

In 1 Corinthians 15:24–26, Paul writes of Christ's reign, "Then comes the end, when he delivers the kingdom to God the Father after destroying every rule and every authority and power. For he must reign until he has put all his enemies under his feet. The last enemy to be destroyed is death." The Son will reign until every enemy of God is destroyed and he will be vindicated in his judgments, as we'll see in Revelation 20. At the end of Revelation 19, Christ is victorious over the Antichrist and his armies, yet one enemy in particular remained conspicuously at large. Verse 2 of Revelation 20 describes him as "the dragon, that ancient serpent, who is the devil and Satan." Satan is still on the loose, but fear not.

The Thousand-Year Reign of Christ Will Bring Final Victory

Let's first consider from the text how this victory will bring glory to God: Christ's reign will glorify God by humiliating a proud adversary.

From the very beginning of the biblical account, God's foremost adversary has been Satan, whose very name means "adversary." Certainly, Satan's rebellion against, and opposition to, God was accompanied by those angels and the mass of humanity over history who joined him. But as Revelation 20 shows, Satan's ringleading role in deceiving the nations is vital in transforming sinful humanity into an organized rebellion against God once again.

But once again, Satan is only effective because God permits him the latitude to operate. In truth, the book of Revelation reveals Satan, that dragon and ancient serpent, to really be nothing more than what he has been from the beginning: a liar and deceiver who is relatively powerless before God. Twice God will dispatch Satan without even directly lifting a hand against him. The angel Michael will cast him out of heaven before the great tribulation, as we know from Revelation 12:7–9, and this angel in Revelation 20:1–3 will take hold of him, bind him up, and shut him in prison, powerless to escape. And when the thousand years of Christ's reign ends, as verses 7–10 indicate:

> Satan will be released from his prison and will come out to deceive the nations that are at the four corners of the earth, Gog and Magog, to gather them for battle; their number is like the sand of the sea. And they marched up over the broad plain of the earth and surrounded the camp of the saints and the beloved city, but fire came down from heaven and consumed them, and the devil who had deceived them was thrown into the lake of fire and sulfur where the beast and the false prophet were, and they will be tormented day and night forever and ever.

In Revelation 16, 17, and 19, John described the great final battle of this present age. The Antichrist rallies the armies of this earth to battle against God and his people, but when God acts through Christ, it will be a swift and anticlimactic end, as we know from Revelation 19. Might Satan somehow be proudly deluded enough to think that the outcome will somehow be different with himself in the lead? Satan repeats history at the end of the millennium and again, once God acts, the end is equally swift and anticlimactic. The great deceiver of the nations, despite all his delusions of supplanting God to bring glory and worship to himself, is nothing more than a petty deceiver before our God. He will be unceremoniously dispatched to an eternal reunion with the remainder of his false trinity to "be tormented day and night forever and ever." Christ's reign will bring the great and final victory over the foremost enemy of God, and as his people accompanied him in his return and victory over the Antichrist and his forces, so they will join him in his kingdom in the work of bringing the enemies of God under Christ's subjection. Christ's reign will bring the blessings of victory to God's people of all ages.

In verse 6, John describes the blessing of the saints' resurrection—"Blessed and holy is the one who shares in the first resurrection!"—then goes on to describe those blessings. The second death, which verse 14 indicates is the eternal judgment in the lake of fire, will have no power over us. His faithful people of all ages will serve God as priests, making us a kingdom of priests, as he promised both to his people Israel in Exodus 19 and to the church in Revelation 1:6. And finally, we will be blessed with the high honor of reigning with him for a thousand years; and commensurate with that reign, John says in verse 4, "Then I saw thrones, and seated on them were those to whom the authority to judge was committed." In other words, we will exercise the latitude to stand in judgment on Christ's behalf.

If you think John must be referring to someone else here, consider the following texts. In 1 Corinthians 6:2, Paul asks the Corinthian church, "do you not know that the saints will judge the world?" In Luke 22:30, Jesus tells his disciples they will "sit on thrones judging the twelve tribes of Israel." Perhaps even more convincingly, Revelation 19:15 says of Christ during his future return that "he will rule [the nations] with a rod of iron"; and yet Jesus tells the church at Thyatira in Revelation 2:26–27, "The one who conquers and who keeps my works until the end, to him I will give authority over the nations, and *he will rule them with a rod of iron,* as when earthen pots are broken in pieces, even as I myself have received authority from my Father."

God's people of all ages will be resurrected by Christ into the victory of his millennial kingdom. In this final age of human history under Christ's reign, we will serve him as his priests to the nations, representing his word, his will, and his rule, and acting in judgment as his representatives to bring the earth into conformity to his will. This will be our role in the victory won for us in Christ. And in that role, we will both see and experience vindication.

The Thousand-Year Reign of Christ Will Bring the Full Vindication of God's Judgment

Once again, this will be vindication for both God and his people. This time though, let's first consider from the text how God's people will be vindicated.

Christ's reign will bring vindication to God's people. You may be wondering from the previous point "who in the world will we be judging and ruling over in the millennium?" Remember in Matthew 24:22, Jesus said of the tribulation, "if those days had not been cut short, no human being would be saved. But for the sake of the elect those days will be cut short." The implication of this statement is that some percentage of humanity will survive the tribulation. Remember as well that the universal slaughter of the Antichrist and his armies was just that—his armies. There are several places in Scripture that indicate that both Jews and Gentiles, although in greatly diminished numbers, will survive and inhabit the earth during the millennium; and if we keep with the narrative from Revelation, this will include every person, great and small, who took the mark of the beast and worshipped him. Furthermore, Paul teaches the Corinthians in 1 Corinthians 6:3, "Do you not know that we are to judge angels?" perhaps referring to the demons who have not been bound at this time as Satan has.

This all gives an explanation to why Christ's reign in the millennium, and our reign as his representatives, will have to be administered "with a rod of iron." God's people will be vindicated in the millennium because

Christ will bring to pass what God had intended for his faithful image-bearers from the very beginning: to "fill the earth and *subdue* it, and have dominion" over everything, as the Lord said in Genesis 1:28. This word "subdue" in Genesis is a military term, used to describe an action of bringing a hostile force in subjection to your will.

What could possibly be a hostile force in need of subduing in a very good creation (which it was before the fall)? "Do you not know that we are to judge angels?" Perhaps a world also inhabited by Satan and his demonic compatriots who were consigned to this very good creation after their rebellion in heaven, as John describes in Revelation 12:4? Perhaps a proud adversary who wanted nothing to do with being subjected to these frail creatures made out of the dust, and who thought he had destroyed the very purpose of God by deceiving Adam and Eve into trading their dominion for his rebellion? "Do you not know that we are to judge angels?" Perhaps God, in promising his adversary Satan that an offspring of a woman would come into the world to reverse the damage and restore his plan for creation, will actually bring that to pass in Christ. "Do you not know that the saints will judge the world? . . . Do you not know that we are to judge angels?" (1 Corinthians 6:2–3).

God's people will be vindicated in Christ's millennial reign because they will stand in righteous judgment over the likes of those who have always brought them persecution and torment because they hold to "the testimony of Jesus and . . . the word of God" (Revelation 20:4). Our judgment will be the judgment we exercise over the nations in the millennium with the authority Christ will give us, as Christ told the church at Thyatira. But the final judgment God exercises will be his and his alone, and it will be an eternal judgment. And in so doing, Christ's reign will vindicate God in his final judgment.

Verses 11–15 describe what is often referred to as the "great white throne" judgment: the final judgment of God which seals the fate of all for eternity, either for blessing or the horror of the second death, which is the lake of fire mentioned in verses 14–15. We've already seen this is the eternal fate of Satan, the Antichrist, and the False Prophet; and in verse 13, Death and Hades will be thrown into the lake of fire as well. Who will that be? John gives us an idea in verse 15: anyone whose name is not written in the book of life.

In Revelation 3:5, Jesus tells the church at Sardis, "The one who conquers will be clothed thus in white garments, and I will never blot his name out of the book of life," and as we know from Revelation, the one who conquers is the one who holds fast to a faithful testimony of Jesus. In Daniel 12:1–2, Daniel makes a similar assertion about faithful Jews during the tribulation: "But at that time your people shall be delivered, everyone whose name shall be found written in the book. And many of those who sleep in the dust of the earth shall awake, some to everlasting life, and some to shame and everlasting contempt." As Daniel teaches, and as John teaches here in Revelation 20, we will all be resurrected and judged. The judgment for the faithful found written in the book of life will be everlasting life. The judgment for those whose names are not found there will be shame and everlasting contempt.

This stark reality often provokes a harsh backlash against the notion God could so judge. But the fact is, he will act to ensure he is clearly vindicated. During the tribulation, John records four times in Revelation that people did not repent despite the harsh judgments God brought upon them, in order to turn them to him. They chose instead to continue to worship Satan and the Antichrist and to live the life of grave immorality that such worship inspires. As John writes in Revelation 16:9–11, "They did not repent and give him glory. . . . People gnawed their tongues in anguish and cursed the God of heaven for their pain and sores. They did not repent of their deeds." And in the millennium—despite all the blessings that will come to the world under the visible thousand-year reign of Jesus Christ, the risen Savior and King, the Son of God—humanity will need a rod of iron to submit to his will. And at the first opportunity, all the nations of the earth, represented in the references by John to Ezekiel's account of the battle of Gog and Magog in verses 8–10, will flock once more to Satan's deception and call to rebellion.

God is not rash, unfair, or arbitrary in his judgment. Christ's reign will vindicate him; his judgments are true and just. In verse 4, John revealed that after Christ's thousand-year reign, Satan *"must be* released for a little while." The verb translated "must be" is a divine imperative: the verb the New Testament writers use to indicate God is commanding himself to act. Satan must be released because God must be vindicated. He will unequivocally prove that he is true and just in his judgments. As one commentator writes, "After a thousand years of experiencing Christ, the unbelieving nations throw themselves after Satan the first chance they get. The message is that in a billion years, a trillion years, they would do the same! Thus, they must suffer the same penalty as the one they worship, namely, eternal torment." [44] Those bent on rejecting Christ will do so and not even the direct, daily presence of God for an eternity will change that. So, all of these insights and conclusions beg a question.

Where Do You Stand?

The psalmist writes, "Therefore the wicked will not stand in the judgment, nor sinners in the congregation of the righteous" (Psalm 1:5). John speaks similarly of eternal life in Revelation 21:7–8 as he records God's words: "The one who conquers will have this heritage, and I will be his God and he will be my son. But as for the cowardly, the faithless, the detestable, as for murderers, the sexually immoral, sorcerers, idolaters, and all liars, their portion will be in the lake that burns with fire and sulfur, which is the second death."

We are saved by grace through faith in Jesus Christ, but as Jesus himself says several times in the gospels, "a tree is known by its fruit." Genuine faith will bear the fruit that marks it, as Alan Johnson contends in his commentary on Revelation 20:

> Works are unmistakable evidence of the loyalty of the heart; they express either belief or unbelief, faithfulness or unfaithfulness. The judgment will reveal through the records whether or not the loyalties were with God and the Lamb or with God's

enemies. John's theology of faith and its inseparable relation to works is the same as Jesus' and Paul's (John 5:29; Romans 2:6–16). This judgment is not a balancing of good works over bad works. Those who have their names in the Lamb's book of life will also have records of righteous deeds. The opposite will be true as well. The imagery reflects the delicate balance between grace and obedience.[45]

How we live matters. I'll leave you with Paul's thoughts on this point with respect to eternity from Galatians 6:7–9: "Do not be deceived: God is not mocked, for whatever one sows, that will he also reap. For the one who sows to his own flesh will from the flesh reap corruption, but the one who sows to the Spirit will from the Spirit reap eternal life. And let us not grow weary of doing good, for in due season we will reap, if we do not give up."

Chapter 26

God Is Making All Things New
(Revelation 21:1–8)

In his book *The Wonder of It All: Rediscovering the Treasures of Your Faith*, author and pastor Bryan Chapell tells a story of an African student named Lawrence delivering his first sermon during a Preaching 101 class at an American seminary. Lawrence chose a text describing the joys we'll share in eternity with Christ and he explained his choice of text this way:

> "I've been in the United States for several months now," he began. "I've seen the great wealth that is here—the fine homes and cars and clothes. I've listened to many sermons in churches here, too. But I've yet to hear one sermon about heaven. Because everyone has so much in this country, no one preaches about heaven. People here don't seem to need it. In my country, most people have very little, so we preach on heaven all the time. We know how much we need it."[46]

Do we know how much we need it? In Matthew 13:45–46, Jesus taught about the nature of this eternity with him and the perspective we ought to have toward it now in a parable: "Again, the kingdom of heaven is like a merchant in search of fine pearls, who, on finding one pearl of great value, went and sold all that he had and bought it." If the perception of this young African seminary student is true, the church in America today may be too distracted to understand this parable. Through faith in Jesus Christ, we've been given the promise of the kingdom of heaven, but instead of investing our lives and hope now in the infinite value of his kingdom, we prefer instead to dabble with the trinkets of our possessions, passions, and worldly interests.

Can we truly claim to have found one pearl of great value if we've put it on a shelf like it's just another collectible? Verse 5 of Revelation 21 states that God is making all things new! Therefore, whatever else we choose to cling to in this life apart from him and what he has in store for us in eternity will become former things which will pass away. Rather than clinging to trinkets, we'll see in Revelation 21 that God himself challenges the church from his very throne to embrace our inheritance as his children. As Jesus told a man in Luke 9:62 who sought to defer his commitment to following the Messiah in favor of meeting his worldly obligations, "No one who puts his hand to the plow and looks back is fit for the kingdom of God." As Christ's followers, we plow in this life with our focus on its eternal purpose for new things lie ahead, not behind.

God Is Making All Things New by Making the Former Things Pass Away (vv. 1–4)

What constitutes "former things" is pretty all-encompassing. Even the old creation will pass away. At the end of Revelation 20, John gives us the awesome image of God seated upon a "great white throne" as he enters into the final and everlasting judgment of all humanity, and in the midst of that awesome and terrifying scene, John writes in 20:11, "From his presence earth and sky fled away, and no place was found for them." John hints at some cataclysmic effect on creation in conjunction with this final judgment, but in 2 Peter 3:10 and 12, Peter describes this moment more elaborately: "the heavens will pass away with a roar, and the heavenly bodies will be burned up and dissolved, and the earth and the works that are done on it will be exposed . . . the heavens will be set on fire and dissolved, and the heavenly bodies will melt as they burn!"

In Romans 8:20–21, Paul teaches of this event as well, not so much in terms of the effect as in terms of God's purpose: "the creation was subjected to futility, not willingly, but because of him who subjected it, in hope that the creation itself will be set free from its bondage to corruption." As Genesis 3 indicates, when sin entered into creation through humanity's rebellion against God's will, the nature of all creation changed as a consequence. A futility and corruption entered into nature as the new reality for humanity's interaction with it, but as Paul indicates in Romans 8, God's renovation of creation in eternity will set his creation free from this bondage imposed upon it for the sake of our hope: we would someday forever experience new life within it.

You get a hint of this hope in verse 2 of Revelation 21: "And I saw the holy city, new Jerusalem, coming down out of heaven from God, prepared as a bride adorned for her husband." We will get into the splendor of this city and the magnificence of life within it in the next chapter, but contrast it with the present Jerusalem. This was the city where God had chosen to dwell amongst his covenant people Israel, with the charge to them to faithfully follow and serve him, yet their repeated failure brought repeated judgment.

Yet it was in the midst of facing one of those instances of judgment, at the hands of the Babylonians, that God promised through Jeremiah that a time would come when he would make a new covenant with his people Israel, and that a day would come when God will say of Jerusalem "this city shall be to me a name of joy, a praise and a glory before all the nations of the earth," as Jeremiah writes in Jeremiah 33:9. The present creation will pass away, as John writes in Revelation 21:1, but a new creation would serve little purpose if the very problem of humanity's sin remained to corrupt creation and human existence all over again. Therefore, more than creation must pass away—the power and presence of sin and death itself must pass away.

John writes in the second half of verse 1, "and *the sea* was no more." This seems a bit out of place. What's wrong with the sea that it needs to go away? Hard to say, but it's very possible that John is speaking figuratively here.

Throughout the book of Revelation, the sea is frequently used to describe the place from which evil originates. In Revelation 12 and 13, the Antichrist arises from the sea, apparently called from there by Satan, and in chapters 17 and 18, Satan's evil worldwide system of rule, religion, and economy rests upon "many waters" and conducts its activities upon the sea. And finally, the sea, along with Hades, are the two places identified from which the wicked dead are resurrected to face and receive their final and everlasting judgment. John is very possibly indicating that the absence of the sea on the new earth is the absence of the very presence and power of sin.

Paul teaches in Romans 6:23, "For the wages of sin is death, but the free gift of God is eternal life in Christ Jesus our Lord." Jesus Christ paid the wages of our sin through his death upon the cross on our behalf, and through faith in him, we receive the free gift of eternal life in a creation remade forever new and forever free from the presence and consequences of sin. An eternity in a creation made new where, as John writes in the second half of verse 4, "death shall be no more, neither shall there be mourning, nor crying, nor pain anymore, for the former things have passed away." In other words, all of creation and all of humanity who have been redeemed by Christ will live forever freed from the corrupting and destructive presence and power of sin— an outcome only possible if one more thing has passed away.

Broken relationship between God and humanity will also pass away. John writes in verse 3 and the first part of verse 4, "And I heard a loud voice from the throne saying, 'Behold, the dwelling place of God is with man. He will dwell with them, and they will be his people, and God himself will be with them as their God. He will wipe away every tear from their eyes.'" For we who have trusted Jesus Christ as our Savior, we have this reality today in part—God dwells within us through his Holy Spirit. But as Paul indicates in Ephesians 1:14, the presence of the Spirit in the life of the believer today "is the guarantee of our inheritance until we acquire possession of it."

As one commentator writes about our present reality and our future inheritance, we presently know this reality spiritually, but in this final age of eternity, "we will know them in terms of final physical reality."[47] God himself will dwell among us as our God, and God himself will wipe away every tear from our eyes. We will spend eternity as the redeemed resurrected people of God, living intimately with him in his presence, delivered forever from the presence and power of sin in a creation made new for all the former things will have passed away. This is the inheritance we faithfully and hopefully wait to acquire possession of, as Paul writes in Ephesians 1:14.

God Invites Us to Embrace His Offer of All Things New as Our Inheritance (vv. 5–8)

Verse 5 is one of the most stunning transitions in all the Bible. In verses 1–4, John records what he saw in this vison of eternity, things that will come to pass in the future. But in verse 5, the narrative dramatically shifts to the present tense, with God himself making a series of pronouncements about eternity from his throne, speaking of the future but addressing the church in the present. And the heart of his address is his promise in verse 7: "The one who conquers will have this heritage." The idea here is an inheritance, as the NASB brings out more clearly: "He who overcomes will *inherit* these things." The tone of God's address as a whole here is that of an invitation or even a challenge to embrace his offer, because God's offer is "trustworthy and true."

God sums up the nature of eternity in verse 5: "Behold, I am making all things new." He then he commands John, "Write this down, for these words are trustworthy and true." Notice God says "I am making," not "I will make." Remember that Jesus said in John 5:17, "My Father is working until now, and I am working." God the Father, the Son, and the Holy Spirit have always been and always are working to bring this eternal redemption of everything to pass, and as God's people we know this. Scripture teaches that through our faith in Christ, he makes us new creations—a work he began and promises to finish through our resurrection. He can be trusted with the task because he is "the Alpha and the Omega, the beginning and the end."

He is the Lord of all things at all times and in his present work in our lives, and through our future resurrection, we are part of "all things new!" And we know this is trustworthy and true because we are being transformed into the likeness of Christ's character "from one degree of glory to another" by the Holy Spirit, as Paul teaches in 2 Corinthians 3:18. God is presently proving the validity of his offer of our inheritance in eternity through his work in our lives. We should embrace it because it is trustworthy and true, and we should embrace it because God's offer is free to those who embrace it by faith.

In the fourth chapter of John's gospel, Jesus, while sitting at a well, tells a Samaritan woman whose life is a sinful mess, "Everyone who drinks of this water will be thirsty again, but whoever drinks of the water that I will give him will never be thirsty again. The water that I will give him will become in him a spring of water welling up to eternal life" (John 4:13–14). In essence, Jesus is offering this woman, steeped in a life of sin, forgiveness before God. We see this inheritance of eternal life in Revelation 21. Jesus will do everything necessary for her, for you, and for me to make it possible. As the eternal Son of God who took on human form for our sakes, lived a sinless life, and offered that life as the One and Only Son of God and perfect sacrifice on our behalf, God can rightly judge us as forgiven because Christ took our punishment; and God can rightly promise we will be resurrected into Christ's sinless likeness because Christ was resurrected to make it so for us. By the very power of God that raised Christ from the dead, God the Son, Jesus Christ, will raise us to be like him.

And so, because his One and Only Son paid the infinite price to save us from judgment and save us for eternity, God the Father can say in Revelation 21:6–7, not unlike what Jesus said to the Samaritan woman, "To the thirsty I will give from the spring of the water of life without payment. The one who conquers will have this heritage, and I will be his God and he will be my son." And as we know from a broad reading of Revelation, "the one who conquers" refers to those who place their faith and trust in Jesus as Savior and holds fast to it. We can embrace God's offer of all things new as our inheritance because it is trustworthy, true, and free to all who embrace it by faith in Jesus Christ. And we must embrace God's offer, because God's judgment is inevitable for those who reject his offer.

In a stark contrast to the message thus far, God shifts to the consequences of eternal judgment for those who reject Christ, as we saw at the end of Revelation 20. The Lord concludes his pronouncement in verse 8: "But as for the cowardly, the faithless, the detestable, as for murderers, the sexually immoral, sorcerers, idolaters, and all liars, their portion will be in the lake that burns with fire and sulfur, which is the second death." In other words, the likes of those whose lives are characterized in this way will not inherit this eternity of life with God in his kingdom.

Paul makes this point in a very similar way in 1 Corinthians 6:9–10, when he tells the Corinthian church, "Or do you not know that the unrighteous will not inherit the kingdom of God? Do not be deceived: neither the sexually immoral, nor idolaters, nor adulterers, nor men who practice homosexuality, nor thieves, nor the greedy, nor drunkards, nor revilers, nor swindlers will inherit the kingdom of God." Although Paul's list of character qualities is somewhat different from the list here in verse 8, the point is the same: to reject Christ is to reject the power of God to make us new creations through faith in him. Through the power of the Holy Spirit who comes to dwell in us, God does a transforming work in our lives to deliver us from the power of sin and the ungodly lives it produces. But those who reject Christ will not experience this change, nor inherit the kingdom. They will not be present in eternity: "their portion will be in the lake that burns with fire and sulfur, which is the second death."

But notice what Paul says next to the Corinthian believers about people who are sexually immoral, idolaters, adulterers, homosexuals, thieves, the greedy, drunkards, revilers, swindlers and the like: "Some of you were once like that. But you were cleansed; you were made holy; you were made right with God by calling on the name of the Lord Jesus Christ and by the Spirit of our God" (1 Corinthians 6:11, NLT). And so, there is no manifestation of our sin nature which places us beyond grace and hope.

You Too Can Be "All Things New!"

In his film *The Passion of the Christ*, Mel Gibson takes some creative license with Revelation 21:5 where God says "Behold, I am making all things new," by placing these words in Jesus' mouth in a much different setting: during Jesus' journey to the cross as he carries his own cross, stumbles under the weight of it, and as his mother rushes to his side. In that tender encounter at the worst of times, Jesus tells his mother, "See mother, I make all things new."

Is it out of place to attribute the making of all things new to Jesus Christ? In a magnificent passage from Ephesians 1:3–7, Paul tells the Ephesian church that "the God and Father of our Lord Jesus Christ . . . has blessed us in Christ with every spiritual blessing." Paul then goes on to enumerate what "every spiritual blessing" entails. Because of what Christ has done, the Father "chose us . . . that we should be holy and blameless before him." He adopted us "to himself as sons" and daughters. Through the love and grace he demonstrated by Christ's death on our behalf, "we have redemption through his blood, the forgiveness of our trespasses [sins]." Because of Christ, Paul says we have obtained the inheritance Revelation 21 speaks of. As he goes on to write in Ephesians 1:13–14, "In [Christ] you also, when you heard the word of truth, the gospel of your salvation, and believed in him, were sealed with the promised Holy Spirit, who is the guarantee of our inheritance until we acquire possession of it."

Through Jesus' life, death, resurrection, and future return to resurrect the faithful to eternal life in his kingdom, and to consign the faithless to eternal judgment, Jesus Christ will accomplish everything necessary for the Father to assure his people of the eternity he has planned for us. It's a plan Paul says God has revealed to us: "A plan for the fullness of time, to unite all things in [Christ], things in heaven and things on earth" (Ephesians 1:10). A plan to make all things new!

Chapter 27

The City of Eternal Glory and Life (Revelation 21:22–22:5)

In the latter part of the thirteenth century, the now-renowned Italian explorer Marco Polo set forth on part of what would become a twenty-four-year expedition to China. The details of his travels have been preserved in his book *The Travels of Marco Polo*, but to his contemporary thirteenth-century Europeans, these details were impossible to believe. Through an amazing set of circumstances, he became a court favorite of the powerful Chinese ruler Kublai Khan, and in China, Marco saw magnificent cities that made European capitals look like roadside villages. The Khan's palace dwarfed the largest castles and cathedrals in Europe; its massive banquet room alone could seat six thousand diners at one time, each eating on a plate of pure gold. Marco also saw the world's first paper money, marveled at the explosive power of gunpowder, and witnessed a steel manufacturing capability that would take Europe another five hundred years to match.

When he arrived home, people dismissed his stories of China as mythical; it was too fantastical in their minds, an impossible reality. At his deathbed, his family, friends, and priest begged him to recant his tales of China for the lies they believed they were, but setting his jaw and gasping for breath, Marco spoke his final words: "I have not even told you half of what I saw."[48] Do you think John may have been able to say

244 • The Gospel

the same thing after writing down what he saw in his vision of the New Jerusalem?

How unfathomable it is for us to comprehend life forever devoid of the presence and power of sin, but I pray we at least believe that it will be wonderful! It may be just as unfathomable for us to comprehend an eternal life where every aspect of it is eternally permeated through and through by God's glory—even more so than it was for Marco Polo's contemporaries to believe his descriptions of a glorious Chinese culture which defied their comprehension.

What we're attempting to take in is the description of the city in Revelation 21–22 that will be the hub and focus of life in eternity on the new earth: the New Jerusalem. Cities embody the fullness of a culture: what we learn and believe and pass on to others; the social customs and norms we practice and observe; the values that we share; our acts of worship and our acts of work; the diversions we enjoy, and much more. Now, if you can, imagine all these things experienced through a life resurrected in Christ's sinless likeness, and infused by the glory of God in the center of everything where he, as Paul writes in Ephesians 2:7, "in the coming ages . . . might show the immeasurable riches of his grace in kindness toward us in Christ Jesus." This will be eternal life lived out, with the New Jerusalem as the God-centered hub and focus of life and culture forever: a city of eternal glory and eternal life.

And when I say "glory," I don't just mean a glorious city—I mean a city that actually possesses the very glory of God as John indicates in verses 10–11 of Revelation 21: "the holy city Jerusalem coming down out of heaven from God, having the glory of God, its radiance like a most rare jewel, like a jasper, clear as crystal."

The New Jerusalem Will Be a City of Eternal Glory (21:22–27)

As we just heard from John's description, the New Jerusalem will be glorious in the form of its coming and in its design, and its glorious design will give it matchless splendor that points to God's matchless purpose of redemption and restoration. It will embody the glory of God's salvation.

In the verses preceding this latter part of Revelation 21, we get a stunning description of the purposeful design of the New Jerusalem, which must be understood in light of the Jewish temple of the old covenant built by Solomon. In that temple, God's presence dwelled within the Holy of Holies, an inner chamber that was a thirty-foot cube. As the author of Hebrews teaches, "only the high priest goes, and he but once a year, and not without taking blood, which he offers for himself and for the unintentional sins of the people" (Hebrews 9:7). But it goes on to teach that Christ "entered once for all into the holy places, not by means of the blood of goats and calves but by means of his own blood, thus securing an eternal redemption . . . so that those who are called may receive the promised eternal inheritance" (9:12, 15).

Only the high priest entered God's presence once a year in the Old Testament temple, into a thirty-foot cube and under the fear of judgment, but through Christ's sacrifice and the eternal redemption he secured, we who place our faith and trust in him will receive "the promised eternal inheritance." Again, this is an eternal inheritance of eternal life in a creation made completely new, and at the center of that creation is a magnificent cube God's people can freely enter and freely live in his presence—not a thirty-foot cube, but the New Jerusalem.

This city, as the NLT indicates in Revelation 21:16, will be "as wide as it was long. In fact, its length and width and height were each 1,400 miles." In other words, its city walls will form a boundary that would cover half of the United States, and those walls will rise to a height of 1,400 miles! But it won't just be big; it will be stunningly beautiful. Looking at these verses, we can imagine our approach to the city, clearly visible from a tremendous distance. Each of the four city walls will have three gates, and each gate will be "made of a single pearl" (v. 21) built into walls "of jasper" built upon twelve foundations "adorned with every kind of [stunningly beautiful] jewel" (vv. 18–19). And when you enter the city, you enter the city and find your way to the main thoroughfare made of "pure gold, like clear glass" (v. 18). A city mind-bogglingly magnificent in size and beauty, but also eternally embellished with the glory of God's great work of salvation—the gates marked with the names of the tribes of his people Israel through whom the Messiah came, and the foundations marked with the names of the Messiah's apostles upon which he built his church. Sounds pretty glorious thus far, but there's more.

The New Jerusalem will be filled by the glory of God's salvation. In verses 22–26 we read:

> And I saw no temple in the city, for its temple is the Lord God the Almighty and the Lamb. And the city has no need of sun or moon to shine on it, for the glory of God gives it light, and its lamp is the Lamb. By its light will the nations walk, and the kings of the earth will bring their glory into it, and its gates will never be shut by day—and there will be no night there. They will bring into it the glory and the honor of the nations.

There is no temple in the city. The city is now a massive Holy of Holies, with the Father and the Son dwelling in it as the temple. As the voice from the throne declared in Revelation 21:3, "Behold, the dwelling place of God is with man," and it is a dwelling filled with his glory. No other source of light will ever be necessary within the city nor will night ever be experienced there because, as John writes in verse 23 "the glory of God gives it light, and its lamp is the Lamb."

Notice the purpose of this glory. In verses 23–24, the light of the city comes from God's glory and the nations walk by this light. Then, in the second half of verse 24 and verse 26, we see that that the kings of the earth will bring their glory, and the glory and the honor of the nations, into the city. There is a lot of glory going around here, but it is all either emanating from or moving to the same point: God the Father and Jesus Christ, the light of the world.

Back in Revelation 5:9, those around God's throne declare of Jesus, "for you were slain, and by your blood you ransomed people for God from every tribe and language and people and nation." Those ransomed by Christ are ransomed to God's glory and they themselves are God's glory: a glory they turn and bring to him, freely in his presence, into a city whose gates will never be shut, as we see in verse 25. The New Jerusalem will be an endless parade of kings and nations he has redeemed through Christ, bearing the glory of so great a salvation into God's presence because there will be nothing in eternity to bear the presence or power of sin through those open gates: "only those who are written in the Lamb's book of life," will pass through them as John indicates in verse 27. But the New Jerusalem will be an eternal city glorious in more ways than one.

The New Jerusalem Will Be a City of Eternal Life (22:1–5)

Whereas the glory of God and his great salvation is the dominant theme in describing the New Jerusalem in Revelation 21, the theme shifts to life in this city in the first part of Revelation 22. But this isn't life in the sense of how we live it, but rather the reality of what our life truly entails. In Genesis 3, Adam and Eve's rebellion led to life giving way to death and in Genesis 3:22–24, after sin enters into creation through Adam and Eve:

> Then the LORD God said, "Behold, the man has become like one of us in knowing good and evil. Now, lest he reach out his hand and take also of the tree of life and eat, and live forever"— therefore the LORD God sent him out from the garden of Eden to work the ground from which he was taken. He drove out the man, and at the east of the garden of Eden he placed the cherubim and a flaming sword that turned every way to guard the way to the tree of life.

In Eden , Adam and Eve were not prohibited from taking of the tree of life; but because of their sin, God barred the way to eternal life lest Adam and Eve gain immortality, forever to live apart from relationship with God, and so be consumed forever by the presence and power of sin. If you think about that for a moment, you come to realize that death is actually, in one sense, a gift that saves us from the torment of such an immortality. In exchange God promised, from the moment sin entered into creation, to deliver us from the consequences of our sin and to save those who trusted him to do so by faith "so that they might obtain a better resurrection" as the author of Hebrews writes (11:35, NASB). And as we know, God's means of deliverance is Jesus Christ, through whom we have obtained that better resurrection and resurrected life.

Remember that in verse 6 of chapter 21, God promised, "To the thirsty I will give from the spring of the water of life without payment"; in 22:1–2, this water is "bright as crystal," flowing through a main thoroughfare of "pure gold, like transparent glass." And this river of water is life-giving because its fountainhead is the very "throne of God and of the Lamb," as we see in verse 1: a perpetual flow of life sustaining water from God from which we will never be barred access. If Eden was paradise lost, the New Jerusalem is paradise restored, with the tree of life once again in the dwelling place of God and humanity—always in season, bearing a variety of fruit and the healing of the nations of the redeemed, as we see in verse 2.

That word "healing" in verse 2 is the Greek word θεραπεία, from which we derive our word "therapy," which ought to convey to you—especially those who are hurting both inside and out—the eternity of tender loving care from our good and compassionate heavenly Father that awaits those who are Christ's. As John writes in Revelation 21:4, "He will wipe away every tear from their eyes" and the pain and sorrow of the curse from our failure in Eden will be wiped away as well, as John writes in 22:3: "No longer will there be anything accursed, but the throne of God and of the Lamb will be in it."

Life in the New Jerusalem is a picture of life fully restored from the fall. The eternal life God gives to the redeemed community will be perpetually available, sustain the well-being of every believer, and cure eternally every memory, every hurt, and every sorrow wrought upon us by the consequence of sin. So then, with this everlasting provision of God to heal and sustain us in every way, we will be restored to live as the faithful image-bearers of God Christ saved us to be.

The New Jerusalem will be a city where salvation is fully realized. At the end of verse 3, after John has described this great eternal life sustaining provision of God, the first act of the redeemed is in light of that provision. "His servants will *worship* him." About half of modern English translations use "worship" here, and about half use "serve." It's not the verb typically used for worship in the New Testament, but rather is a verb that closely ties the concept of worship and service. It conveys the idea that, as God transforms our lives into the likeness of Christ, our right response to his work in our lives is to serve him—and in serving him in this way, it is an act of worship. Hebrews 9:14 is a good demonstration of this: "how much more will the blood of Christ, who through the eternal Spirit offered himself without blemish to God, purify our conscience from dead works to serve the living God."

We do this now, yet hindered by sin, but we will meaningfully serve him in eternity completely unhindered. Every act, activity, work, etc., will have a redeemed quality to be carried out in his presence as his people who are his prized possession, for John says the redeemed "will see his face, and his name will be on their foreheads" in verse 4. In Revelation 3:12, Jesus promises the church at Philadelphia, "The one who conquers, I will make him a pillar in the temple of my God. Never shall he go out of it, and I will write on him the name of my God, and the name of the city of my God, the new Jerusalem, which comes down from my God out of heaven, and my own new name."

Remember there is no temple in the city: "the Lord God the Almighty and the Lamb" are its temple. We are his. We will bear his name. As he told the faithful among Israel who keep his covenant in Exodus 19:5, we are his "treasured possession" who will serve him as a kingdom of priests, always in the joy of his delighted presence, never to walk in darkness again, as John says in verse 5. The Father and the Son will reign over all of creation restored forever new, and we will meaningfully serve them. How meaningfully? Well, how vast and majestic will a fully restored creation under the reign of God be?

Speaking of God's redeemed servants, John closes this passage by saying "they will reign forever and ever." Try to wrap your mind around that—but only tightly enough to fill you with the joy, excitement, and hope of life forever where God is making all things new! As Paul says in Romans 5:5 (NASB), this is a hope that "does not disappoint."

Hope in God's Promise of Life Restored

It's interesting that Paul describes this "disappointment-proof" hope in Romans 5 as one that comes by persevering in Christlike character through times of struggle. I think it's equally interesting that God will remove from us the kind of hurt that mourning, crying, and pain over the reality of death represents.

Researcher and neuroscientist Matt Lieberman conducted a study to determine the body's reaction to the pain of social rejection, and discovered that the brain processes this type of emotional, soul-wrenching pain a lot like physical pain: "a broken heart can feel like a broken leg."[49] I've been physically hurt quite a bit in my life, but apart from when an ache or pain reminds me of it, I don't deal with the nagging memory of these things. But the kind of hurt that comes from great loss, betrayal, or rejection and such—either when I was on the giving or the receiving end of them—leaves the kind of scars that pierce as far as the division of soul and spirit, with a hurt that can cause these very depths of who we are to shudder like no physical pain can. I know many of you reading this at this moment have this kind of hurt, not unlike the psalmist who said "O my God, I cry by day, but You do not answer; and by night, but I have no rest" (Psalm 22:2). But that same psalmist would go on to say, "The afflicted will eat and be satisfied; those who seek him will praise the LORD. Let your heart live forever!" (v. 26).

For those of you hurting in this way, let John's vision of eternity lift your hope. God knows your hurt and he will pour out his healing grace and love upon you. We will likely bear some kind of deep hurt of soul and spirit for the balance of our days, but "He will wipe away every tear from their eyes." I pray for each of us the blessing of his eternal comfort and good hope through his sufficient and marvelous grace.

Chapter 28

An Epic Epilogue! (Revelation 22:6–21)

Years ago, the early twentieth-century president Calvin Coolidge returned home from church one Sunday and was asked by his wife what the minister had talked about. Coolidge replied, "Sin." When his wife pressed him as to what the preacher said about sin, Coolidge responded, "I think he was against it." That's an interesting summary. Coolidge could discern the preacher's topic but couldn't confidently summarize it. This raises an interesting question as to where the fault lies: Was it with the preacher or the distinguished member of his audience? We'll never know, but if I know human nature, most of you reading this would be inclined to blame the preacher!

Revelation 22 is unique in all the Scriptures. It is both God's closing thoughts to us in his message for us in the book of Revelation and in his Word as a whole. He has just finished tying all the loose ends together in his story of redemption and restoration and revealed to us how it will all end, and in these final verses, he gives us his epilogue to it all. *Webster's Dictionary* defines the word "epilogue" as "a concluding section that rounds out the design of a literary work,"[50] and so, with these verses, God rounds out the design of his story of redemption and restoration by reminding all of humanity about some essential truths: truths about his Word, truths about his one and only Son Jesus Christ, and truths about his salvation. Now these three topics are not neatly laid out in order in this text; John cycles through each repeatedly. But this is the order in which they appear in the text, so let's begin where John begins—purposefully, I believe: with God's Word.

This Epic Epilogue Reminds Us of Essential Truths about God's Word

My church's doctrinal statement begins with God's word as well: "We believe the Bible to be the verbally inspired word of God, authoritative, without error, infallible and God breathed, and therefore, the only rule of faith and practice."[51] Our statement goes on to cite some of the many passages one could cite to affirm that this statement isn't innovative, but rather affirms the claims the Bible makes of itself. Everything about our faith and practice rests, first and foremost, upon accepting what God himself says of his Word. It is the testimony he has chosen to reveal to us and preserve: a testimony that God himself declares in Isaiah 55:11 (NIV) "will accomplish what I desire and achieve the purpose for which I sent it." In reminding us of what is essential, it makes perfect sense for God to begin with his word that serves as the basis for what we believe to be essential, and he begins by communicating to John, through his angel, that God's word is trustworthy and true.

The angel says this very thing in Revelation 22:6, but remember, he's repeating what God himself said of his word from his throne in Revelation 21:5 when he commanded John, "Write this down, for these words are trustworthy and true." Now one might be inclined to argue that God is only characterizing John's account here in Revelation, but in 22:6, the angel goes on to say, "And the Lord, the God of the spirits of the prophets, has sent his angel to show his servants what must soon take place." In referring to the Lord as "the God of the spirits of the prophets," the angel is lumping John in with the host of human authors God has inspired to bring us his Word. Because of his nature, what God declares of his Word here is applicable to every word he has inspired as "the God of the spirits of the prophets"; therefore, we can also conclude from this epilogue that God's Word is complete.

And when I say "complete," I mean that it is precisely what he believes we need. Revelation is the piece of God's story that ties up the loose ends and brings us conclusively to the end he has in store. It reveals the ultimate aim of his work begun in eternity past and the significance of that revelation to all humanity. As such it offers, as one commentator notes, a uniquely rich opportunity for false teachers "to restructure the Christian faith"[52] by altering it—a reality reflected in Christ's warning in verses 18–19: "I warn everyone who hears the words of the prophecy of this book: if anyone adds to them, God will add to him the plagues described in this book, and if anyone takes away from the words of the book of this prophecy, God will take away his share in the tree of life and in the holy city, which are described in this book." If Christ is warning against adding to or deleting from God's Word in Revelation, he's not applying a unique standard to his Word here. Because of who he is, this is a standard that applies to all of his Word which, in these verses, merits a particular warning.

But not only is God's Word trustworthy and true and complete; it is also eternally profitable. In 2 Timothy 3:16, Paul states, "All Scripture is breathed out by God and profitable" and then explains in the next verse that this profitable quality brings the result "that the man of God may be complete, equipped for every good work." A careful read of Revelation 22 likewise speaks to the importance of keeping the words of this book. In verse 9, the angel rebukes John by reminding him that God's servants are "those who keep the words of this book" and in verse 7, Jesus says, "Blessed is the one who keeps the words of the prophecy of this book." Now it's not abundantly clear what that blessing is; it may be that we're "equipped for every good work" by doing so, as Paul teaches in 2 Timothy. But Jesus' warning in verse 19 indicates that the blessing is the very thing those who alter God's Word will lose: our "share in the tree of life and in the holy city, which are described in this book." In other words, the blessing is the eternal life promised by Jesus as described in this book.

This, then, is the trustworthy, true, complete, and eternally profitable quality of God's Word, which points us to the central figure in God's story of redemption and restoration—who won this eternity for us.

This Epic Epilogue Reminds Us of Essential Truths about Jesus

Let's begin with what the text says about who he is. First and foremost, Jesus is fully God. In verse 13 Jesus declares of himself, "I am the Alpha and the Omega, the first and the last, the beginning and the end." As you read through the book of Revelation, you'll recognize parts of this statement, but this is the only place in the book where all three parts are combined to describe one person. In 1:8, the Lord God makes the statement, "I am the Alpha and the Omega." In 1:17 and 2:8, Jesus refers to himself as "the first and the last"; and in 21:6, God proclaims from his throne "I am the Alpha and the Omega, the beginning and the end." So then, Jesus' statement in verse 13 indicates that he possesses the very attributes God alone possesses, and that these attributes affirm he, along with the Father, and the Spirit, is Lord over all of history. And within history, and humbly so as God the Son, Jesus took on human form to become the central figure in human history. This epic epilogue reminds us that Jesus is the Christ.

In verse 16, Jesus emphatically proclaims, "I, Jesus, have sent my angel to testify to you about these things for the churches. I am the root and the descendant of David, the bright morning star." As we've seen earlier on in the biblical account, being "the root and the descendant of David, the bright morning star" is a reminder that Jesus is the Messiah; the Christ. He is not only fully God; he is the fully human man God promised as humanity's deliverer in Genesis 3:15 who would be born of a woman. And as God's revelation to humanity unfolded, the prophecies of the Messiah unfolded, revealing him to be a descendant of David who would be born of a virgin, bring victory over sin and death through his life, death, and resurrection, and will ultimately rule forever over a restored kingdom of Israel and the kingdoms of the world. In short, he completely fulfilled the prophecies of the Christ up to the present age, but there remain some vital aspects of God's work of redemption and restoration in Christ to be fulfilled—most notably, that Jesus is coming in judgment.

In verse 12, Jesus says "Behold, I am coming soon, bringing my *recompense* with me, to repay each one for what he has done." The word "recompense" here refers literally to compensation for work done, and as such it can refer to punishment as well as reward. [53] Revelation records frequently the reality that we all will be judged according to our works, and this includes those who are in Christ. With respect to the faithful, this "recompense" is typically with the favorable connotation of reward; but in 2:23, Jesus ominously tells the church at Thyatira, in the midst of rebuking them for tolerating false teaching, sexual immorality, and idolatry in their midst, "I will give to each of you according to your works." As one commentator notes, the promise of Jesus' coming is meant to prompt God's people to repentance and faithfulness, and so, it is a promise with a sense of urgency.

Jesus is coming soon. Jesus makes this point three times in this passage, each emphatically, but what does "soon" mean? After all, it has been some two thousand years. In Matthew 24, Jesus indicates that his return would come unexpectedly; and the New Testament writers followed suit, frequently stressing that Jesus' return was imminent. The long delay seems to present a problem to this teaching, but Peter anticipates it in 2 Peter 3:4 when he states the question of the cynics who ask, "Where is the promise of his coming?" Peter responds by reminding his readers "do not overlook this one fact . . . that with the Lord one day is as a thousand years, and a thousand years as one day. The Lord is not slow to fulfill his promise as some count slowness, but is patient toward you, not wishing that any should perish, but that all should reach repentance" (2 Peter 3:8–9).

So then, from God's perspective, whether it's two thousand years, five thousand years, or whenever, the period between John's time and Christ's return will always be "soon." Jesus wants his people to regard his coming as imminent—not to build a calendar but to build character. As Jesus says in Matthew 24:45–46, in the midst of teaching that his return can come at any time, "Who then is the faithful and wise servant, whom his master has set over his household, to give them their food at the proper time? Blessed is that servant whom his master will find so doing when he comes." Perhaps Paul had something similar in mind in

Philippians 2:12 when he wrote "work out your own salvation with fear and trembling," for salvation is a work in progress we play a part in.

This Epic Epilogue Reminds Us of Essential Truths about His Salvation

We come back to where we began this chapter: salvation is rooted in faithful obedience to God's Word. As we discussed earlier in considering what this passage teaches about God's word, the text emphasizes that a mark of God's faithful people who will inherit eternal life is that they "keep the words of this book." If that's so, it logically follows that our lives will reflect this obedience. Not surprisingly, Jesus makes the point in verse 14 that salvation is reflected by the righteous works of God's people: "Blessed are those who wash their robes, so that they may have the right to the tree of life and that they may enter the city by the gates." Those who inherit eternal life will have irrevocable access to the New Jerusalem and the tree of life; Jesus describes these as "those who wash their robes."

Back in 7:14, John was told that "the ones coming out of the great tribulation . . . have *washed* their robes and made them white in the blood of the Lamb," indicating that one washes their robes through faith in Christ. But the verb "wash" here is in the present tense, indicating that this life of faith in Christ is not just a past event—it is an ongoing activity that characterizes the life of the believer. The same can be said from the previous point, where keeping "the words of this book" is also present tense.

This life of faith is the prevailing quality of the believer, building to a third point about our character in Christ: salvation will be realized through the persistent faithfulness of God's people—an explicit point made in this passage. In verse 11 the angel tells John, "Let the evildoer still do evil, and the filthy still be filthy, and the righteous still do right, and the holy still be holy." This is actually a series of four commands where the angel is declaring that there will be a difference between the wicked and the righteous. Genuine believers will persevere in their walk; and apart from Christ, those who reject him will remain in a life characterized by sin. You see this same side-by-side comparison in verses 14–15, where those who are "outside" in verse 15 are described in the same way as those destined for the lake of fire in 21:8. Daniel makes this very same point in Daniel 12:10: "Many shall purify themselves and make themselves white and be refined, but the wicked shall act wickedly. And none of the wicked shall understand, but those who are wise shall understand."

The marks of genuine saving faith in Christ are obedience to God's Word and a life that persists in reflecting that obedience. As John teaches throughout his letter of 1 John, God's work will be effective in transforming the believer, and this is an evident work he does in us for our assurance in our salvation.

But Revelation 22 teaches one more essential truth about our salvation: it is evident where God's people long for Christ's return. Verse 17 reads, "The Spirit and the Bride say, 'Come.' And let the one who hears say, 'Come.' And let the one who is thirsty come; let the one who desires take the water of life without price." The latter part of the verse is clearly an invitation to come to Christ, but many commentators take the first half to indicate that the Spirit and the church are longingly calling to Christ to come, and that Jesus' statement in verse 20 "Surely I am coming soon" is Jesus' response to their appeal. Even if that's not the case, the response at the end of verse 20, "Amen. Come, Lord Jesus!" is clearly an indication of the desire of his people. It ought to be our great and consuming longing for his return, knowing that the work he is doing in us now will be a work he completes at his return. We are participants in his work through our life of obedience; but ultimately, the faithful know that salvation in every sense is only possible by the grace of the Lord Jesus.

And so, ever fittingly, John concludes this epic epilogue saying "The grace of the Lord Jesus be with all. Amen." As Alan F. Johnson comments on verse 21, "Nothing less than God's grace is required for us to be overcomers and to triumphantly enter the Holy City of God, where we shall reign with him for ever and ever."[54] There is a tension in the

258 • The Gospel

Scriptures teaching between the assurance of our salvation in Christ, our obligation to walk in obedience, and the reality that grace will change us, both now and forever. In Titus 2:11–14, Paul puts it all together for us in the same context our passage today presents this tension: in light of our hope and longing for the Lord Jesus to come quickly:

> For the grace of God has appeared, bringing salvation for all people, training us to renounce ungodliness and worldly passions, and to live self-controlled, upright, and godly lives in the present age, waiting for our blessed hope, the appearing of the glory of our great God and Savior Jesus Christ, who gave himself for us to redeem us from all lawlessness and to purify for himself a people for his own possession who are zealous for good works.

God's grace toward us through Jesus Christ brings us salvation. This salvation results in a life in the present age which abandons the ways of the world and embraces the ways of God. Such a life waits for the blessed hope of the glorious return of our Savior. Knowing this is his aim in redeeming us, we live knowing we are his own possession, and as his possession, we are zealous for good works. If this is truly who we are, I invite you to join me now by expressing the great desire of his people God chose to conclude his Word with: "Amen. Come, Lord Jesus!"

Chapter 29

The Gospel:
A Redemption and Restoration Story

Way back when I was a young Air Force officer, the service impressed upon me the importance of closing your message to an audience with a summary of the highlights in sufficient detail to leave your audience with the substantive "gist" of what you hoped to communicate. In this journey through *The Gospel: A Redemption and Restoration Story*, we have moved through the story by moving through selected passages from Genesis, Exodus, 2 Samuel, Ezekiel, Isaiah, Matthew, Acts, 1 and 2 Thessalonians, and the book of Revelation. I pray that as we've done so, you've gained an appreciation for how the gospel is more than just a simple message. It is a message that runs through the whole counsel of God like a driveshaft and is deeply rooted in every major movement in the biblical account.

And so, what I'd like to do with this last chapter is leave you with the substantive "gist," using a common and well-established framework for these major movements: Creation, Rebellion, Redemption, and Restoration. And so, let's begin this recap where the Scripture begins: in the beginning.

Creation

God is the sovereign Creator and Redeemer of his very good creation; and in his work of creation, he teaches us about himself. He teaches us that he created everything. In Genesis 1:1, he "created the heavens and the earth," and in 2:1, "Thus the heavens and the earth were finished." And as if to emphasize that this included everything, 2:1 concludes "and all the host of them."

Because God created everything, we can infer from this text that God transcends his creation. He is not a created being but has eternally existed apart from his creation, Therefore, although his creation operates according to his design, he can act within creation supernaturally, that is, in ways which are impossible for any other being—most notably, in the very act of creation itself. This, then, ties the very nature of our faith to God as Creator, as Hebrews 11:3 teaches: "By faith we understand that the universe was created by the word of God, so that what is seen was not made out of things that are visible." This verse points us to another aspect of God's nature that he teaches us through creation: his word has the power to bring his perfect will to pass.

Every stage of creation in Genesis 1 is prefaced by the statement, "And God said," indicating the means by which all of creation came to pass. His very word has the power to speak the entire universe into existence; therefore, everything must be under his control. If that is so, then God is sovereign over all the universe; and as such, our sovereign God makes true distinctions.

In Genesis 1 God created by separating things from one another, most notably light and darkness. Throughout the Scriptures, light and darkness represent a distinction between good and evil—and it is, very notably, the first distinction God makes in all the Scriptures. Our sovereign, transcendent God who created everything by speaking it all into existence uses the very act of creation to make a distinction that points to his great work and purpose, which would inevitably and necessarily come to the fore in his work in human history. God's creative work brings about redemption.

In Genesis 1:2, the text reads "The earth was without form and void," a phrase that essentially means "an empty wasteland." God begins with something that is good for nothing; and as we know from

Genesis 1–2, in a very orderly fashion, he transforms the formless wasteland of earth into something "very good" (Genesis 1:31). As Allen Ross notes about this pattern, "God's creative work brings about redemption. It begins by taking a formless and void waste place and ends with a marvelous creation at rest, blessed and sanctified by God. The pattern of God's redemptive work first begins to unfold at creation." It's a pattern modeled in creation, but with a particular purpose for the pinnacle of God's creation. Humanity was created to partner with God in his meaningful work. In the key text of Genesis 1:26–28, the scripture reads:

> Then God said, "Let us make man in our image, after our likeness. And let them have dominion over the fish of the sea and over the birds of the heavens and over the livestock and over all the earth and over every creeping thing that creeps on the earth."
>
> So God created man in his own image, in the image of God he created him; male and female he created them.
>
> And God blessed them. And God said to them, "Be fruitful and multiply and fill the earth and subdue it, and have dominion over the fish of the sea and over the birds of the heavens and over every living thing that moves on the earth."

We were created for the unique purpose within his creation of joining with him in his creative work. As his image-bearers, he created us to be his faithful representatives. As his faithful representatives, we were charged to reproduce as his image-bearers, filling the earth and exercising a dominion of creative care over his creation. And in so doing, we were to subdue everything in his creation to keep it subject to his good and perfect will. And as we moved through the Scriptures, we came to see that our work of subduing may have been intended to entail a rebellious angelic host who had been consigned to earth . . . without a dominion.

262 • The Gospel

Rebellion

Twice in Genesis 1:26–28, God indicates that humanity's dominion was to be over every living thing on the earth. And so, in Genesis 3, Satan takes the form of a creature under humanity's dominion, and tempts Adam and Eve to reject God's will and embrace their own pride-fueled desire instead. In so doing, humanity ceded its dominion to Satan—now "the ruler of this world," as Jesus refers to him three times in John's gospel. And in joining in Satan's rebellion, humanity reaped the sweeping repercussions of its sin.

In Genesis 3, not only is dominion lost but life is lost. Life as God defines it. Eternal life in his presence in right relationship with him, with all the blessings that come with it. Instead, death and judgment would now reign as the inevitable end for humanity, and the marred life we would now possess until that death would be consumed by the power of sin unleashed on all creation. Relationship with God was broken. Relationship with one another was now marked by strife. Creation was subjected to a curse of futility, making life in it a hardship and often a tragedy. And Satan was given latitude to pursue his hostility toward these now-marred image-bearers of God he so despised.

As we continued through the Genesis narrative, we saw the horrible consequence of such a life as God brought the worldwide judgment of the flood. In Genesis 6:5 and 7, "The LORD saw that the wickedness of man was great in the earth, and that every intention of the thoughts of his heart was only evil continually. . . . So the LORD said, 'I will blot out man whom I have created from the face of the land, man and animals and creeping things and birds of the heavens.'" As Paul teaches in Ephesians 2:3, we are all "by nature children of wrath"; and as the flood narrative proves, when left to our own devices, we merit wrath. We merit worldwide judgment. "Every intention of the thoughts of [our] heart [are] only evil continually."

But in this tragic story of rebellion and its consequences, the grace of God's redemption walks hand in hand with the reality of judgment and wrath.

Redemption

Grace did not and does not tarry in the midst of our perpetually great failure of exchanging "the truth about God for a lie" (Romans 1:25). From the very outset of our rebellion, redemption was revealed immediately. In Genesis 3:15 God pronounced Satan's doom as the consequence for the rebellion he inspired. An offspring of a woman "shall bruise your head, and you shall bruise his heel," foreshadowing the limited harm Satan would bring against this deliverer God would send and the conclusive defeat he would experience at the hands of this offspring of a woman in return. And it was, once again, in the midst of God's terrible judgment that we next saw God's gracious redemption in the Genesis story.

Redemption was demonstrated in God's deliverance of Noah. As God set about destroying the earth through the flood, Genesis 6:8 states, "Noah found *favor* in the eyes of the LORD." The word "favor" here is the Hebrew word for "grace." Noah found grace, and this grace did for Noah what grace has always done in the lives of those who come to God *on his terms* by faith. The next verse says of Noah, "Noah was a righteous man, blameless in his generation. Noah walked with God." And so, Noah and his family were delivered from the consequences of God's wrath.

But the same old pattern of wickedness predictably came to the fore once again after the flood. So yet again in the midst of God's judgment, redemption was demonstrated through the creation of the nations. In Genesis 9–11, the scripture revealed once again that, left unrestrained, humanity embraced a proud rebellion against God. In Genesis 9:1, after the flood, God renews a creation mandate from Genesis 1 as he commands Noah, "Be fruitful and multiply and fill the earth." But in Genesis 11, the entire human race unifies in rebellion against this command. With a common language, they gather in the land of Shinar with every intention of staying there, as 11:4 indicates: "Then they said, 'Come, let us build ourselves a city and a tower with its top in the heavens, and let

264 • The Gospel

us make a name for ourselves, lest we be dispersed over the face of the whole earth.'" As a judgment against their rebellious pride, God confused their language and divided humanity into nations, to restrain us from the sin of pride.

The creation of the nations was also an act of God's common grace, to keep us from the worst of what our corporate pride could bring. The nations would be God's instrument to restrain humanity from the proliferation of wickedness. Remember the creation of nations follows quickly after the pre-flood history of humanity living without this civilizational structure: no nations and no government. And as the flood account proves, this resulted in such widespread evil that God acted in worldwide judgment. In Romans 13:1–4, Paul writes:

> Let every person be subject to the governing authorities. For there is no authority except from God, and those that exist have been instituted by God. Therefore, whoever resists the authorities resists what God has appointed, and those who resist will incur judgment. For rulers are not a terror to good conduct, but to bad. Would you have no fear of the one who is in authority? Then do what is good, and you will receive his approval, for he is God's servant for your good. But if you do wrong, be afraid, for he does not bear the sword in vain. For he is the servant of God, an avenger who carries out God's wrath on the wrongdoer.

With the nations came the ruling authorities that Paul teaches have been instituted by God as an agent of his wrath against wickedness. In other words, the nations emerge in God's redemptive plan as a central feature of his plan. But the nations represent more than just God's common grace as a force to restrain evil. The Scriptures also teach that the nations become the object and vehicle of God's work of eternal redemption.

Consider again the following train of thought: God creates the nations from the families descended from Noah in Genesis 10–11. In

Genesis 12, God calls Abram, promises to make a great nation from his descendants, and promises to bless all the families of the earth through him. In Genesis 22:18, God then promises Abram, "in your offspring shall all the nations of the earth be blessed." This singular offspring would come through the great nation that God would make of Abraham—Israel—and this offspring is progressively revealed in Scripture as the Messiah, a man who would be a descendant of David who would rule over Israel on David's throne forever per 2 Samuel 7, whose rule would extend over the nations forever, per Isaiah 49.

And how can he rule over all forever? Because he will bring the salvation of eternal life for all to dwell with him forever in his kingdom, as Isaiah 49:6 indicates: "It is too light a thing that you should be my servant *to raise up* the tribes of Jacob and to bring back the preserved of Israel; I will make you as a light for the nations, that my salvation may reach to the end of the earth."

So then, the gospel of Jesus Messiah—Jesus Christ—is one he commands we take and "Go therefore and make disciples of all nations" (Matthew 28:19); "for you were slain, and by your blood you ransomed people for God from every tribe and language and people and nation, and you have made them a kingdom and priests to our God, and they shall reign on the earth" (Revelation 5:9–10). And as we saw toward the end of this gospel story, redeemed nations will endure as a feature of eternal civilization. In Revelation 21:24–26, John describes the new Jerusalem on the new earth and says of the city, "By its light will the nations walk, and the kings of the earth will bring their glory into it, and its gates will never be shut by day—and there will be no night there. They will bring into it the glory and the honor of the nations." This is the outcome of the great salvation the gospel has the power to bring.

The gospel is a message of redemption: our deliverance from wrath and for the glory of his kingdom. Jesus' perfect sacrifice on our behalf saves us from God's justifiable wrath against us, because Christ bore God's wrath against us fully. And by his resurrection, we who have placed our faith and trust in him are now joined to his destiny of human life resurrected to glory. As Paul says in Romans 6:5, by God's grace through our faith in Jesus Christ, "we shall certainly be united with him in a resurrection like his"; and again in 2 Timothy 2:11–12, "If we have died with him, we will also live with him; if we endure, we will also reign with him."

This is why Jesus refers to the gospel of the kingdom more than one hundred times in the Gospels. Rooted in God's age-old promise to his people Israel, to whom the gospel repeatedly came first throughout the New Testament, Jesus will restore them to the land of their inheritance forever. So then, Jesus describes the gospel most frequently in terms of what we were saved for. And this points to the culmination of his work.

Restoration

Let's go back to the beginning. We were created as God's image-bearers to rule over his very good creation, to live in his presence forever in right relationship with him and to be forever blessed by him. But our rebellion led to tragedy. Death instead of life. Banishment from his presence, broken relationship with him, and barred from the tree of life. Objects of wrath instead of his blessing. A futile life in a cursed creation subject to futility. Satan- and sin-empowered to bring misery. A hopeless existence under judgment and ravaged by sin and death.

But from the start, God gave hope through the promise of a redeemer whom the Scriptures would ultimately reveal to be Jesus, the eternal Son of God who took on human form, to fulfill every prophecy of the Christ, accomplishing every necessary work to redeem and restore . . . everything.

And so, as God's story of redemption and restoration ends, we saw that, as Paul taught in Ephesians 1:10, from before the foundation of the world, God had "a plan for the fullness of time, to unite all things in [Christ], things in heaven and things on earth"; and we saw of this plan of restoration fulfilled in Revelation 20–22: Satan and all who followed him forever consigned to wrath under God's judgment. God declaring, "Behold, I am making all things new!" (21:5). "A new heaven and a new earth" (21:1). The New Jerusalem as the glorious heaven-sent center of a new earth. God once again, but now forever, dwelling among his people. Sin's presence and power forever eradicated. The curse upon creation forever lifted. Irrevocable access to the tree of life and God's presence forever granted.

The nations Christ died and rose again to redeem now bearing the glory of God's salvation. And as his resurrected image-bearers, we now faithfully bearing the sinless likeness of Christ, as his people reigning forever as his representatives over his forever new and forever good creation. Amen and amen.

Endnotes

1. "transcend," Merriam-Webster.com, https://www.merriam-webster.com/dictionary/transcend?src=search-dict-hed (accessed January 17, 2020).

2. K. A. Mathews, *Genesis 1–11:26*, The New American Commentary, vol. 1A (Nashville: Broadman & Holman Publishers, 1996), 128.

3. Allen P. Ross, *Creation and Blessing* (Grand Rapids: Baker Academic, 1996), 103.

4. Steve Farrar, *Finishing Strong* (Sisters, OR: Multnomah Publishing, 1995), 90.

5. Haddon Robinson, *Biblical Preaching* (Grand Rapids: Baker Academic, 2001), 100.

6. Abraham Kuruvilla, *Genesis: A Theological Commentary for Preachers* (Eugene, OR: Resource Publications, 2014), 81.

7. Philip Yancey, *Vanishing Grace* (Grand Rapids: Zondervan, 2014), 63–64.

8. Kay Warren, "The Only Hope for Monsters," *Christianity Today*, October 2008, 98.

9. John Ortberg, *Love Beyond Reason* (Grand Rapids: Zondervan, 1998), 141–42.

10. John Ortberg, *Waiting on God*, Faith Builders Book 1 (Carol Stream, IL: Christianity Today International: Kindle Edition) 137–142.

11. J.I. Packer, *The New Encyclopedia of Christian Quotations*, ed. Mark Water (Ada, MI: Baker, 2000), 190.

12. H. D. M. Spence-Jones, ed., *2 Samuel*, The Pulpit Commentary (London; New York: Funk & Wagnalls Company, 1909), 189.

13. Juliana Penaranda-Loftus and Alejandra Nash, "Landfill Harmonic," video, 3:34, https://vimeo.com/groups/focusforwardfilms/videos/51890020 (accessed January 23, 2020).

14. Nancy Guthrie, ed., *Jesus, Keep Me Near the Cross* (Wheaton, IL: Crossway, 2009), 136.

15. Gary V. Smith, Isaiah 1–39, The New American Commentary, ed. E. Ray Clendenen (Nashville: B & H Publishing Group, 2007), 131.

16. "James Hudson Taylor Quotes," *Goodreads*, https://www.goodreads.com/author/quotes/4693730.James_Hudson_Taylor (accessed February 9, 2020).

17. Ruth A. Tucker, *From Jerusalem to Irian Jaya* (Grand Rapids: Zondervan, 2004), 137.

18. Tucker, *From Jerusalem to Irian Jaya*, 139.

19. Timothy Keller, *Walking with God through Pain and Suffering* (New York: Dutton Adult, 2013), 120.

20. Craig Blomberg, *Matthew*, The New American Commentary, vol. 22 (Nashville: Broadman & Holman Publishers, 1992), 172.

21. William Arndt, Frederick W. Danker, and Walter Bauer, *A Greek-English Lexicon of the New Testament and Other Early Christian Literature* (Chicago: University of Chicago Press, 2000), 882.

22. Arndt, Danker, and Bauer, *Greek-English Lexicon*, 1002.

23. Arndt, Danker, and Bauer, *Greek-English Lexicon*, 252.

24. The Joshua Project, https://joshuaproject.net (accessed May 22, 2017).

25. Irenaeus of Lyons, "Against Heresies," in *The Apostolic Fathers with Justin Martyr and Irenaeus*, eds. Alexander Roberts, James Donaldson, and A. Cleveland Coxe, The Ante-Nicene Fathers, vol. 1 (Buffalo, NY: Christian Literature Company, 1885), 562.

26. Papias, "Fragments of Papias," in *The Apostolic Fathers with Justin Martyr and Irenaeus*, eds. Alexander Roberts, James Donaldson, and A. Cleveland Coxe, The Ante-Nicene Fathers, vol. 1 (Buffalo, NY: Christian Literature Company, 1885), 153.

27. Papias, "Fragments of Papias," 154.

28. Richard N. Longenecker, Luke–Acts, "Acts" of The Expositor's Bible Commentary, vol. 10, rev. ed, eds. Tremper Longman III and David E. Garland (Grand Rapids, MI: Zondervan, 2007), 720.

29. Blomberg, *Matthew*, 170.

30. John B. Polhill, *Acts*, The New American Commentary, vol. 26 (Nashville: Broadman & Holman Publishers, 1992), 111.

31. Sasha Goldstein, "Orlando Boy Shoots, Kills Younger Brother, 12, after Mistaking Him for a Home invader," New York Daily News, https://www.nydailynews.com/news/national/boy-shoots-brother-12-thinking-intruder-article-1.1297242 (accessed January 25, 2020).

32. Nancy Guthrie, *Holding onto Hope: Drawn by Suffering to the Heart of God* (Carol Stream, IL: Tyndale House, 2002), 9–11.

33. C. S. Lewis, *God in the Dock* (New York: HarperOne, 2014; Kindle edition), 1227.

34. Elie Wiesel, "The Perils of Indifference," April 12, 1999, https://www.americanrhetoric.com/speeches/ewieselperilsofindifference.html (accessed January 30, 2020).

35. D. Michael Martin, *1, 2 Thessalonians*, The New American Commentary, vol. 33 (Nashville: Broadman & Holman Publishers, 1995), 167.

36. Arndt, Danker, and Bauer, *Greek-English Lexicon*, 696.

37. Robert L. Thomas, "2 Thessalonians," *The Expositor's Bible Commentary: Ephesians–Philemon*, vol. 12, rev. ed., eds. Tremper Longman III and David E. Garland (Grand Rapids, MI: Zondervan, 2006), 471.

38. Clark Cothern, "Honesty is the Best Policy," *Preaching Today*, https://www.preachingtoday.com/search/?query=Honesty%20is%20the%20best%20Policy&type= (accessed January 30, 2020).

39. Arndt, Danker, and Bauer, *Greek-English Lexicon*, 178.

40. "The Martyrdom of Polycarp," *New Advent*, http://www.newadvent.org/fathers/0102.htm (accessed February 9, 2020).

41. "The Martyrdom of Polycarp."

42. "The Martyrdom of Polycarp."

43. "Only God Is Great," Bible.org, https://bible.org/illustration/only-god-great (accessed February 9, 2020).

44. Grant R. Osborne, *Revelation*, Baker Exegetical Commentary on the New Testament (Grand Rapids, MI: Baker Academic, 2002), 716.

45. Alan F. Johnson, "Revelation," in *The Expositor's Bible Commentary: Hebrews–Revelation*, vol. 13, rev, ed., eds. Tremper Longman III and David E. Garland (Grand Rapids, MI: Zondervan, 2006), 775.

46. Bryan Chapell, *The Wonder of It All: Rediscovering the Treasures of Your Faith* (Wheaton, IL: Crossway, 1999), 189.

47. Osborne, *Revelation*, 735.

48. Dr. Robert Peterson, "All Things New: Our Eternal Home," sermon, Covenant Presbyterian Church, Naples, FL, November 8, 2009.

49. Matt Lieberman, "Ouch! In the Brain, Social Rejection Feels Like Physical Pain," *Discover*, https://www.discovermagazine.com/mind/ouch-in-the-brain-social-rejection-feels-like-physical-pain (accessed February 11, 2020).

50. "epilogue," Merriam-Webster, https://www.merriam-webster.com/dictionary/epilogue (accessed February 14, 2020).

51. "Our Beliefs," Leptondale Bible Church, https://www.leptondale.org/about-us/our-beliefs (accessed February 14, 2020).

52. Osborne, *Revelation*, 795.

53. Arndt, Danker, and Bauer, *Greek-English Lexicon*, 653.

54. Johnson, "Revelation," 789.